Human Settlements and Energy

United Nations Economic Commission for Europe

Some other titles from Pergamon Press

HOUSING FOR SPECIAL GROUPS

BEHAVIOUR OF WOOD PRODUCTS IN FIRE

PROTEIN AND NON-PROTEIN NITROGEN FOR RUMINANTS

FROZEN AND QUICK-FROZEN FOOD

FACTORS OF GROWTH AND INVESTMENT POLICIES

COAL: 1985 AND BEYOND

NON-WASTE TECHNOLOGY AND PRODUCTION

THE GAS INDUSTRY AND THE ENVIRONMENT

BUILDING RESEARCH POLICIES

AIR POLLUTION PROBLEMS OF THE INORGANIC CHEMICAL INDUSTRY

STATISTICAL SERVICES IN TEN YEARS' TIME

Human Settlements and Energy

An Account of the ECE Seminar on the Impact of Energy Considerations
on the Planning and Development of Human Settlements
Ottawa, Canada, 3 - 14 October 1977

Edited by

C. I. JACKSON

Ministry of State for Urban Affairs, Canada

Published for the
UNITED NATIONS
by
PERGAMON PRESS

OXFORD · NEW YORK · TORONTO · SYDNEY · PARIS · FRANKFURT

U.K.	Pergamon Press Ltd., Headington Hill Hall, Oxford OX3 0BW, England
U.S.A.	Pergamon Press Inc., Maxwell House, Fairview Park, Elmsford, New York 10523, U.S.A.
CANADA	Pergamon of Canada Ltd., 75 The East Mall, Toronto, Ontario, Canada
AUSTRALIA	Pergamon Press (Aust.) Pty. Ltd., 19a Boundary Street, Rushcutters Bay, N.S.W. 2011, Australia
FRANCE	Pergamon Press SARL, 24 rue des Ecoles, 75240 Paris, Cedex 05, France
FEDERAL REPUBLIC OF GERMANY	Pergamon Press GmbH, 6242 Kronberg-Taunus, Pferdstrasse 1, Federal Republic of Germany

First edition 1978

British Library Cataloguing in Publication Data

Seminar on the Impact of Energy Considerations
on the Planning and Development of Human
Settlements, Ottawa, 1977
Human settlements and energy.
1. City planning 2. Regional planning
3. Power resources
I. Title II. Jackson, Charles Ian
III. Economic Commission for Europe
711.4   HT166   78-40137
ISBN 0-08-022427-X
ISBN 0-08-022411-3 Pbk.

Printed in Great Britain by Page Bros (Norwich) Ltd, Norwich and London

CONTENTS

ACKNOWLEDGEMENTS

ECE and Pergamon Press are grateful to the Government of Canada for making available the services of the editor, Dr. C. I. Jackson, and for other assistance in the publication of this book. The editor accepts personal responsibility for the selection of quotations from texts by various authors and for the opinions expressed in those parts of the book that are not directly based on the Seminar documentation.

PART I

INTRODUCTION

Although the Economic Commission for Europe (ECE) organizes approximately twenty seminars and similar meetings each year, the Ottawa Seminar in October 1977 was unusual in a number of respects. It was, as the speech of welcome points out, the first event of its kind to take place in Canada since the country became a full member of the ECE in 1973. Secondly, and of most significance, the subject of energy use (and misuse) in human settlements is one that is of great and continuing importance throughout the ECE region in view of the large proportion of total national energy use that is accounted for by human settlements in all ECE countries.

The Seminar was also distinctive in its emphasis on the long-term future rather than immediate problems, and on policy development and implementation rather than technical matters. Bodies such as the International Council for Building Research, Studies and Documentation (CIB) at the international level, and similar agencies within individual countries, have in recent years done much to analyse the nature of energy flows within human settlements and to devise practical techniques to improve the efficiency of energy use. Since the energy crisis of 1973, however, there has been a growing recognition that major changes in energy-use patterns are likely and indeed necessary throughout the rest of this century. If these are to be reconciled with continued progress in the improvement of the quality of life in human settlements, the trend of change needs to be identified in some detail, and comprehensive national policies and strategies need to be developed and implemented on a continuing and consistent basis. It was with matters of this kind that the Ottawa Seminar was primarily concerned.

Although the initiative for such a seminar came mainly from the host country and from the ECE Committee on Housing, Building, and Planning (CHBP), the subject-matter of the seminar clearly extends well beyond the normal interests of the CHBP and of the housing, building, and planning authorities in member countries. The substantial work undertaken by the ECE Secretariat in preparation for the Seminar involved a special task force that represented most of the Divisions in the Secretariat. The national delegations at the Seminar itself similarly reflected the wide-ranging implications of energy use in human settlements and the need for comprehensive and integrated policy development. The Seminar was a major element in the extensive programme of work on energy matters at present being carried out by the ECE.

Yet another distinctive feature of the Seminar was the unusual volume of substantive documentation. Since the emphasis was on policies rather than techniques, contributions were invited on a national basis rather than from individual experts. The response was gratifying. In addition to a seminar theme paper written, on behalf of the host country, by the present editor in co-operation with the ECE Secretariat, approximately fifty specialized papers were prepared by member countries and international organizations. A substantial proportion (fifteen) of these were contributed by Canada; five came from France and the others from a total of seventeen other member countries and four international organizations including the ECE Secretariat itself. In addition, several countries prepared and distributed "response papers" describing the particular situation and prospects in regard to energy use in human settlements in the country concerned.

Such a large amount of material represents both a valuable resource and a difficult problem for an editor of the seminar proceedings. In view of the general neglect of energy issues in human settlements planning in the past, the specialized and other papers prepared for the Ottawa Seminar are clearly valuable contributions to knowledge and to policy development that deserve much wider circulation. However, the sheer volume of material makes it impossible to reproduce all the papers in complete form. It may be noted here that they were not prepared with such publication in mind, nor were they "read" in Ottawa; they were designed as background documents that could provide a basis for the discussions in Ottawa, could indicate the nature of the conclusions and recommendations that the Seminar might adopt, and could assist the implementation of these recommendations in the years ahead.

One way of making these specialized background papers available to a wider audience is noted on p. 161 of the present volume. Eighteen of the papers will be published in a special issue of the journal *Habitat International* during 1978. A second way is through the present volume, which is divided into three sections. Following this introduction are the texts of the welcoming address at the opening of the Seminar by the Parliamentary Secretary to the Minister of State for Urban Affairs of Canada, and of the address by the Executive Secretary of the ECE. Each of these, in different ways, puts the Seminar in a broader context of national and international concern for energy supply and use, now and in the future.

The second part of the volume utilizes the specialized papers and other material to provide a summary survey of the issues with which the Ottawa Seminar was concerned. Such an approach can in no sense be regarded as a substitute for the specialized papers themselves. The extracts from these papers that are quoted do, it is hoped, convey some of the concerns expressed by governments and other bodies, but the extracts are necessarily very brief when compared to the substantial amount of data and other material included in the full papers. In addition, in order to provide as coherent and comprehensive an account as possible, it must be kept in mind that the main themes of an individual paper are not necessarily reflected in the extracts from it that are included in the present volume. The aim in Part II is not so much to provide a précis of the specialized papers as to produce a reasonably comprehensive and useful survey of the main interactions between energy policies and human settlements policies.

To use the word "useful" is to beg the question "useful to whom?" Part II will, it is hoped, be of assistance to the many human settlements planners at work in all ECE countries, especially at the regional, municipal or community levels of government. Such people seldom have the opportunity to participate in international meetings like the Ottawa Seminar, where of necessity small national delegations tend to consist primarily of representatives of central government. Yet the daily work of such planners constantly involves them in situations where, explicitly or implicitly, their views or decisions have major implications for energy use or misuse. It was recognized by every-one who participated in the Ottawa Seminar (and is reflected in the conclusions and recommendations) that although the key energy decisions tend to be taken at the national or international level, the character and form of human settlements and the buildings they contain owe much more to individual decisions taken mainly at the local level. The local human settlements planner is generally aware of the potential significance of his role in promoting energy conservation and improving the efficiency of energy use, just as, a decade or so ago, he was similarly aware of his new responsibilities for pre-serving and improving environmental quality. Now, as then, what is lacking is prac-tical advice and experience to assist the planner in discharging such responsibilities. The specialized papers prepared for the Ottawa Seminar are full of such advice and practical experience, and the aim of Part II is to convey as much of this as possible to those who will bear the main responsibility for implementing the conclusions and recommendations of the Seminar.

These conclusions and recommendations, together with an analytical summary of the discussions in Ottawa that led to their adoption, form the principal element of Part III. In a strict sense, the recommendations are part of the report of the Seminar to the ECE Committee on Housing, Building and Planning which sponsored the Seminar. The governmental representatives who constitute that Committee will review this report during an in-depth discussion of the Seminar theme in September 1978, and the Com-mittee will also decide what further action by the ECE is desirable. In many respects, however, the conclusions and recommendations need no further endorsement; they are the findings of a highly expert group drawn from twenty-four countries in all parts of the ECE region and from the international organizations which were represented in Ottawa. The majority of recommendations need no further action by the ECE to make them effective; their success depends on the effectiveness with which they are imple-mented in individual countries and communities.

The immediate relevance of the recommendations is made particularly clear by the format in which they were adopted, which follows the model used for the recommenda-tions of the UN Conference on Human Settlements (Habitat) in Vancouver in 1976. Each recommendation consists of three parts: (a) a brief statement of a specific prob-lem, (b) the recommendation itself, and (c) a list of ways and means by which the re-commendation may be implemented and the problem solved or ameliorated. Inter-national meetings are sometimes criticized on the grounds that their proceedings are difficult to understand from the outside or because the recommendations they adopt seem to have little or no practical significance. It would be difficult to criticize the Ottawa Seminar recommendations on the latter grounds, and the structure adopted for this volume will, it is hoped, illustrate how the conclusions and recommendations resulted from the documentation and other preparations for the meeting. In particular, the present editor has tried to link Parts II and III by providing references in the margins of Part II which link the contents of that part to the relevant conclusions and recommen-dations of the Seminar listed in Part III.

ADDRESS* ON BEHALF OF CANADA

by JEAN-ROBERT GAUTHIER, MP

Parliamentary Secretary to the Minister of State for Urban Affairs of Canada

Ottawa, 3 October 1977

Ladies and gentlemen, delegates, experts, observers, and other distinguished partici-pants. I am very honoured to welcome you today to Ottawa at the beginning of this important meeting of the United Nations Organization, prepared under the auspices of the Committee on Housing, Building and Planning of the Economic Commission for Europe.

Canada has been a member of ECE since 1973 and is proud of having participated for many years in the important work of this Commission. We value the studies, recom-mendations, and co-operation of the Commission and all its specialized committees very highly. I am pleased to recognize in this audience members of several delegations whose perception and co-operative spirit I had an opportunity to appreciate during the conferences in Vancouver and Mar del Plata † Moreover, I am particularly happy to welcome so many eminent visitors at a time of year when Canada's trees are exception-ally beautiful. Even those of you who have visited Canada several times have perhaps not seen the extraordinary variety of colours with which our forests are adorned in the fall. One would think that nature wishes to compensate for the formidable winter in store for us, for there is no doubt that the winter is severe and that energy resources for that reason hold and have always held a most important place throughout our history.

The famous Viking mariner, Leif Ericsson, already knew our Atlantic coast a thou-sand years ago. But it would appear that Jacques Cartier, who came to settle here in 1534, was the first European to do so. When he returned from his voyages which had led him up the St. Lawrence River to the present site of Montreal, Cartier extolled in vain the richness of the vegetation and the abundance and variety of the fish and game. Before Champlain, who came here in 1608, no one wished to face the snow and cold-ness of our winter.

The history of European settlement on the vast expanses of Canadian territory was in large part one of ingenuity in building and in the use of energy in such a winter en-vironment. The first houses were of Breton and Norman design and they were heated with huge quantities of wood which was burned in the large fireplaces located at each end of the ground floor.

---

* Based on the English-language notes issued in the Seminar documentation as HBP/SEM.17/CRP.1.

† Vancouver and Mar del Plata were the sites of the United Nations conferences on Human Settlements (1976) and Water (1977).

While the wood was blazing, the house stayed quite comfortable, although most of the heat was lost in the chimneys. But when the embers were dying, the chimneys stopped drawing, the air current was reversed and gusts of cold air blew into the house. Over a century went by before this primitive system could be replaced. In order to achieve this it was necessary to await a very important event—the installation in the country of a small blast furnace which was used to process iron ore and cast it. From that time on it was possible to manufacture large iron cooking stoves, heated with wood, whose cooking surface was sometimes as large as two square metres. It was first noted that the fire lasted longer in the stoves than in the fireplaces and that the surface itself helped to heat the house. Then, instead of connecting the exhaust pipes directly to the chimneys, the stoves were placed in the centre of the ground floor and large sheet metal pipes were installed near the ceiling to spread the heat from the stove throughout the entire floor. Then all that had to be done was to block the hearth in order to prevent cold air from entering. Thus efficient central heating, revolutionary for that era, was invented. From that time on, houses in Canada became very comfortable throughout the winter, and Canadian homes built after 1760 were designed to be heated by box stoves rather than the open fireplaces formerly used.

About 1850 the Industrial Revolution brought the use of coal, first in box stoves and later in furnaces installed in the basement, to supply hot water to the radiators, which would henceforth be installed in every room of the house. Then, in this century, all these furnaces were converted or replaced so that oil could be burned instead of coal.

But the Industrial Revolution, which had begun with coal and had been so stimulated by the abundance and versatility of oil, assumed that there was no limit to the quantities available. Oil was so cheap that it was unnecessary to insulate houses heated with it, huge cars could be built without concern for their gas consumption, and electricity could be manufactured cheaply in hungry oil-fired thermal generators. From that time onwards oil became the world's most prized resource. Such a state of affairs was evidently not without risks. The rapid rise in the price of oil and its consequences for many countries have made us reconsider our attitude towards oil resources that we once thought to be inexhaustible.

According to the most optimistic predictions, including those of this Commission, oil production will no longer meet the demand between now and the year 2000, and shortages could begin to be felt between 1985 and 1995. It is clear that we will have to think of replacing this fuel and that the more quickly we decide where and how this can be done, the better. For oil is more than a source of energy. It is an essential feedstock of modern industry, and this type of use must have priority. During the period of transition, oil will continue to play a very important role. However, we must recognize that after rapidly reaching the peak of consumption, oil production will decline to an appreciable extent.

It is clear that oil is only one example among many others, although most of our consumers think that this is only a passing crisis, linked solely and directly to oil. We are all inclined to forget that other non-renewable resources, like gas, are also threatened. Water, which we neglect, coal and wood: all these riches which will be invaluable to us tomorrow must be conserved, preserved and put to better use. These resources are directly related to our human settlements, to our way of life, and to the quality of life.

In a few years all the countries represented here, which together now consume some three-quarters of the world's energy, will have to make fundamental decisions regarding the quality of life of their citizens. In addition, it will be increasingly necessary for these decisions to harmonize and combine with the aspirations and needs of the developing countries. In co-operation with these countries, we must find solutions which will make it possible for them to make rapid progress towards efficiency in the use of energy and indeed towards a standard of living in harmony with their rightful aspirations. As for conserving energy, we have no choice. However, in order to find new energy sources, we will have to choose from the possible options those which will suit our needs best without our incurring ruinous debts or sacrificing the environment.

A mere glance at the Seminar programme reveals that the whole range of energy questions related to human settlements will be examined. We all have a great deal to learn, and we will do this by learning from one another. We hope that the discussions beginning today will produce a number of promising ideas and techniques. Perhaps they have not yet all been tested but there will be cases when their application could produce unexpected and extremely advantageous solutions. Nevertheless we will not find miraculous, overall solutions, and our progress will be laborious.

However, next week, the study tour in Quebec, Ontario, and Prince Edward Island will give you an opportunity to evaluate some efforts that have been made in our country to apply new ideas that could prove to be solutions to a number of housing and energy problems.

Partly because of our climate, we Canadians consume more energy *per capita* than any other nation in the world. We will be eagerly awaiting innovative suggestions from delegations and their experts. We are convinced that you can help us to make better energy plans for our future, so that we may ensure that our descendants living in this snow-bound country have as full a life as we do.

On behalf of my fellow Canadians, I wish you a pleasant stay in our country. I also wish you stimulating and productive discussions.

ADDRESS*

by JANEZ STANOVNIK

Executive Secretary of the United Nations Economic Commission for Europe (ECE)

Ottawa, 3 October 1977

Distinguished delegates and ladies and gentlemen: There are few areas which show such tangible results of economic growth as that of human settlements. Growth over the three decades since the Second World War cannot be better illustrated than from an aircraft looking down on the cities which have all acquired "doughnuts" around their traditional centres. This is equally true for this continent and for the old continent over the Atlantic Ocean. It is in these human settlements that economic growth is seen in its true dimension. It is through human settlements that people experience the beneficial results of increasing production, known to us as economic growth.

Settlements are built to last for years to come, for decades. Whatever we build today establishes a solid infrastructure for the rest of our lives and probably for those of our children, and maybe even of our children's children. Settlements in a way predetermine what will happen tomorrow. It is a particularly sensitive area because if we are wrong in our calculations, in translating our visions into brick and stone, we may very well lay the foundations of future tension—if what we have done comes into conflict with actual trends. It is important that we approach this subject with the utmost care and feeling of responsibility not only to our own generation, but also to the generations to come. I would, therefore, like to invite you to have a true sense of history and responsibility.

I often meet people who say: "How far into the future can you really see? Ten years? Twenty years? All the rest is Utopia." Perhaps so, but if we cannot predict the future there are certain elements of the future of which we can already be quite sure. If there are any of you who have doubts about the dimension of change, may I invite you to gather with me for a short trip back into the period after the Second World War—into the early 1950s, for instance—and mentally foresee what will happen during the 25 years up to 1975. You would have been amazed if I had told you that we would conquer the law of gravity, that we would reach to the moon. You would have been surprised if I had told you that we would decipher the genetic code. You would have been surprised if I had told you that in these 25 years, whatever happened on the earth—in whatever corner, would immediately be seen and heard everywhere else. That we would increase our production approximately threefold. That the production of steel in our Economic

---

*Taken from the English text issued in the Seminar documentation as HBP/SEM.17/CRP.2.

Commission for Europe region would increase threefold from 200 million to 600 million tons. That the increase in the use of energy would be threefold and that we would burn in these 25 years as much energy as the human race had burned since Adam and Eve. In 25 years. That there would be fantastic economic growth without parallel in human history. Because never before have we had a period of 25 years of uninterrupted economic growth at the high rate of 5 per cent, or even more—never before. But there would not only be successes, there would be problems. We would end these 25 years with 4 billion people as against 2 billion in 1950. There would be other problems. There would be inflation.

And in the early 1970s we would face one crisis after another. There would be an environmental crisis, a population crisis, a food crisis, a monetary crisis and an energy crisis. All these would be the subjects of big international conferences. There would be a very important conference in Vancouver where we would reflect on this process of urbanization.

At the beginning of this century there were only 11 cities with one million inhabitants and 6 out of these 11 were in Europe. The number had grown to almost 200 in 1975, of which more than half were in the developing world. I would have had to foretell in 1950 that there would be a terrific difference between cities in the developed world and those in developing countries. Cities in the developed world would be the consequence of industrial growth, but cities in the developing countries would not grow necessarily as a result of economic progress; they would grow because there was no employment in agriculture. They would be more a sign of pauperization than of progress and would create growing problems.

However, this forward view would show that the food problem might be overcome as a result of the marvellous discoveries of science. There would be other problems, among which, of course, would be the problem of energy—a matter of the greatest concern. So great would be the problems by the beginning of the 1970s that the majority of mankind would demand a new international economic order, an order which would be built on the principles of justice, equality, sovereignty and interdependence.

On the basis of past progress and problems, we should now take a look into the future. Shall we have more of the same? Or shall we have a different kind of development in the future? There are material and political factors at work which tell me—and this is a personal view—that the future will not be just a continuation of the past. The Moloch of gross national product will cease to be all-powerful. There will be demands for a somewhat different kind of development for a different kind of growth.

But before we say anything about what the future might hold, it would be wise to consider why things have been happening in the way they did. Why did this tremendous progress occur? Why has progress created such terrific problems? The economists will tell you that a singularly important factor influencing economic development has been technology. So important that we all thought technology could resolve everything. Everything was dependent on technology—only technology was dependent on itself. Technology seemed to be autonomous, independent of the human will which gave it direction.

Developments in technology have become so energy-intensive that what we have considered as being the results of technology might very well be considered as the product of energy. Only 1 per cent of the driving force in modern manufacturing industries is human energy, while 99 per cent is geochemically stored and transformed energy. Why have we used so much energy? The immediate answer is that it was so cheap, relatively speaking. Labour was becoming increasingly expensive while energy was cheap. Market forces had fixed the relative prices of human and natural energy. Organized labour was powerful in the industrialized countries and was able to gain for the workers an increase in the distribution of income. The bargaining power of the developing countries, on the other hand, was weak. As a result, the prices of primary materials, and particularly of energy, were depressed over this period while the prices of the goods we produced with the same energy in our manufacturing industries were growing.

Statistics in the ECE study* on energy economy and efficiency show beyond any doubt, for all the industrialized countries, that prices of energy have been either stable or declining while prices and wages in the industrialized countries have been constantly growing over this period. As might have been expected, energy was freely substituted for human labour.

We have developed various energy-intensive structures in the economy, and we have moved from one source of energy to another. These developments have profoundly affected human settlements. It is not only industry that has become energy-intensive. Everything has become energy-intensive.

Settlements are widely spread out because one of the marvels of the abundance of energy is the private automobile. The private car has become a necessity to move us from the places where we live to the places where we work. Therefore, transportation has become an integral part of the way in which settlements are planned and built.

We have been using energy so abundantly that, representing only 25 per cent of humanity, we burn about three-quarters of the total energy used today. If everybody in the world wanted to have the same *per capita* consumption of energy as we have today in our region, then the developing countries would have to consume nine times as much energy as they actually do. The unequal distribution of energy reflects the great inequalities which prevail in the world today.

We are deliberating something which concerns not only us, it concerns everybody. The developing countries very rightly ask how they will industrialize if we burn all the geochemically stored energy beforehand. While considering problems in the regional framework, we must be constantly aware that those we are faced with have profound global implications and touch on the sensitive questions to be answered in considering demands for a new international economic order. If the future cannot be just more of the same, but should be in many respects different from the past, the question arises: What kind of economic development are we to have in the future? Firstly, economic growth, not zero growth. There must be growth, but growth with distribution. In the past, we believed that if there were a higher GNP, the product would be automatically more evenly distributed. This has not happened. There must be a deliberate policy effort to arrive at a more just distribution within and between nations. If economic growth is to make the slightest contribution to our civilization, then it must promote

---

* *Increased Energy Economy and Efficiency in the ECE Region*, E/ECE/883/Rev.1, United Nations, New York, 1976.

human values. Keynes rightly said that any economic system, to be viable, must be economically efficient, socially just, and promote individual freedom.

We can accept that economic forces will work for greater efficiency. But the same forces which work for greater productivity and efficiency will not necessarily work for a more just distribution, or for greater individual freedom. We must therefore make a deliberate effort to achieve three aims: economic efficiency, social justice and individual freedom.

This must not be economic growth as it was in the past. It must be a "conservation" growth in which resources are used rationally and in which Nature is not destroyed. Non-waste and low-waste technology should become part and parcel of the model for future growth. This does not mean that those who are economically powerful should concentrate on their territories whatever they desire. Why should a nation which has neither bauxite nor energy have aluminium industries? Why should industries not be more equitably distributed in the world? The developing countries at the Lima conference asked for 25 per cent of the world's industrial capacity by the end of the century. Why not?

In recent years our countries have increasingly imported manufactured products from developing countries because we have lost our comparative advantages in a number of industries. This is not only for energy reasons but also because our labour costs are rising. It pays to import more manufactured products from developing countries. This development leads us to a more equitable distribution of industry in the world.

What matters in the future is not just that we have higher GNP figures but how these GNP figures are distributed. In the first and second development decades, the developing countries overall attained a 5 per cent rate of growth of GNP, but when you examine the situation, you find that a few achieved not 5 per cent but 10 per cent or 15 per cent growth and that one billion people, on the other hand, achieved practically no growth at all. This question of growth distribution should be given much greater attention.

In the future, we must be much more environmentally minded. Civilizations have been great in history not because they left behind piles of tin cans and empty containers but because they left behind cathedrals and cultural values of a more permanent nature.

How, in this context, will the energy outlook appear? Will there be enough energy to ensure this new pattern of growth? There are some who think that we are coming to the end of the rope. Some oil companies argue there is no need to worry, that there is plenty of energy. At the World Energy Conference recently in Istanbul, eminent nuclear scientists agreed that there is no reason to worry because the prospect of nuclear energy is just before us. I think that the truth on this future energy question is somewhat evenly divided between the optimists and pessimists. Geochemically stored, recoverable resources of energy are limited. Some people will tell you that if we rely only on oil as the primary source of energy we have enough to live in our kind of civilization for another 30 to 40 years. Others will point out that we have coal—enough to live for almost another 70 years. Finally, there are some who remind us that there is natural gas and that there is enough gas for another 10 years. If we compare these projections made by various companies and research institutes, we find pessimists who say we have enough energy for 50 years, and optimists who say we can go on for 150 years.

I do not care who is right. One thing is quite sure: conventional energy resources are finite and exhaustible. If conventional sources of energy are exhaustible, what then?

Some nuclear optimists tell us that while we have enough uranium-235 only for a short time, it will last for 230 years if it is used to make plutonium. Nuclear pollution is a controversial subject and I will not deal with that, but I would point out that the breeder, of necessity, breeds plutonium, and plutonium is a very dangerous substance indeed. I do not say that for that reason we should not use any particular source of energy, but we must be aware that in using this source of energy, we shall have to have certain international safeguards and controls. Accordingly, if we want to have nuclear energy, we should not complain if more international controls are instituted and sovereignty is limited in the interests of protecting human lives.

The crucial question is that, if we want more and more energy, clearly there is only one source which can provide us with this additional energy in the present state of knowledge and this is the nuclear source. We must realize that there will be more nuclear plants, not just conventional reactors, but also breeder reactors.

Is there any alternative? Yes, there is the appealing alternative of conservation. We could use less energy. We could waste much less energy. We should invest more of our intellectual and research capacities in the search for renewable sources of energy. The final answer for our civilization is neither energy from conventional nuclear reactors nor from breeder reactors, because even they have a limited life span. Only renewable energy—solar energy, geothermal energy and photosynthetic energy—has an unlimited life. These three sources have, so far, often been ignored and neglected. I suggest that they must be given much greater attention and more resources in future than was the case in the past.

We are in a period of transition so far as energy is concerned. I am not preaching the collapse of our civilization. Far from it. I hope I have conveyed my thoughts clearly. I do not think that we have come to the end of the rope. But we have choices to make. The choice is basically between nuclear proliferation and conservation. I should like to suggest that conservation is a very realistic option. It must be taken more seriously than was the case in the past.

I am therefore deliberately using this occasion and this forum to say as clearly as I can that there must be more public participation in these efforts if we are to succeed in achieving results in conservation. If people will change their behaviour, if there is a more willing participation by the people in this terrific effort which confronts our civilization, then there will necessarily and logically be less state intervention. But if there is no participation, our civilization must still survive, and the result will be more regulatory action by the public authorities. I believe that international organizations, and not least the ECE, have a very special responsibility in this respect. In a week's time, on Monday next, I shall be speaking to the Belgrade Review Meeting of the Conference on Security and Co-operation in Europe, and what I say to you today, I will say again in a week's time in Belgrade. I think that the time has come when international co-operation cannot remain only at the level of governments. It must take place also at the level of business people and of the man in the street. People must change their behaviour if we are to have the full success that we need.

This is of direct relevance to the subject-matter of your conference. You will be thinking of the human settlements of the future. In the developed regions of the world, it is in human settlements that we are today using practically half the total energy consumed. But, what is even more interesting is that human settlements are largely using the type of energy which is the scarcest of all—liquid fuels. And it is also interesting that the area of human settlements is where the greatest potentiality of energy saving occurs. You can economize on energy consumption in industry but not to a tremendous extent. Of course you could save a great deal in transportation, but this already comes close to the question of human settlements. But the greatest savings of all could be made in human settlements properly speaking, and particularly in the heating and cooling of buildings. There is action to be taken in the short term and in the long term. In the short term, of course, steps to improve insulation, the control of temperatures, and other measures of this kind can be taken.

We have seen, both in this continent and in Europe, that when the energy crisis occurred in 1974 we suddenly had an apparent saving of energy. OECD reported remarkable energy savings in 1974. I have some reservations on the subject of this particular saving of energy. First of all, it occurred under the pressure of price measures and, secondly, it occurred at a time when economic activity was declining.

The real test is coming now. Shall we save and conserve energy year by year, not just because of the diminution of economic activity, nor on account of our standard of living, but on account of making rational and more efficient use of energy? This could be done. It could be done in the short-run and on a long-term basis. At this conference you will be more concerned with the long-term aspects—how to plan for the future. In planning for the future, you will not, of course, suddenly start planning settlements now only from the energy conservation point of view. I would certainly not suggest that you should take only energy saving into consideration. There are many many other important considerations that you will take into account when planning settlements for the future. Yet one has to remember that energy was a non-existent, or even negative, factor in planning settlements in the past; it was assumed that energy was so abundant that you could easily sacrifice it for the sake of architectural form. However, when you look into the future of settlements now, you will give due weight to the energy conservation factor which is such a central preoccupation of the economically developed region covered by the ECE.

I feel that we are here confronted with such a basic challenge to our civilization that no time spent in reflecting on the path we must follow is really lost. Whatever we do in this matter will bear not only on our own lives but will be decisive for the lives of those who come after us. We must accept that we are transitory visitors to this earth. We must not leave it in a worse shape than that in which we received it from those who went before us.

PART II

Chapter 1

ENERGY USE AND ENERGY CONSERVATION
IN HUMAN SETTLEMENTS

The immediate effects of the 1973 energy crisis were relatively short-lived, but the crisis provoked a re-evaluation of the use of energy in all sectors of national economies, a re-evaluation that is still going on. Prices of most forms of energy have risen markedly, imposing severe burdens on individual family budgets, on the provision of public services, on the level of activity of national economies and on external balances of payments. Behind such problems there is the prospect that energy supplies, at any price, will become very scarce in the future. As the Executive Secretary of ECE remarked in his opening address to the Seminar:

> If we compare these projections made by various companies and research institutes, we find pessimists who say we have enough energy for 50 years, and optimists who say we can go on for 150 years.

> . . . One thing is quite sure: conventional energy resources are finite and exhaustible. (CRP.2, see also pp. 14-15)*

Human settlements, however these are defined, account for a large part of total energy use. As pointed out in the U.K. contribution (R.43), houses and other dwellings are particularly important because in total they account for more than half the primary energy used in buildings, and because they are occupied by individuals who normally cannot pass on the costs of scarce or interrupted energy supplies to others, as is possible to a considerable extent in the industrial and other sectors. Human settlements are also extremely durable. A community, a city or a village may last for centuries. The individual buildings in it may have an average life of 60 to 100 years. Transport systems are also long-lived, even though the cars, buses or other units of which they are composed may need replacement in a time frame of 5 to 15 years. If there is a clear prospect that conventional energy supplies will be depleted within 50 to 150 years, this will affect many of the buildings and other elements of the human settlements we have now and that we will create in the near future.

The Ottawa Seminar, therefore, was concerned with the future as well as with the present: with the implications of long-term energy supply prospects as well as with the needs and opportunities that are evident in the human settlements of today. Certainly the Seminar was concerned with the situation up to the end of the present century.

---

* References in this form, immediately following the quotation, are to the official documentation of the Ottawa Seminar (see pp. 161 - 166). Where possible, references are to paragraphs; alternatively, they are to the page numbers of the English-language versions of the documents. Minor corrections to style, etc., have been made by the editor. References to other sources are made as footnotes.

THE PRESENT DEMAND FOR ENERGY IN HUMAN SETTLEMENTS IN THE ECE REGION AND ANTICIPATED TRENDS

"The future starts in the present" (R.15, para. 46), and the use of energy in the human settlements that exist at present must be the basis for any forecasts of how the situation may change in the future.

Human settlements, defined in ECE Energy Statistics as "households and other consumers" (including commerce and tertiary activities) absorbed in 1974 36 per cent of the total final energy consumption in the ECE region (see Table 1). The tonnage involved in direct use was about 1,425 million tce (tons of coal equivalent), but in order to make the deliveries of secondary forms of energy possible, another 700 to 800 million tce had to be committed by the energy conversion industries. These are huge quantities, making the domestic sector second in importance after "industry", the transport sector ranging behind.

TABLE 1. *Percentage breakdown of total final energy consumption, 1974*

Region	Industry	Domestic sector	Transport	Total final consumption
Western Europe	43	37	20	100
Eastern Europe	55	36	9	100
North America	33	36	32	100
ECE region	41	36	23	100

Not merely are the proportions of energy used by the domestic sector very similar in all three subregions, the figures for individual countries are also usually similar to the regional average.

This would seem to indicate that the differences in climate, national income, degree of industrialization, primary energy pattern, energy consumption habits, building regulations, types of dwellings, social and economic systems etc. either outweigh each other or are of lesser importance than the common factors (urbanization, urban planning, heating technologies, energy requirements for light, cooking and warm water etc.).   (R.42, para. 2.)

Despite the overall similarity in relative importance of the domestic sector, there are substantial differences among ECE countries in the *per capita* consumption of energy. There are also marked differences in the dominant fuel:

Western Europe, whose total energy demand is strongly based on oil, exhibits an equal preference for oil in the case of household demand: 48 per cent of total household requirements are for heating oil. North American households, in line with the general energy pattern, rely on natural gas to an extent of 43 per cent, whilst eastern European households, as well as the economies at large, are still coal-based (42 per cent if hard and brown coal are combined).   (R.42, para. 3.)

In the early 1970s the ECE region therefore showed the effect of a period of development which had begun about 50 years earlier. This period was marked by the rapid expansion of electricity, oil and natural gas demand and distribution systems, and by the use of the internal combustion engine in road vehicles. The apparent difference between eastern Europe, with its continuing dependence on solid fuel, and the remainder of the ECE region which was, by the early 1970s, heavily dependent on fluid hydrocarbons, is mainly a difference of timing: the proportion of solid fuel is expected to decline substantially in eastern Europe also in the next two decades.

The substantial differences that exist among ECE countries in their levels of *per capita* energy use are not easily explicable, and in particular are not necessarily evidence of waste. As a Finnish contribution to the Ottawa Seminar recognized:

> In practice the comparisons are very difficult to make because there are not enough statistics available. Differences between countries exist in the ways of calculating dwelling areas, energy consumptions and even degree-days. Nevertheless when the comparison is made based on the available material it can be noticed that the relative energy consumption in Finnish dwellings is only 50 - 70% of that in some middle European countries.   (R.23, p. 3.)

There is little doubt that fuel economy in Finland, especially in dwellings, is much more effective than in the vast majority of other ECE countries. But more detailed comparisons are difficult because of climatic differences between and within countries, differences in proportions of housing of different type, levels of income, etc. It is, therefore, very difficult to "prove", at the level of international comparisons, energy waste, the effect of poor insulation standards, etc.

The "huge quantities" of energy used in the domestic sector in the early 1970s were to a considerable extent a reflection of consumer reaction to a period of little more than a decade in which energy prices, and especially the price of oil, had been relatively low in comparison to earlier times, and particularly in comparison to world prices since 1973. In the United Kingdom, for example, *per capita* consumption of energy for all purposes in 1952, at about 4.3 tce per year, was practically identical to the level in 1900: in the intervening period, growth in demand to meet new energy uses had been matched by improvements in the efficiency of energy use. By 1973, however, *per capita* consumption had increased over 40 per cent in two decades to reach 6.2 tce per year, with the low prices providing little incentive to economy or efficiency.*

The same phenomenon was observable in other countries and in other forms of energy. Woodson,[†] for example, has compiled a table (Table 2) that clearly indicates the incentive to increased use of electricity in the domestic sector in the U.S.A. during the last two decades.

---

* United Kingdom, Royal Commission on Environmental Pollution, Sixth Report: *Nuclear Power and the Environment*, Cmnd 6618, 1976, fig. 21.

† T. T. Woodson, Residential energy use, *in* Craig B. Smith (ed.), *Efficient Electricity Use*, Pergamon Press, New York, 1976.

TABLE 2

	1950	1960	1970
Per capita disposable income (Constant $1967)	1881	2155	2950
Average residential electricity price ¢ kWh)	2.88	2.47	2.10
Consumer price index (1967 = 100)	72.1	88.7	116.3
Household appliance consumer price index	138.3	117.9	104.1

In the U.S.A., and throughout the ECE region, households became more affluent, and the price of both energy and energy-using domestic appliances remained steady or decreased in real terms.

Viewed against this background, therefore, the problem of increasing the efficiency of energy use in human settlements is one involving changes both to a long-term trend towards dependence on sources of fossil fuel (especially oil and gas) that have only a limited life in terms of known or anticipated resources, and to a more recent situation when the price of energy in all its forms was such as to encourage use and to neglect economy and efficiency. The magnitude of the changes needed was indicated in another background paper prepared by the ECE Secretariat. Even if a slower rate of growth in energy demand is assumed in the years ahead than was characteristic of the 1960s, the dependence on oil and gas is likely to increase rather than decrease:

> . . . only one region is likely to reduce its relative direct dependence on hydro-carbons: North America. All others are likely to increase their relative dependency, even those regions which, like eastern Europe and western Europe, have practically no, or rather limited, hydrocarbon reserves. For ECE as a whole, the dependency ratio will grow from 56 per cent in 1974 to 63 per cent in the year 2000. The amounts of hydrocarbons consumed will increase by 3.3 times.

> . . . *as with the direct dependency on hydrocarbons, the indirect dependency (via electricity and heat) will increase in the ECE region in absolute and relative terms,* i.e. the vulnerability to supply disruptions and/or substantial price increases will grow. The absolute tonnage of hydrocarbons necessary to cover the needs of households for electricity and heat would increase by almost six times.
>
> (R.44, paras. 25, 28.)

On the basis of such calculations, the Secretariat paper concludes that:

> The desirable disconnexion of energy supplies to human settlements from rapidly depleting hydrocarbons, with the help of electricity, heat, synthetic liquids and gases, will not materialize during the next twenty to thirty years. The main reasons are inadequate growth rates of supplies of steam coal, inadequate growth rates of supplies of hydroelectricity and too small initial shares of nuclear power in the electricity balance. (R.44, para. 31.)

The ECE Secretariat paper also concludes that world energy supplies, mainly from conventional sources, will suffice to meet energy demand in the ECE region during the remainder of the twentieth century, although prices may be expected to rise and the region will become more vulnerable to supply interruptions. There are, however, many reasons why steps should be—and are being—taken to reduce the growth of energy demand in the region to levels well below the rates assumed in the ECE Secretariat paper. These include, for example, the very great burden of current fuel prices on the external trade balances of countries that currently import a large proportion of their fuel needs, such as France, Czechoslovakia, Sweden and Finland. In a wider context, another reason for economy was mentioned by the Executive Secretary in his address to the Ottawa Seminar:

> We [in the ECE region] have been using energy so abundantly that, representing only 25 per cent of humanity, we burn about three-quarters of the total energy used today. . . . The unequal distribution of energy reflects the great inequalities which prevail in the world today.
>
> . . . The developing countries very rightly ask how they will industrialize if we burn all the geochemically-stored energy beforehand.
>
> (CRP.2; see also p. 13.)

Certainly few countries in the ECE region feel energy-rich at present; some, like Canada, have been forced to abandon such an attitude even during the present decade. The United Kingdom, and a few other countries around the North Sea, have in the same period gained access to offshore oil and gas resources that temporarily ease the impact of shortages and price rises. However, the United Kingdom contribution recognizes that "Although the U.K. is moving into net energy surplus the case for active energy conservation is as compelling as throughout the developed world" (R.43, p. 3). By the end of the century it is anticipated that the United Kingdom will again be a net importer of energy.

THE PRINCIPAL USES OF ENERGY IN HUMAN SETTLEMENTS

Although the "domestic sector", as defined in ECE and similar statistical sources, represents a major element in total energy use, it does not include all energy use in human settlements as the latter term is normally understood. In particular, the large amounts of energy used in transportation within individual human settlements must be taken into account; some might argue that inter-urban transportation is also an integral part of the energy needs of human settlements. It is, indeed, unrealistic to draw rigid divisions between the forms of energy use; after all, much of the energy consumption by "industry" is also essential for the functioning of human settlements, since it is this industry which provides much of the employment. If office employment is included, for energy statistics purposes, in the domestic sector, it seems rather arbitrary to separate from the domestic sector buildings used for other types of employment.

When viewed in terms of the ways the energy is actually used, the arbitrary nature of his division is less marked, however, since the energy needs of the human settlements

sector may conveniently be defined as energy used in buildings and energy used in transportation, especially urban transportation. Further, in homes, shops, offices and other
similar buildings, space and water heating, cooling and lighting account for the over-
whelming proportion of energy use, in contrast to the industrial sector where substantial amounts of energy are used in the industrial processes themselves. This can be
illustrated from Fisk's summary of net energy consumption "per dwelling" in the
'Composite Ten'* countries in 1973 (Table 3).

TABLE 3. *Annual net energy consumption per dwelling
in the 'Composite Ten' 1973*

	Gigajoules	Per cent
Space heating (74) ⎫ Space cooling (2) ⎬	76	65
Water heating	18	15
Television, lighting, etc.	17	14
Cooking	7	6
	118	100

The figures in Table 3 indicate only the broad proportions of consumption. It is not
clear, for instance, whether the data from each country refer only to residential buildings, or to the "domestic sector" as a whole, including offices and other buildings in
the tertiary sector. Similarly, Fisk notes that although most uses of energy are comparable throughout the "Composite Ten", the figure of 17 GJ for television, lighting
and miscellaneous uses would drop to only 6 GJ if North America were excluded.
Despite these data problems, the CIB analysis confirms the view that

> For the ECE region as a whole, between 70 and 90 per cent of the energy used in
> this ["household and other consumers"] sector is for space heating. Lighting
> proper, excluding other electrical appliances, accounts for only 2 - 3 per cent of
> energy consumption in this sector. . . . The remainder is used for appliances (using
> mostly electricity and gas, but also some coal) and for water heating.†

The ECE Secretariat provided a similar table to that of Fisk in one of its contributions to the Ottawa Seminar (R.42, para. 5), and used it to emphasize the important,
and often ignored, point that

> . . . energy conservation efforts are likely to yield a much better result if directed
> towards heating, ventilation and insulation, than towards other uses.
>
> (R.42, para. 6.)

---

* This phrase was coined by Fisk to indicate the ten countries that submitted monographs concerning
national energy use in buildings to the CIB Energy Conservation Symposium in 1976. These countries are:
Belgium, Canada, Denmark, France, Ireland, the Netherlands, Norway, Sweden, the United Kingdom and
the U.S.A. See D. J. Fisk, A comparative summary of national energy consumptions and potential savings
in buildings, *in* Roger C. Courtney (ed.), *Energy Conservation in the Built Environment*, CIB, 1976.

† Economic Commission for Europe, *Increased Energy Economy and Efficiency in the ECE Region*,
E/ECE/883/Rev.1, United Nations, New York, 1976, para. 124.

The dominant roles played by space heating and cooling, and to a lesser extent by water heating, have another significance in the context of the long-term supply and use of energy. Space or water heating needs can in principle be satisfied in a number of ways, as indeed they are in most countries at present. A variety of fuels can be used: peat, lignite, coal and other solid fuels, oil, gas and electricity either in "primary" form from hydroelectric or nuclear resources, or through the conversion of other fuels into electricity. The heat may be generated by "decentralized" burning at the point of end-use, as in fireplaces, stoves or domestic furnaces, or it may be supplied from a centralized source such as an electricity generating station or a district heating plant. The space and water heating needs can be met through dependence on a single form of energy or by utilizing multiple forms. A single house, for example, may use oil or gas for central heating, have supplementary electric heaters for both space and water needs, and a fireplace for aesthetic reasons. Further, unconventional forms of energy generation (including solar, wind and solid waste sources, heat pumps, etc.) can also be utilized to provide space or water heating, and some of these unconventional forms may be particularly suited for such applications. This great degree of flexibility means that the domestic sector is likely to have a particular importance for future energy planning, since similar flexibility is not characteristic of many of the other principal demands for energy that comprise national needs. In other words, if national energy planning requires substantial shifts from oil, gas or other fuels, these shifts may be concentrated in the human settlements sector.

There is a strong contrast between the flexibility with which space and water heating needs can be met and the relative inflexibility of the other principal use of energy in human settlements: urban transport systems. Surveying the transport sector as a whole, the ECE Secretariat found that:

> The most important primary form of energy for the transport sector is oil in the form of gasoline, diesel fuel and kerosene. These products account for approximately 85 to 95 per cent of the sector demand, with gasoline accounting for the major share. The remaining 5 to 15 per cent of the demand is for electricity and, in particular in eastern Europe, for coal. . . . The trend is towards a more or less complete elimination of solid fuels in favour of electricity and diesel fuel, and towards a further absolute and relative increase in the use of petroleum products.*

Within urban areas, the dominance of gasoline and diesel fuels in transportation is even greater, with electricity playing a relatively insignificant role. In its paper for the Ottawa Seminar, the ECE Secretariat suggests that hydrocarbons account for 99 per cent or more of the transportation energy used in urban areas in all three ECE sub-regions (R.44, table 4). Little change in this pattern is foreseen in the remainder of the century, although other contributions to the Seminar suggest that electric vehicles may play an increasing role (see Chapter 2).

THE CASE FOR CONSERVATION

As noted already, the ECE Secretariat sees the disconnection of human settlements from their present heavy dependence on rapidly depleting hydrocarbons as desirable

---

* *Ibid.*, para. 80.

but unlikely, at least in the present century. To the extent that it is capable of being achieved at all, such a disconnection appears to depend mainly on a rapid expansion of nuclear-generated electricity, and there are many who would regard this as an undesirable alternative. The other option is to reduce the growth of energy use:

> The crucial question is that, if we want more and more energy, clearly there is only one source which can provide us with this additional energy in the present state of knowledge and this is the nuclear source. We must realize there will be more nuclear plants, not just conventional reactors, but also breeder reactors.

> Is there any alternative? Yes, there is the appealing alternative of conservation. We could use less energy. We could waste much less energy. We should invest more of our intellectual and research capacities in the search for renewable sources of energy. . . .

> . . . The choice is basically between nuclear proliferation and conservation. I should like to suggest that conservation is a very realistic option. It must be taken more seriously than was the case in the past.

> (CRP.2, see also p.15.)

The Ottawa Seminar was not wholly concerned with energy conservation in human settlements but with the whole range of interactions between energy and human settlements, including the impact of new energy supply technology on human settlements. Nevertheless, conservation was necessarily a major theme, not least because of the enormous waste of energy that takes place in human settlements. Losses, it is true, take place elsewhere in the chain of energy supply through to the point of end-use. There are substantial losses in extraction and much smaller ones in transport, distribution and storage of energy. Other losses are "technological"; for example, the inefficiencies endemic in internal combustion engines or in electricity generating stations. What distinguishes energy waste in human settlements, normally at the point of end-use, is that such waste is much more easily eliminated. It includes

> . . . losses due to bad insulation, bad load shaping, wastage, i.e. losses which were not imposed by nature or technology, but which were tolerated by man, and which might be called "human-decision induced" . . . the distinction made is . . . a useful indication: improvements are more likely to materialize with respect to losses induced or tolerated by man than with respect to naturally induced losses. . . .*

As a result of its preliminary survey on *Increased Energy Economy and Efficiency in the ECE Region,* the ECE Secretariat concluded that the scope for improvement in efficiency in the ECE area in the "households and other consumers" sector was greater than in any other part of the flow of energy except at the stage of extraction. An improvement of 15 to 40 per cent was seen as feasible by the early 1990s. In the light of subsequent, more detailed, analysis within the framework of the CIB's Working Group on Energy Conservation (W67) and other bodies, such an estimate seems likely to be on the conservative side so far as technical feasibility is concerned: it may be more realistic in terms of the institutional and similar problems involved in implementing large-scale

---

* *Ibid.,* para. 145.

programmes of action to achieve such increased efficiency within this time-frame.

HOW, NOT WHAT

The need for conservation can be more easily expressed than conservation can be achieved. This is not because feasible means of achieving the necessary savings or improved efficiency are not available but because at the present time most countries in the ECE region lack the political commitment and the public acceptability required for such savings, and consequently lack also the programmes and systems through which such savings must be realized. The situation is, significantly, perceived particularly keenly by those who are most concerned with the identification of the "What?"—the technical means needed to achieve the savings. The CIB paper for the Ottawa Seminar, for example, urged that:

> Even if there is a firm need for further research, energy conservation will only come about as a result of action. . . The need for further research should not . . . be used as an excuse for postponing action, when such actions would appear to make both technical and economic sense. . . .

> It is difficult to imagine that the building stock can be brought into harmony with the energy supply and the fuel prices of the future, if early and efficient efforts are not made to cope with the situation. There is a need for strong political decisions, aimed at reducing energy consumption in buildings.

(R.15, paras. 44, 60.)

1.4   Similar concern was expressed in other contributions to the Ottawa Seminar, and particular emphasis was placed on the lack of public perception of the situation that is likely to develop in the years ahead: political initiative, it was felt, requires a stronger level of public acceptance for such initiatives than exists at present. One of the French contributions, for example, asked—and answered—this question:

> Ne va-t-il pas falloir inventer autre chose, analyser et peut-être remettre en cause les "tendances lourdes naturelles" de croissance de la consommation d'énergie? Voilà quelques-unes des interrogations importantes qui vont se poser aux hommes politiques et aux planificateurs. S'ils semblent avoir quelque réticence à les entendre jusqu'à présent, peut-être est-ce qu'ils devinent que les réponses qui pourront leur être apportées risquent parfois d'être en contradiction avec les aspirations des citoyens à une meilleure qualité de vie. C'est bien là que se situe le noeud du problème. . . .*   (R.11, p. 7.)

The validity of this answer was strongly emphasized by the Deputy Minister of Energy, Mines and Resources of Canada, in his banquet address to the Seminar participants:

> . . . without public acceptance of this secular change in the energy supply picture,

---

* *Editor's translation:* "Should we not do something different: investigate and perhaps call into question the "strong natural trends" of growth in energy use? These are some of the major questions that are arising for politicians and planners. If they seem rather reluctant to hear them up to now, this may be because they are aware that the answers which might be given to such questions are sometimes liable to be at variance with the desire of citizens for a better quality of life. This is the real crux of the problem. . . ."

and the need to adapt our patterns of energy use to it, any proposals for change, no matter how imaginative, will be imperfectly implemented. And the vulnerability of our way of life will remain. . . .

Recently, I have been travelling across Canada with some of my colleagues, endeavouring to increase awareness of energy problems and gauge acceptance of the current situation and of the policies we are implementing. It is often a frustrating and somewhat depressing experience—awareness and acceptance levels are far less than we had hoped for and reactions have frequently reflected only a regional perception of the problems with little recognition of the national or global perspective. . .

Public perceptions are slow to change and social habits even slower. While we may be good urban planners and good energy analysts, all that will be to no avail if we fail to communicate effectively with those who in turn must respond positively to our policies to make them truly effective. That is the immediate crisis, a crisis of communication. Failure to meet it effectively will guarantee an energy crisis within the next decade.*

Or, as the United Kingdom's paper summarised the situation:

. . . it is the lack of individual interest in achieving energy saving measures compared with the collective imperative of doing so that is at the root of the problem.
(R.43, p. 23.)

The Ottawa Seminar, therefore, was less concerned with *what* should be done to increase economy and efficiency in energy use in human settlements than with *how* such techniques can be implemented effectively. It was concerned with problems of policy development, of programme implementation, and with information and advice to national populations that, in many cases, remain unconvinced about the long-term need for such conservation, but whose co-operation is essential if action on the necessary scale is to be successful.

UNCERTAINTY

The difficulties involved in altering present patterns of supply and use are increased greatly by the considerable uncertainties involved in forecasting or defining desirable future patterns. Such uncertainties are most widely recognized in regard to energy supply, but the situation in regard to energy demand is equally problematic. On the supply side, for example, the traditional pattern of gearing exploration for fossil resources to the current pace of energy use means that some of the estimates of the life of oil, gas or coal reserves may be misleading: the "years' supply" figures normally quoted merely represent what it has been thought worthwhile to explore and prove at the present time. There have, however, been several authoritative suggestions in recent years that the long-term indications are that such new resources are becoming increasingly

---

* Gordon M. MacNabb, Notes for an address . . . to the ECE Seminar on habitat and energy, 13 October 1977, unpublished.

more difficult and expensive to find. Although fossil fuel reserves are unlikely to become *exhausted* in the foreseeable future, they may become *depleted* in the sense that the costs of extraction and transportation become excessive. Uncertainties also clearly exist in regard to the massive international trade in energy resources that is required by the present heavy dependence of the ECE region on hydrocarbons. The 1973 crisis was a clear indication of the vulnerability of advanced industrial economies, and the human settlements associated with them, to short- or longer-term interruptions in supply. Other significant uncertainties on the supply side include environmental pressures (affecting, for example, the speed of nuclear power development or the use of solid fuels or tar sands) and the prospects for new forms of energy.

1.3   On the demand side, however, the uncertainties are greater still, although they have gone largely unrecognized until recently in most countries. There has been, in many countries, little detailed analysis of demand; since energy was cheap in the 1960s the main task was to define a total demand and then to find ways of meeting it. To a great extent the energy supply utilities were in competition with one another to expand their relative shares of the market (e.g. in home heating by solid fuel, oil, gas or electricity), and there was little attempt to distinguish between *demand* at the going price and real energy *needs*. Pricing policies were, with few exceptions, based on historic costs rather than on long-run marginal costs (although admittedly there are great difficulties involved in defining the true long-run marginal costs of energy resources).

What is more disturbing is that to a considerable extent the situation has not changed significantly even now. Energy supply utilities still define their role primarily in terms of meeting demand, and the gestures made by such utilities towards encouraging energy savings generally fall far short of adequate demand analysis, let alone of demand management through pricing and similar policies. Pricing is used, for example, to distribute demand more evenly in terms of the load on facilities; but it is seldom used to discourage energy use. Lacking such demand analysis, estimates of future changes in demand tend to be based either on extrapolation of past trends, or are derived estimates, made, for example, on the basis of assumptions about the rate of future economic growth in the countries concerned and about the relationship between economic growth and energy consumption.

There are many reasons why demand forecasting of this superficial kind is likely to be erroneous, particularly at a time when demand and supply relationships are changing rapidly, in contrast to the earlier period of comparative stability. Since that period was one of low energy prices and rapid growth in demand, it seems likely that current estimates of future demand that are based on extrapolation of such trends (including those used by the ECE Secretariat in its papers for the Ottawa Seminar) are likely to exaggerate the actual growth in demand. Such estimates, for example, do not take account of the following factors that are likely to influence future demand in human settlements.

(a) Reduced Energy Demand in New Buildings

As is discussed in Chapter 5 there has already been a marked improvement in the insulation standards for new houses and other buildings in many countries in the ECE region, and further improvements are imminent. The effect of such standards will depend on the rates of demolition and new building during the remainder of the century, but it seems reasonable to expect that, by the year 2000, between a quarter and a third of the building stock in many ECE countries will have been constructed to insulation standards that imply only about 60 per cent of the energy needed for space heating in buildings of similar size and design constructed during the 1960s. Using Fisk's table (Table 3) as a basis, this would imply that residential dwellings in the "Composite Ten" might require 42 to 48 GJ net per annum for space heating, instead of 70 to 80 GJ.

Such savings relate only to the benefits to be gained from improving the thermal characteristics of the building envelope (e.g. insulation, double glazing, limits on fenestration). They do not take into account the effects of other conservation techniques such as ventilation control, nor of techniques to improve the efficiency of energy use, such as heat pumps.

(b) Slower Population Growth and Reduced Rates of Building

Estimates of energy demand growth in human settlements are liable to use as a basis a period when construction rates were unusually high:

> The 1960s witnessed a boom in construction. . . . Housing production reached record levels; the European average was some 8 dwellings per thousand inhabitants in 1970.*

That boom has now passed. Sweden, for example, was building houses at a rate of 13.7 per thousand population in 1970, only 6.8 per thousand in 1976. Some countries, particularly in eastern Europe, are maintaining fairly steady rates of construction, but throughout the ECE region there is a recognition that, in broad terms, we have reached or are approaching a situation where there is *enough* housing; what is now required is *better* housing. One important manifestation of this awareness is that there is a growing preference for rehabilitation and modernization of the building stock rather than for its replacement—and such modernization is likely to include insulation and other improvements to the energy economy of existing buildings.

These trends are reinforced by the stabilization of the European population. Between 1950 and 1975 the population of the ECE region grew from 758 millions to 1001 millions (32 per cent); between 1975 and 2000 it is expected to add only another 214 millions (21 per cent). "Europe as a whole could approach near-zero natural increase of population in about a demographic generation from the present."†

(c) Slower Growth as Demand Approaches Satisfaction

There are other grounds for believing that the 1950s and 1960s are unreliable as guides to the future growth of energy demand. These decades were, for example, periods when unprecedented investments were made by large numbers of people in home-heating systems and in private cars. There are, however, real limits to the temperatures at

---

* Economic Commission for Europe, *Human Settlements in Europe,* ECE/HBP/18, United Nations, New York, 1976, p. 3.

† Economic Commission for Europe, *Economic Survey of Europe in 1974* (Part II), United Nations, New York, 1976.

which man is comfortable and, when these have been achieved, demand will tend to stabilize. Similarly, there appear to be limits to the number of cars that populations can absorb and also to the amount that they are driven each year. The 1950s and 1960s may well represent the middle of an S-shaped energy growth curve in human settlements that was unprecedented in terms of past experience and equally unsuitable as a guide to the future. A large proportion of the European population may already be close to satisfying its needs for such items as space heating and personal transportation. Though other energy-related demands may develop and grow (e.g. long-distance travel), energy consumption in human settlements may tend to stabilize.

(d) Response to Rising Prices for Energy

The 1950s and 1960s were times when, as Woodson's table (Table 2) indicates, the prices of energy and energy-using appliances were decreasing in real terms. The same was true of the gasoline required in transportation. Those days have passed; energy consumption is strongly influenced by price. If, "in the long run, an energy price increase of 1 per cent should decrease consumption by 0.5 per cent",* then the sharp break in the energy growth curve experienced in many countries since 1973 is presumably in part an expression of demand elasticity, in human settlements as well as in other sectors. Since energy prices seem likely to rise in real terms for the remainder of the century, they too are likely to contribute to reducing energy demand below the levels suggested by extrapolation of past trends.

These are just some of the problems that exist at present because of inadequate analysis of energy demand in human settlements in the past. Similarly, there are problems in estimating the probable effect of conservation measures. Measures taken in buildings, for example, may be less effective than anticipated for many reasons: (a) because benefits from insulation are taken in the form of improved comfort (i.e. higher room or house temperatures) rather than as energy savings; (b) because we may underestimate the extent to which remedial measures have already been taken and may therefore overestimate the potential benefits of insulation programmes;† (c) because the occupants of buildings do not understand or fail to utilize techniques designed to save energy (see Chapter 6); (d) because large-scale programmes frequently fail to provide optimum treatment for each dwelling unit; (e) because different improvements often do not have a cumulative effect; or (f) because demand elasticity reduced the potential for savings (i.e. consumers use less energy because it costs more and therefore reduce the potential benefit of insulation or a similar improvement). Conversely, there may be factors that will lead to increased conservation: much higher prices; technical breakthroughs in the development of conservation measures (e.g. for insulating solid walls); or increased priority to reduce vulnerability to interruptions in supply.

In short, we do not know. The inherent uncertainties of future energy supply and demand, reinforced by the neglect of demand analysis in human settlements during the period of cheap energy, mean that it is difficult to interpret past trends. It is difficult

---

* *Increased Energy Economy and Efficiency in the ECE Region, loc. cit.,* para. 63.

† U.S. Government estimates of potential savings have been challenged on these grounds by insulation manufacturers.

to know whether past trends would have continued in the future even if supplies were assured and prices remained at their pre-1973 levels. It is difficult to know what are the most effective conservation measures (especially in regard to encouraging fuel substitution), and we have a much less assured basis than is normally assumed for forecasting their direct effects on energy use, let alone their indirect effects on society and economy as a whole.

III.4
THE INTERRELATION OF ENERGY POLICIES WITH OTHER HUMAN SETTLEMENT POLICIES

Difficult though it may be to assess the impact of energy and energy conservation policies on human settlements, the matter is one of vital concern to human settlement planners. One of the central themes of the Executive Secretary's address to the Ottawa Seminar was that it is in human settlements that the effects of energy consumption, and of the tremendous economic growth in the ECE region since 1945, are most evident. The impact is apparent, even if we do not understand adequately how it is achieved. The quality of life enjoyed by the population of the ECE region is very closely linked to the availability of energy. As one American remarked a few years ago,

> At last everybody in the home can have a long hot shower, and at last the corners of the home are finally warm.*

In broad economic terms, the interrelationship between energy use and social and economic development is shown in the strong statistical relationships beween gross domestic product (or similar indices) and the use of energy. There are, it is true, reasons to believe that this correlation may not be immutable: that economic growth and improvements in the quality of life are compatible with reduced or stabilized energy con-
II.4 sumption. Nevertheless, those responsible for maintaining and improving the quality of life in human settlements are naturally concerned that the need to conserve energy
III.3 should so far as possible be reconciled with other long-standing objectives. Measures to conserve energy should be taken with an understanding of the effects, indirect as well as direct, that they are likely to have. Pricing, for example, is a technique that has to be applied with care, since

> ". . . the consumption habits of the poor are relatively energy intensive (energy used per dollar of income) compared with those of the rich."†

Price rises, therefore, are likely to be socially regressive if they are not compensated for in other ways. Measures such as higher prices may also not be matched by significant energy savings; as the U.K. contribution to the Ottawa Seminar pointed out:

> . . . a quite large sector of the population uses comparatively little fuel and therefore will save little or no energy through insulation. . . .   (R.43, para. 4.2.)

---

* John C. Fisher, *in* National Academy of Sciences, *Energy: Future Alternatives and Risks,* Washington D.C., 1974.

† *Increased Energy Economy and Efficiency in the ECE Region, loc. cit.,* para. 42.

The need to reconcile energy conservation with other human settlement policies was a major theme in the Ottawa Seminar, and is reflected in the conclusions adopted at the end of the Seminar:

> While there are many potential areas of conflict, there is also evidence that human settlements objectives and energy conservation objectives are often and to a great extent compatible. Therefore, long-standing human settlement objectives must not be sacrificed to respond to the urgent need, in many countries, to reduce growth in energy use. . . . Many opportunities exist to improve the quality of life in human settlements in parallel or in combination with determined efforts to reduce energy demand in such settlements. What is necessary, however, is that these objectives be reconciled through careful consideration and co-ordination of energy and human settlements policies within the context of national economic and social develop-ment policies.   (See p. 142.)

It may in fact seem self-evident—now—that human settlements policies and energy policies need to be planned in conjunction with each other, and indeed that both need to be set in the context of national economic and social development plans and objec-tives. But such integrated planning has been rare in most countries in the past. Energy has usually been regarded as a utility: as a service that needed to be provided to human settlements, but that could be left to technical experts to arrange. Human settlements planners have paid similarly little regard to the implications for life-styles of either the form or the amount of energy used.

II.4

The opposite has indeed seemed to be more frequently the case. Kozierski,* for example, has pointed out that the energy loss per square metre of usable floor space is much the same in Germany, the United Kingdom, Denmark, France and Poland, de-spite the considerable climatic differences. Cheap and apparently unlimited energy was, in effect, used as a substitute for good construction and insulation methods. The Austrian paper for the Ottawa Seminar similarly pointed out that one reason for the long neglect of adequate insulation standards was the argument that to adopt such standards would increase construction costs; it made more sense to build cheaply and to use more energy in heating and other recurring costs of building operation (R.3, p. 1). In the urban planning field, massive expansion of urban transportation was a price that had to be paid in order to achieve the separation of functions in cities that has been an important element of city planning for the last three or four decades.

In a still wider context, energy use in human settlements has great significance for employment policy and activity levels in the economy as a whole. Continuation of pre-1973 trends in energy demand growth implies capital and other requirements for supply facilities that would place (and, in the early 1970s, were placing) great strain on national resources, especially when external trade balances are involved. Conversely, reduc-tions in energy demand through successful conservation policies can, if not carefully planned and allowed for in energy policies, lead to expensive over-provision of supply facilities, especially in view of the long lead-time necessary in the provision of such facilities. The U.K. electricity industry, currently experiencing a situation in which

---

* J. Kozierski, Principles of energy conservation in building heating based on Polish experience, paper 2.7 *in* Roger C. Courtney (ed.), *Energy Conservation in the Built Environment*, CIB, 1976.

supply facilities are substantially in excess of present demand, is an example of such a situation, although conservation measures are only partly responsible for the disparity. On the labour side, energy conservation programmes tend to be labour-intensive, and are an obvious way of generating new employment. In the Netherlands, employment generation has been a specific reason for national energy conservation programmes (see p. 79), and the Danish paper similarly reported that investments in energy conservation policy are "the main tool in present employment policy" (R.10, para. 15).

The integration of human settlements and energy policies in a wider socio-economic framework encounters one particular problem of great importance. Energy policies and the key energy supply decisions are normally made at the national or even international level, and the dominant trend in energy supply and energy management in the past has been towards a centralization of decisionmaking. The creation of national or international electricity distribution grids and the construction of long-distance oil and gas pipelines have encouraged this trend; the importance, in much of the ECE region, of energy imports has made it inevitable. As the Hungarian paper for the Ottawa Seminar expressed it:

> . . . the main trend of national energy policy and development deviates from that of the demand of towns. . . . This is due to the fact that the main development trend of the energy system of the national economy is determined by the interaction between the energy economy and other sectors. This main development trend is characteristic of the entire energy system, but the regional projections differ. They depend on regional specifications, as well as on aspects which are primarily on the town planning level. Nowadays, the determination of the energy requirement of a town and the supply district belonging to it and the projection of the development trend on the basis of past tendencies no longer coincide.
>
> (R.36, para. 17.)

Meanwhile, human settlements decisions are characteristically taken at the regional or local level, either through the exercise of local governmental powers or through individual decisions. Most of the responsibility for the management of community form and building design is delegated by national governments to the community level, and this trend is accelerating rather than diminishing, in response to demands for public participation. One result of this situation was noted in a Canadian contribution to the Ottawa Seminar:

I.4
> In terms of the effect on people's life styles, decisions on energy use planning are as important as decisions on the physical layout of the community. While it is generally accepted that local citizens can participate in the development of physical plans for their community, there are no opportunities for them to participate in the energy use plan for their community.   (R.40, pp. 15 - 16.)

The implications of this separation between national energy planning and community settlement planning extend well beyond the question of public participation. The decisions taken at the community level on such matters as community form, building design and transportation planning have, cumulatively, an enormous influence on national energy use. Energy conservation policies for human settlements must in most cases be implemented through this decentralized structure of administration. In most countries this involves hundreds of units and thousands of individuals, whereas major shifts in energy policy can in principle be achieved much more quickly and expeditiously. As the International Energy Agency* has pointed out, many countries have, since 1973, given more emphasis to increasing their energy supply alternatives than to energy conservation. This may in part be due to a perception that energy supply measures can be implemented more quickly and effectively than conservation measures because of the complex and decentralized system of human settlements planning and decisionmaking.

THE INDIVIDUALITY PROBLEM

If the problem of decentralized decisionmaking is a major one for an effective energy conservation programme, the twin problems of the number of units involved and of individual behaviour may be even more significant. On the one hand, each existing building is, to a great extent, unique in its energy budget characteristics, and conservation policies must somehow take this into account. This individuality is naturally most evident in the case of buildings that have been erected for some time, and that have therefore been modified over time by their occupants or have developed faults with the passage of time. But the individuality is also true of new buildings; apparently identical houses, for example, may have very different rates of air infiltration due to faults in construction.

The individuality of the building is normally increased by diversity in the energy-related behaviour of building occupants: how many occupants there are, their diurnal and seasonal occupation of the building, etc. The CIB paper for the Ottawa Seminar reported that:

> The results of extensive research into individual consumption in many countries are available and underline this fact. For example, monitoring carried out in 1968 by the Norwegian Building Research Institute in electrically heated flats of similar design and size, but differently located within the block of flats, showed a difference in energy consumption between the extremes of 2,000 to 25,000 kWh per flat per year. Material from other countries indicates that lowest and highest individual consumptions in similar dwellings can vary by factors of from 5 to 10. This indicates that a main determinant of energy consumption in buildings is human behaviour itself. There is thus room for a reduction in energy consumption in buildings even before alterations in envelope or installations are considered.
>
> (R.15, para. 12.)

It also indicates that behaviour patterns may well nullify or reduce the effect of physical improvements to building energy budgets. Conservation policies that are only aimed at the physical structure are inherently sub-optimal, since they are liable to lead to over-investments in structures in which little energy is in fact used. Or, conversely, they may be irrelevant to the principal wastes of energy, which might be avoided by changes (relatively costless in financial terms) to individual behaviour patterns.

---

* *Energy Conservation in the International Energy Agency, 1976 Review,* OECD, Paris, 1976, p. 8.

ACTION DESPITE UNCERTAINTY

I.1

III.8

To an extent that was perhaps rather surprising, the participants in the Ottawa Seminar affirmed the need for urgent action in regard to energy use in human settlements, despite the very great uncertainties that exist about the future. The need for further research was well recognized, but, like the CIB (see p. 27), the participants did not feel it possible to wait for the results of such research. Much is known already that is not being utilized, and the best way to encourage further research may well be through the use of what has already been discovered. Similarly, the major inadequacies of data, especially in regard to energy use in human settlements, were not used to argue that action now may be in wrong or sub-optimal directions. Instead it was urged, especially by the Irish delegation, that action in such a situation of uncertainty needs to be carefully monitored in order that the uncertainty can be progressively reduced.

This insistence on immediate action probably stems from a number of considerations. At the professional and technical level it may be due to an awareness of the very great energy wastes that are at present characteristic of human settlements, and of a similar awareness of the variety of techniques by which such wastes may be reduced. At the governmental policy and decisionmaking level, the urgency of action probably reflects a variety of concerns (balance of payments, unemployment, etc.) that are the aftermath of the 1973 energy crisis. On a longer view it was also recognized that what the planner does—or does not—do at the present time is likely to have continuing effects because of the durability of human settlements and of the systems they contain.

The participants in the Ottawa Seminar were, it is true, concerned that action in human settlements should not foreclose energy supply and demand options in the future. But the need to keep as many options open as possible was again not seen as an excuse for inaction. In human settlements the main need is not so much to respond to the specific problems caused by the 1973 energy crisis. Rather it is to deal with an inherited burden of inefficient energy use that has gradually accumulated and increased throughout the twentieth century. As the representative at the Ottawa Seminar of the International Union of Architects expressed it:

> All this leads us to conclude that the "energy crisis" is a real blessing and that its seemingly negative aspects can be turned around in modifying our attitudes towards the planning and development of human settlements. . . .

> Of course, we cannot assume . . . that the existence of a need will automatically assure the launching and support of a program to solve that need. In our political decision-making process, there must be a sufficiently irresistible combination of facts and pressure to offset the usual tendency toward maintaining the status quo. It is important that the facts be placed on the table. This is the object of the seminar. . . .*

---

* Jean-Louis Lalonde, Energy and human settlements, the impact of energy considerations on the quality of life in human settlements, Montreal, 28 September 1977, unpublished.

Chapter 2

ENERGY ISSUES RELATED TO
PHYSICAL PLANNING

THE LEGACY OF THE PAST

Ainsi en moins de 30 ans la France, comme beaucoup d'autres pays industrialisés, a connu deux changements profonds de sa politique énergétique. Ces changements ont eu des répercussions profonds sur la distribution des activités sur le territoire français et plus généralement sur l'organisation des établissements humains dans notre pays.*

(R.12, p. 2.)

At the end of the 1950s the gradual shift from coal to oil that had begun between the two world wars was markedly accelerated as the decline or exhaustion of French coal-mines coincided with the introduction of cheap imported oil:

L'instauration en 1959 de quotas d'importation de pétrole aux Etats-Unis par l'administration Eisenhower a fait de l'Europe et du Japon le champ de bataille des compagnies pétrolieres qui doivent écouler la production bon marché en provenance du Moyen-Orient. L'Europe va ainsi progressivement subir l'invasion des produits pétroliers et substituer dans de nombreux usages industriels le pétrole au charbon.†

(R.12, p. 3.)

In France, as in other ECE countries, the change led to large industrial developments at the oil-importing ports: Marseilles, Le Havre, Dunkirk, Bordeaux and Nantes. During the post-war period large hydroelectric developments in the French Alps similarly provided the basis for industrial and urban development in the region, affecting such cities as Grenoble. The development of natural gas resources in south-western France provided the basis for the growth of the chemical industry around Lacq.

The French paper emphasizes, however, that the locational effects of such energy developments were much less rigid than those resulting from the original Industrial Revolution based on coal. Oil and gas pipelines and electricity grids supplied existing centres, as well as encouraging local industrial and urban development around their point of extraction or conversion. In the French view, whatever form the new revolu-

---

* *Editor's translation:* "So, in less than 30 years, France, like many other industrialized countries, has undergone two fundamental changes in its energy policy. These changes have had major repercussions on the location of human activity throughout France and, more generally, on the pattern of human settlements in the country."

† *Editor's translation:* "The creation, in 1959, of petroleum import quotas for the U.S.A. by the Eisenhower Administration made Europe and Japan a battlefield for oil companies that had to dispose of the cheap output of the Middle East. Europe therefore experienced a flood of oil products, and substituted oil for coal in many industrial processes."

37

tion will take, it is likely to be even less of a locational imperative than were the energy changes of the 1960s:

> Ainsi l'énergie, longtemps facteur de concentration et de polarisation des activités industrielles, contribue désormais à leur dispersion.*   (R.12, p. 4.)

Despite the relatively brief period of cheap oil, the overall effect on French energy use patterns was profound. By 1972 imports accounted for 77 per cent of energy use in France (R.12, p. 2). A similar pattern was evident elsewhere: more than half the countries in the ECE region depended on imports for more than half their national energy requirements. Since the period was one of rapid population growth and of post-war rebuilding, the human settlements of the ECE region reflect this brief period of cheap oil as much as they do the much longer period when energy supplies were dominated by coal and other solid fuels.

CENTRALIZED AND DECENTRALIZED ENERGY SUPPLIES, AND THE CHOICE OF FUEL

During the twentieth century, and especially in the post-1945 period, there has been a strong tendency in the ECE region to centralize the conversion and distribution of energy resources. In the nineteenth century such centralization was almost totally absent; fuel, in solid form, was delivered to individual homes and other buildings and its conversion—burning—took place at the point of end-use. The change to a more centralized system of supply began with the creation of municipal gas systems in the late nineteenth century, and was enormously increased by the growth in the use of electricity since the beginning of the twentieth century. This extension of the electricity distribution network has been a major task of governments and electricity utilities, a task that was essentially completed by mid-century. Virtually the entire population of the ECE region is now linked to an electricity generation and distribution system that is highly centralized and that is becoming continental rather than national in scope in both Europe and North America.

The centralization of electricity generation may not, it is true, be so permanent as recent developments would indicate. One of the possibilities for the future is the development of "total energy systems" in which all the forms of energy required by a building, including electricity, are generated within the building itself, in the same way that cars, ships and aircraft act as total energy systems at present. For the foreseeable future, however, the use of electricity in human settlements is likely to involve dependence on highly centralized and ever-larger units of generation or conversion. This, it may be noted, is likely to be true also of electric vehicles if they are introduced on a large scale in the future. Most research and development at present is oriented to linking them, through batteries or roadside and overhead cables, to national electricity systems, rather than to developing them as total energy systems.

Because of the problems of storage, gas is also a fuel that requires an expensive basic infrastructure so that it can be supplied to the point of end-use as required. By contrast,

---

* *Editor's translation:* "Energy, for so long a factor encouraging concentration and polarization of industrial activity, will in the future assist in its dispersion."

the use of oil is much more decentralized. Like coal, it can be stored safely and conveniently in relatively small amounts close to the point of end-use (e.g. an individual dwelling). Like coal, such storage points can be supplied by a flexible distribution system—oil pipelines, rail and road tankers, etc.—that can be gradually enlarged and extended without, normally, massive investments in fixed infrastructure. The relative simplicity of oil distribution systems, which of course also affects the supply of energy for urban transportation, is a major reason why oil has tended to replace the less convenient coal as the ubiquitous fuel in the ECE region. Just as there are few households without electricity in the ECE region at present, there are similarly few that do not have easy access to supplies of oil. Gas supplies are much more restricted to areas where population density warrants the creation of a gas distribution system, and the swift decline of coal, on grounds of convenience, cost and sometimes of availability, means that it has in most countries reversed its role, or is in course of doing so. Instead of being a form of energy that is used on a decentralized basis, it is more and more becoming a fuel that is supplied mainly to major consumers such as electricity power stations and the iron and steel industry.

This trend towards centralization has brought many benefits to human settlements in the ECE region: greater choice of energy form, cheaper energy, convenience, and an improved environment. But such benefits have been achieved only at the cost of introducing rigidities and other problems. The ECE region has become increasingly dependent on external sources of energy; individual users have become more vulnerable than in the past to interruptions in supply; and dependence on centralized supply, especially of electricity, has entailed high overheads in the form of conversion losses, that may reasonably be regarded as a waste of energy.

(1) The increased dependence of energy users on distant sources is due to a number of factors. One is the inability of conventional and local energy resources to meet rapidly rising demands, demands that to a considerable extent are themselves a function of the cheapness and ease of availability of such distant sources in the recent past. Secondly, there is the obvious convenience of using fluid fuels rather than coal or other solid fuels. A major factor in the dependence of ECE countries on imported oil is also the difficulty of finding a substitute for it in transportation. Lastly the growth in demand, and consequently increased dependence on external sources, is due in part to the increasing similarities in life-style across the ECE region, so that what is the norm in one country became desired and expected elsewhere.

1.1 (2) The increased vulnerability to interruptions in energy supply appears rather paradoxical in a period when the ECE energy user has a much greater choice of fuels and forms of energy than in the days of "King Coal". But the choice may often be more apparent than real. In transport, for example, the dependence on oil is almost complete, and the easy availability of oil for both public and private transportation made possible the "flight to the suburbs" on a scale far beyond that generated by suburban railway networks. Oil also made possible the functional separation of residential areas, industry and other activities within human settlements. If oil supplies are interrupted, as they were in some countries in 1973, or if they become much more expensive, the individual may well be more vulnerable than his nineteenth-century ancestor, who generally had to live within walking distance of his work and other activities.

A similar vulnerability is often to be found in individual buildings, whether industrial, commercial or residential, in the heart of the multi-fuel economies of the ECE
region. The nineteenth-century fireplace or stove could burn a variety of solid fuels,
and solid fuel could also be stored for an indefinite period. Storage is still possible for
oil-based heating systems, but the oil furnace is not so adaptable if the oil does run
out or becomes too expensive. For premises dependent on gas or electricity the vulnerability to interruptions in supply is much greater, and is particularly acute in "all electric" homes. If the electricity system fails, there is no substitute, often not even a fireplace.

(3) The emphasis that has been placed by users on the convenience as well as cheapness of energy has inevitably led to inefficiency in energy use. It is true that the traditional fireplace or stove, burning solid fuel, was not particularly efficient either: much
of the heat disappeared up the chimney without benefit. But newer fuels and newer

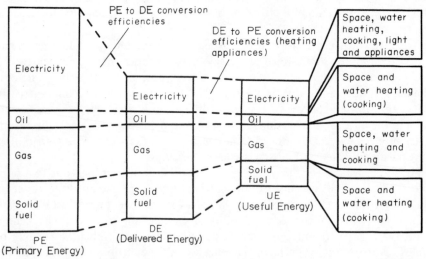

FIG. 1. The conversion efficiencies (or "losses") between primary energy, delivered energy and useful energy.
(Source: R.39.)

technology, although potentially more efficient, have seldom been utilized as effectively as they should have been. This is particularly so in regard to the generation of
electricity. In most respects this is the most convenient form of energy, but it is one
that normally involves a "waste" of energy resources in comparison to alternative
methods by which these resources could be utilized in heating or other uses. The paper
prepared for the Ottawa Seminar by the International Institute for Environment and
Development (IIED) contained a diagram illustrating the general relationship between
the overall (or "primary") energy requirements of the domestic sector, the smaller
amount of "delivered energy" supplied to households after conversion to electricity or
other forms and, smaller still, the actual "useful energy" that was obtained from these
resources (see Fig. 1).

In a more quantitative form, the ECE Secretariat recently prepared a table of current
efficiencies and the prospects for improvement (Table 4).

TABLE 4. *Approximate space heating efficiencies in the ECE region (per cent)[a]*

	Coal		Oil		Natural gas	
	Early 1970s	Practically possible	Early 1970s	Practically possible	Early 1970s	Practically possible
a . *Direct use*						
Used in heating	45	54	63	76	75	80
Overall efficiency	28	35	20	31	50	61
b. *Converted to electricity*						
Used in heating	95	95	95	95	95	95
Overall efficiency	20	24	10	15	20	27
c. *Combined generation*						
Used in heating	95	95	95	95	95	95
Overall efficiency	46	47	23	30	46	52

[a] Based on Table II.12 in ECE, *Increased Energy Economy and Efficiency in the ECE Region,* E/ECE/883/ Rev.1, United Nations, New York, 1976

In direct use, as can be seen from Table 4, coal is less efficient as a fuel than either oil or gas and, in a period of cheap and unlimited hydrocarbons, this has been a factor encouraging the replacement of coal. Overall, however, dependence on oil has meant a reduction in efficiency, since current methods of extraction are little better than 35 per cent efficient, as compared to 70 per cent for coal extraction. More significant, however, is the drop in overall efficiency that results when these fuels are used to produce electricity in conventional power stations. The contrast is particularly great for natural gas and rather less so for oil. For coal, however, its inefficiency in direct use is so great that its use in power stations does not lead to a significant waste by comparison.

In a world where the *efficient* use of high-priced, depleting and often imported energy resources is of great importance, Table 4 has some significant implications for human settlements. In particular it suggests that space heating by electricity involves very large unnecessary waste, especially if the electricity is generated by burning natural gas. In contemporary society electricity is essential, but electric heating based on imported, expensive, and scarce hydrocarbons is not. If oil or gas are to be used for space heating, they are much more efficiently used by direct burning at the point of end use.*

In certain circumstances, however, electric space heating may become a much more efficient use of resources. Space heating, for example, can be a very convenient way of utilizing the off-peak output of base-load thermal power stations, through the use of simple, short-period storage systems. Battery recharging of electric vehicles would also normally be accomplished in off-peak periods (see p. 52).

Electric heating may also be appropriate if the electricity is generated from hydro or nuclear energy resources. The notion of "conversion losses" is inappropriate when considering hydro plants, since the energy (i.e. falling water) cannot be utilized more efficiently at the point of end-use in the same way as oil, gas, or coal. In practice, if the resource is not used to generate electricity, it will not be utilized at all. In those countries where hydroelectricity is a significant factor (e.g. Norway, Canada, Switzerland,

*Increased Energy Economy and Efficiency in the ECE Region, loc. cit., para. 148.

France), the use of electricity may be the most efficient form of energy use in human settlements, especially as the resource is not a depleting one.

Nuclear energy is in a similar, though not identical, position. Like hydro power, there is no practical possibility at present or in the foreseeable future of utilizing it at the point of end-use in human settlements; it is either utilized in large power stations or not at all. The nuclear-electric process, unlike the hydroelectric process, does, however, generate amounts of "waste" heat comparable to conventional thermal generating stations based on fossil fuel, and the possibility therefore exists of utilizing this waste heat for use in district heating systems. If this opportunity can be realized, the overall efficiency of nuclear-electricity generation will be increased considerably. Even if this is not possible, it seems misleading to compare nuclear-electric "overheads" with those associated with conventional thermal electricity.

THE BASIC ISSUES

The Ottawa Seminar was faced with two main issues in the planning and development of human settlements arising from the present pattern of energy use. One is the question of vulnerability. As posed in Annex IV* of the Seminar programme, the question took the form:

I.1
II.1
In view of the major uncertainties in the long-term energy supply situation in many countries, what actions should be taken in the planning and development of human settlements to ensure that they can be adapted to new energy supply situations with minimum disruption and that they conserve energy resources as much as possible?

The second question is that of efficiency and is included in the closing words of the question posed above. It is, however, a question that can be considered separately from that of vulnerability and it might be posed in the following terms. In view of the III.1 fact that as much as 80 per cent of the energy used in buildings is accounted for by space and water heating, which can take a variety of forms and use a variety of energy sources, what methods of space and water heating should be encouraged or required in new, and perhaps also in existing, human settlements? Similarly, what action in the planning and development of human settlements is likely to conserve energy in urban transportation, since transportation is particularly dependent on finite resources of oil?

NEW ENERGY TECHNOLOGIES

The rise in energy prices since 1973 and the long-term prospect of rapid depletion of conventional energy sources have revived interest in other sources of energy. The Ottawa Seminar, which was policy-oriented rather than a meeting of technical experts, was not directly concerned with technical possibilities and problems but neither could it ignore progress in new energy technology, since it is already evident that some of the new sources and forms of energy may be particularly relevant to human settlements,

* By mistake there are two annexes numbered IV to the document (HBP/SEM.17/1) on the programme and organization of the Seminar. This reference is to the annex contained in document HBP/SEM.17/1/Add.3; the other annex numbered IV refers to the arrangements for the Study Tour following the Seminar.

especially for space or water heating. Two papers prepared for the Seminar, by Turkey and the International Council for Building Research, Studies and Documentation (CIB), respectively, contained general reviews of the probable impact of new technologies; a third (R.8) examined the opportunities for using geothermal and solar heat in France during the next 10 to 15 years.

1. Solar Energy

The Turkish paper considered both small-scale applications (where the main focus of research and development is concentrated at present) and also the possibility of large-scale power generation. At the small scale, the most promising developments are for water heating using roof-mounted collectors. This is

> . . . the most advanced system among the thermal applications in buildings (domestic sector, industrial sector and others) and is at present used commercially in the sunny regions of several countries (e.g. Australia, France, Israel, Japan, USSR and the United States.) The technology is well developed and economic feasibility has been established. . . .

> Notwithstanding high initial capital costs, the average costs over 20 years are currently competitive with those of electrical, oil and gas systems . . . and the advent of higher energy prices (especially oil prices) is likely to create new markets for domestic water heating. The problems are essentially commercial such as the large-scale manufacture of collectors which would allow a further reduction in costs and, ultimately, a wider use of the system and public acceptability. Hot water for hospitals, schools, industries, and other institutions, as well as for families, could then become much more widely available. . . .   (R.41, paras. 33, 36.)

The use of solar energy for space heating is likely to follow more slowly:

> In the United States, Japan and elsewhere, solar heating is now under rapid commercial development. However, allowing for socio-economic factors such as consumers' reluctance to accept higher initial construction costs, despite lower operating costs, and the slow rate of housebuilding, much more than a decade will elapse before this form of heating can come into more general use and affect total energy consumption.   (R.41, para. 40.)

So far as large-scale applications are concerned,

> Solar energy for power generation, either in the form of electricity or mechanical work, has been the subject of extensive research in many parts of the world; United States; USSR; Japan; France; Germany, Federal Republic of; Italy and Israel to name a few.

> The two fundamental concepts of electricity generation from solar energy on the earth's surface are the thermal conversion of sunlight by means of solar collectors and direct photovoltaic conversion in solar cells.   (R.41, paras. 43, 44.)

There are at present major economic barriers to the adoption of the thermal conversion process:

. . . the economics of . . . solar power generation, given the very high costs involved, are by no means comparable with those of conventional thermal or nuclear
plants. Very tentative estimates show that a mean kilowatt of capacity would cost
$2500. . . . In the United States it is forecast that 100 MW solar thermal plants
will be demonstrated by the mid-1980s. . . .   (R.41, para. 46.)

Similarly, the process of photovoltaic conversion using solar cells seems likely to be
extremely expensive:

. . . the investment required per kilowatt of capacity is still over 100 times that of
a conventional fuel-fired power plant.   (R.41, para. 48, footnote.)

The research planned at present . . . aims at the generation of electricity by solar
cells at a cost where a complete system—solar conversion, storage, power conditioning and transmission/distribution—can compete on a life-cycle cost basis
with other large-scale energy system alternatives and perhaps be useful even in
small-scale applications in remote rural areas . . . (perhaps as early as the mid-
1980s).

Such applications have generally been in situations where there has been a need for
remote power in the 1-100 W range and where the cost of replacement of batteries,
transportation of fuel or remote power lines is prohibitive, such as remote communication stations, weather-monitoring stations, remote educational-television
sets, navigational and warning lights on lighthouses and on off-shore oil platforms.
                                                            (R.41, paras. 49, 50.)

This generally cautious view of the opportunities for solar energy is generally en-
dorsed in the CIB paper, and the latter is rather less optimistic so far as the cost-effectiveness of solar water heating is concerned. In general it finds that:

The further development of solar energy utilization by active systems seems, at
least for some time, to be less promising than the simple passive systems, like windows. With rising energy prices and diminishing resources the further development of solar collector systems is, however, likely to be important.
                                                            (R.15, para. 30.)

This reference to passive systems reiterates views expressed at the CIB 1976 symposium on energy conservation in buildings. Siviour,* for example, claimed that in lati-
tudes and climates typical of much of the ECE region (the United Kingdom was taken
as the example), the net energy gain through a single-glazed south-facing window is
positive over the year as a whole, and that if the windows are double-glazed the balance
is positive for windows facing east, south and west. Mechanical curtain systems, to
retain such heat at night, may therefore be much more cost-effective than active solar
energy systems.
Despite the cautious approach taken by experts towards the commercial feasibility
of solar energy systems in the short term, they are of particular significance to human

* J. B. Siviour, Designs for low energy houses, paper 2.8 in Roger C. Courtney (ed.), *Energy Conservation in the Built Environment,* CIB, 1976.

settlements, since small-scale applications—to serve one or more individual buildings—seem more promising than large-scale systems, and solar energy seems particularly easy to utilize for space or water heating. One specific approach that may have important implications for both new and existing housing was described in the Canadian "response paper" prepared for the Ottawa Seminar:

> . . . the only way that 100% solar heating can be economically viable is to construct a large storage facility which can supply heat to several houses. The advantages of large-scale storage systems are: (i) fixed construction costs become a smaller proportion of total costs, and (ii) heat losses decline because of the cube - square ratio (that is, the volume of the tank increases much faster than its surface area). This approach of a community scale storage facility providing heat to a number of housing units has become known as the solar mini-utility. One of the main advantages of the solar mini-utility is that it can be used as a retrofit technology to supply heat to existing houses.*

2. Geothermal Heat

As the Turkish paper pointed out, geothermal heat is already in use in several ECE countries:

> In Iceland, for instance, the city of Reykjavik is almost exclusively heated by geothermal water; while in Hungary the land area covered by greenhouses heated by geothermal water exceeded 1.5 million square metres in 1973. . . .

> Representative costs in Europe fall within the range of $1 to $4/Gcal which is about one-half to one-eighth of the cost of such thermal energy at current (1976) local prices for imported oil. . . .

> The main use of geothermal energy has been to generate electricity. . . . The significant power plants known so far are Larderello (Italy) and The Geysers (California), about 400 MW each at the end of 1973. Both construction and operating costs for the geothermal plants installed above these fields have proved to be lower than those for plants using fossil or nuclear fuel.   (R.41, paras. 66, 67, 68.)

In France, geothermal heat is seen at the present time as one of the more promising new forms of energy, though economic considerations are as usual dominant:

> Geothermal energy yields low-temperature water (about 70°C) in most of the aquifers situated in France. Owing to the high cost of developing these aquifers (drilling of extraction and re-injection wells, exchange, distribution), special equipment has to be installed in order to make the most efficient use of this low-temperature water, and long-term financing is required to offset the large initial investment by operational savings.

> Experiments involving several thousand housing units have been conducted at the request of the authorities and with their assistance.   (R.8, English summary.)

---

* Canada, Ministry of State for Urban Affairs, *Habitat and Energy in Canada,* Ottawa, 1977, p. 53.

The opportunities for utilizing geothermal heat naturally tend to be very localized, and it is likely that the main applications will be for district heating or small-scale power generation.

3. Organic Waste

According to the Turkish paper,

> . . . organic waste (such as urban refuse, agricultural crop residues, animal and industrial waste) for the ultimate purpose of producing heat through direct combustion or for producing synthetic fuels through biological and chemical conversions is of particular importance today in view of the partly renewable nature of these resources and because such techniques might represent a solution to the serious environmental problem of waste disposal raised by an increasing population and by densely populated areas.   (R.41, para.55.)

Various techniques are available to produce fuel from waste including pyrolysis ("destructive distillation"), hydrogenation (i.e. chemical reduction) and biological conversion through anaerobic fermentation. Pyrolysis, however, seems to be the most promising approach, and is at present at the pilot-plant stage of development.

> Tests have shown that, in the United States, one ton of dry organic waste could have a net yield of 1.25 barrels of low-sulphur . . . crude oil, or 10 mcf of methane if gasified. . . .The heat required for the process is 25 per cent of the heat content of the gas produced. . . . Oil produced from urban waste with this system has been estimated to cost $8.41 per barrel in a 1000 ton per day plant. . . . Such costs would diminish in a larger scale production plant.   (R.41, para. 59.)

A Canadian paper for the Ottawa Seminar dealt with the choice between utilizing urban wastes to produce energy by combustion, compared to the value of the materials that might be recycled from such waste. It found that:

> If wastes can be collected in segregated form, as might readily be the case with some commercial or light industrial sources, and if suitable markets exist or can be developed, the material recovery option will provide the greatest benefit. Unfortunately, preconditions such as these do not usually exist. . . . Domestic solid wastes are normally mixed at the residence, then further mixed with commercial and institutional wastes in the collection process. Under these conditions, the conversion of the combustible fraction of the solid waste to steam heat energy by the use of bulk incineration has the advantage of simplicity. . . .

> . . . if increased resource recovery from urban wastes is to take place in North America over the next quarter century it is most likely to occur through extension of the energy recovery option since technology is available and the economics are usually better than alternative options.   (R.51, pp. 6, 7.)

4. Wind

The main drawbacks to utilising wind energy are the low density of air (requiring large diameter rotors or blades if a significant amount of energy is to be captured) and the intermittent nature of the energy source, requiring expensive storage systems or, more often, the use of wind energy in combination with other sources. Its principal applications are likely to be in remote communities where the cost of alternative forms of energy, especially in the form of electricity, is high.

Despite the disadvantages, several proposals have been made to meet substantial proportions of national energy needs through wind power,* and some countries are undertaking major experiments. One of these, located in the Magdalen Islands in the Gulf of St. Lawrence, was described in a Canadian paper for the Ottawa Seminar. Unlike the conventional windmill with its horizontal axis, this is a vertical axis rotor linked to a 225 kW generator. The experiment is designed to test the feasibility of similar windmills with a larger capacity, and also the possibility of storing wind energy in the form of compressed air in natural salt caverns in the islands. Although the existing plant is only a pilot-scale project, it is significant that the power utility, Hydro-Québec, anticipates that the system will be competitive with the high cost of the present diesel - electric system used in the Magdalen Islands (Table 5).

TABLE 5

	Wind turbine/diesel system	Diesel system
Discounted present value (1975)	$19,730,060	$21,398,932
Equivalent annual value	$2,249,389	$2,439,586
Unit cost of energy (kWh) 1977 - 96[a]	6 ¢/kWh	6 ¢/kWh

[a] The cost is obtained by dividing the discounted present value of the inflated cash flow by the annual discounted energy production for the period. (R.38, fig. 3.)

A more general survey of the potential importance of wind and other novel forms of energy in remote communities is provided in another Canadian paper (R.40). Although based on the situation in northern Canada, it seems relevant to the problems of other remote regions. It is the great expense of conventional heating systems that makes new methods particularly attractive and potentially competitive. The paper, however, points out a number of problems involved in applying novel methods in remote communities, including the difficulties of adapting systems developed in more densely populated areas to conditions in remote communities. For instance, solar energy systems that depend on electric pumps may be unsuitable since the electricity supply systems in remote areas are liable to interruptions, and in severe climates this may result in freezing or other permanent damage to the system. Similarly:

> The distinction between . . . "technically viable" and . . . "industrially viable" technologies is important. Because of the problems of maintenance and upkeep, any technology which is used in a remote community must be tried and tested. Isolated locations are simply not the place to experiment with prototype models.
>
> (R.40, pp. 9 - 10.)

---

* See, for example, the proposals made for Denmark by Bent Sørensen, Energy and Resources, *Science* **189**, 4199, 25 July 1975.

Against these disadvantages, such small remote communities may be more adapted to the self-reliance in operation and maintenance that many new techniques such as solar and wind energy imply. The energy used at present in these communities is normally generated within the community, whereas the inhabitants of urban regions have become used to decentralized energy supplies or to professional maintenance systems.

Of the methods reviewed above, it may be that energy production from urban wastes, again through some form of district heating system, will have the most widespread impact on human settlements energy supply in the next decade or so. Some other techniques, however, which are not "new" because they are already well established in some parts of the ECE region, or are well understood in technical terms, also seem likely to become widespread in the near future.

HEAT PUMPS

The CIB contribution to the Ottawa Seminar regarded heat pumps as the most promising technical advance in domestic energy supply at the present time.

> Heat pumps utilize heat from the external air or from the ground or from nearby water resources. Those taking heat from the external air seem to be the most likely development in the existing urban stock of buildings. . . . The energy needed for running a heat pump system (electric or gasoline motors etc.) may release three times this quantity of energy for space heating. . . . Small heat pumps may also have a role in low energy design for the extraction of heat from lukewarm domestic water, from energy storage during the winter time, etc. . . . With rising energy prices and industry's determined efforts to satisfy a growing and promising market, it is likely that the economic break-even point for heat pumps is close.
>
> (R.15, para. 23.)

There have also been suggestions that simple short-term storage of heat may be possible by linking heat pumps to storage facilities similar to those used in off-peak electric heating. If air-to-air systems do prove to be the most suitable for domestic applications, this is likely to influence house design, especially in European countries where circulation of hot water has been the normal method of central heating up to now, rather than warm air systems. Local planning may also need to take into account the noise and other characteristics of heat pumps.

DISTRICT HEATING

Like other recent conferences concerned with energy conservation, the Ottawa Seminar produced a large number of papers on district heating, already a technique of substantial importance in many ECE countries. The policy implications are of particular concern to the seminar; although some technical problems exist and new technical developments are taking place, it seems clear that institutional, legal and social barriers to the wider use of district heating are more important than either technology or economics.

There is certainly no shortage of examples of the practicability and efficiency of district heating, and several countries emphasized the importance of such systems in over-all fuel economy when linked to electricity generating stations in combined power and heat production systems. The USSR, for example, has developed combined generation since 1924, to the point that:

> In 1975 the installed energy capacity of the combined power-and-heat generating plants was 49.1 million kW or 32.5 per cent of the total capacity of thermal power stations. They provide heat for about 800 towns.

> . . . the annual fuel economy obtained due to the operation of combined plants . . . is about 27 million tons of conventional fuel.   (R.47, pp. 3, 4.)

About 85 per cent of the consumers in Moscow, for example, are provided with heat from combined plants or large boilerhouses, through a network of mains that is 4000 km in length.

A Finnish contribution also emphasized the importance of district heating and combined generation in conditions of expensive and scarce energy resources.

> The beginning of district heating dates from the 1950s when it was introduced in many localities. At the end of 1973, all the medium-sized population centres in Finland with the exception of one town were producing district heat. . . .

> The trend in the heating of buildings in densely populated areas is distinctly to-wards regional and district heating. Extensively centralised heating achieves sav-ings in both fuel costs (better efficiency of boilers and cheaper fuels) and invest-ment and operating costs compared with individual central heating. Centralised heating achieves better results than individual fuel heating also in the environ-mental sense. . . .

> The year 1973 divides Finland's energy supply into two periods. Distinct energy policy objectives were lacking until the 1970s. The oil crisis of 1973, however, dic-tated the urgent need of energy policy aims: general saving of energy, and saving of foreign currency needed for the purchase of imported fuels and for energy invest-ments. . . . For heat supply, this has meant especial emphasis on, e.g., the role of district heating.   (R.22, paras. 2.1, 3, 6.)

Peat, for example, can be used as a district heating fuel in Finland, whereas it would be much less suitable for individual central heating systems. The Finnish paper also described the gradual development of district heating systems in that country; these normally begin with inexpensive "transportable" heat units (about 2.5 MW) and gra-dually develop through larger permanent stations towards combined heat and power systems.

> Finnish district heating always starts today with a so-called transportable heating plant. Transportable heating plants collect a heat load which can be combined later into a more comprehensive district heating system. The use of transportable heat-ing plants in the early building phase makes it possible to lower considerably the initial investments of the construction project. It is then possible to begin district heating activity for considerably smaller areas than earlier.   (R.22, para. 5.2.)

Canada is not normally identified as a country where district heating is of great importance but several networks exist in the larger cities. In Ottawa, for example, several participants in the Seminar took the opportunity to visit a plant that supplies heat to over forty public buildings in the downtown core, and is also one of the largest district cooling plants in the world. The two Canadian papers on district heating, however, were mainly concerned with the prospects for new installations in Canada, which seem likely to be very different to those that exist today. In particular, the prospect that a new international airport for Toronto will be constructed near to an existing nuclear electric plant led to an investigation of the potential advantages of using the heat from the plant in a district heating scheme for the new community the airport would require. Several advantages were discovered.

> This study . . . found that the incremental costs for establishing . . . optimal insulation standards can be almost entirely offset by savings attributable to reductions in the central system's requirements for boilers, water volume and pipe sizes. For individual heating and cooling systems, furnace cost reductions result in an average savings equal to only 10 per cent of the incremental insulation costs. Therefore the financial benefits of district heating seem to improve relative to individual heating systems under optimal building energy utilization.   (R.30, pp. 4 - 5.)

On economic grounds,

> Given the assumption of the continuing escalation of fossil fuel prices, the study of the North Pickering Community concluded that ". . . any form of district heating appears less costly in the long run than heating of buildings with the individual fired system." . . .

> A companion study to the Pickering off-peak nuclear option . . . extended the life cycle cost analysis to communities of 20,000, 10,000 and 2,500 population, both existing and planned. The study assumed oil fired plants and the climatic conditions of Pickering. The minimum size of community in which the life cycle costs for district heating would equal those for individual heating is about 4,000 population for a non-industrial community.   (R.30, pp. 5, 11.)

Other relevant factors include the location of the plants and the fuel for the system. Sulphur dioxide removal, when using fossil fuels in urban sites, would, for instance, be a major cost consideration. This increases the attractiveness of the nuclear district heating option and, as the other Canadian paper on the subject points out:

> The situation in Ontario is different from that which, in Europe, led to the development of district heating in the early part of this century. There, the driving force was the need to utilize to the maximum the energy of the fossil fuel burned to produce electricity. In Ontario, the incentive to integrate the electrical system with district heating schemes will more likely be found in the increased utilization of capital-intensive nuclear systems and in the possibility of relatively cheap steam during off-peak hours, as the nuclear generating base in the electrical system grows.

> In Ontario, we are coming to believe that the district heating system of the future will be a relatively low-temperature (less than 100°C) hot water system, primarily because of its compatibility with a variety of energy sources and its compatibility with storage of heat on a large scale, including seasonal storage if this technology can be successfully developed.   (R.50, summary.)

The advantages of district heating schemes seem greatest when systems can be incorporated in the design and construction of new communities or neighbourhoods. Unfortunately, less attention was paid in the documentation for the Ottawa Seminar to the feasibility and cost of retrofitting such schemes in existing communities, although such retrofitting is taking place in a number of ECE countries.

Before leaving the subject of district heating and combined generation, it is worth noting a point made in an ECE Secretariat paper contributed to the Ottawa Seminar on the subject. This points out that the notion of district heating systems utilizing "waste" heat from electricity generating stations is normally an incorrect one.

> In order to increase the efficiency of conversion to electricity (Carnot cycle), thermal power stations release their waste heat into the environment at the lowest temperature possible. On the other hand, for technical and economic reasons, water should be supplied to a district heating network or steam to an industrial complex at much higher temperatures. Consequently, in the case of combined heat and electricity production, it is less a matter of utilizing the waste heat from the installation than of improving the thermodynamic utilization of its thermal capacity. This is done to the detriment of electricity output. . . .   (see Table 6).

TABLE 6. *Electricity available for various quantities of steam bled from a 1000 MW(th) pressurized water nuclear power plant*

Equivalent power drawn off in the form of steam (MW(th))	Electric power produced (MW(e))	Useful energy yield of the installation (%)	Thermal discharges from the station (MWth)
0	320	32	680
150	270	42	580
300	220	52	480
600	120	72	280
900	30	93	70
1000	0	100	0

The first three columns of this table are taken from a publication of the Commission of the European Communities. The source is given in document R.28, para. 3.

TRANSPORTATION

At the present time the dependence of transportation within human settlements on oil products is almost total, electricity playing a very minor role indeed. There was little either in the documentation for the Ottawa Seminar or in the discussions in Ottawa to indicate that this dependence is likely to be reduced in the short or medium term. The Polish paper (R.14) did, however, argue that electric forms of public transit (including existing forms such as the tramway and trolleybus) are likely to play a larger role once again, replacing diesel buses. This was echoed in a paper from the United States of America, which drew attention to the Electric and Hybrid Vehicles Act of 1976 in that country:

There are potential markets for electric and hybrid vehicles in both private and commercial applications, such as passenger vehicles, delivery vans, agricultural vehicles and light duty trucks, particularly in the longer term. . . . technologies can be developed to provide electric vehicles with extended daily urban operating ranges of 100 miles or more. As a minimum, this range capability could substantially impact the buying trends of second- and third-car households. At present the number of vehicles owned as second and third cars [in the U.S.A.] is 26 million. This substitution alone would result in a savings of about 400 million barrels of oil annually by the year 2000. . . .

Hybrid vehicles offer an important set of options for meeting personal transportation needs. They may be operated in an all-electric mode for short-distance urban trips, or they may operate in the hybrid mode with unrestricted range at a higher efficiency than conventional vehicles.

In addition to their potential for making significant shifts of the transportation energy base away from crude oil, electric and hybrid vehicles offer an additional benefit. They can make use of existing utility capacity for recharging during off-peak hours. Currently, 40 - 50 percent of utility capacity is idle at night, an amount capable of recharging up to 35 million vehicles without additional capital investment.   (R.26, Annex 1, paras. 10, 11, 12.)

Like district heating systems, the use of electric vehicles is already much more common in some countries (e.g. the United Kingdom) than in others, and there is a growing interest also in electricity-powered light rapid transit systems in and adjacent to major centres of population, as an alternative to expensive mass transit facilities. The role of electric vehicles may therefore be much more significant in the future than in the recent past, when the convenience and cheapness of buses and gasoline-driven cars led to the abandonment of electric public transit systems.

Apart from oil and electricity, the only prospect of other forms of energy affecting the transportation patterns appears to be the possibility of large-scale production of hydrogen through decomposition of seawater using nuclear electricity plants. This, it was suggested in one of the French contributions to the Ottawa Seminar (R.12), may be practicable towards the end of the century, but the first uses of such hydrogen are unlikely to be in transportation. The prospects for electric-powered and hybrid vehicles appear much brighter at present.

COMMUNICATION AS A SUBSTITUTE FOR TRANSPORTATION

As in buildings, conservation appears as an attractive option in the transportation field in reducing dependence on expensive and depleting sources of fossil fuel. A French paper points out that much transport is not desired and that it is important

. . . distinguer la "mobilité souhaitée" (valorisable) de la "mobilité obligée", c'est-à-dire imposée par des contraintes de localisations spatiales. C'est seulement

la réduction de cette dernière que devrait viser une stratégie de conservation de
l'énergie. . . .*   (R.11, p. 5.)

The Polish contribution pointed out that some of these journeys could be replaced
by the wider use of communication systems, including television, telecommunications
(including videophones), automation and computerization of accounting, reservation
and information systems, pneumatic transmission systems and shopping by phone or
mail (R.14, pp. 2 - 3).

Some of the opportunities that can be obtained from such developments were described
in a paper prepared for the Ottawa Seminar by the Department of Communications of
the Government of Canada.

Table 7 illustrates the energy required for two people to make a 400-mile trip for a
3-hour meeting versus the energy required to hold a corresponding conference:

TABLE 7

	Primary energy input (kWh)
Telecommunications	
Telephone	Less than 1
Studio base audio system	2
Viewphone	40
Transport (average occupancy rates)	
Air	2500
Car	1600
Rail	450

(R.37, pp. 4 - 5.)

There is, therefore, considerable scope for communication systems as replacements
for transport, and the Canadian paper described three possible applications: the substitution of teleconferencing facilities for business travel, the use of communications
facilities in remote medical services, and similar facilities used in continuing education
in the medical profession.

From questionnaire surveys it was found that in Canada:

The average business trip for the business traveller lasts 2 - 9 days and involves
1 - 7 hours which are spent in 2 - 7 meetings. . . .

The substitution of telecommunication facilities by 20% of the business travellers
on intercity travel would be reflected in a 3% savings of energy used by the transport sector in Canada. This can be translated to about 1.3% of the national petroleum consumption.   (R.37, pp. 11, 5.)

The telemedicine experiment was conducted in 1976-7 using a geostationary satel-
lite that linked a remote nursing station in northern Ontario, the regional base hospital

---

* *Editor's translation:* ". . . to distinguish "desired mobility" from "forced mobility", the latter being
required by spatial separation of activities. Energy conservation strategies should concentrate only on reducing forced mobility. . . ."

and a university teaching hospital that was approximately 500 air miles from the base hospital.

> The nursing station was linked to the base hospital and the University Hospital by voice, facsimile and EKG. . . .

> The signals sent from the base hospital to the University Hospital included real-time video, voice, facsimile, EKG and electronic stethoscope. Return links to the base hospital were audio and facsimile only. Cameras at the base hospital could be controlled remotely. . . .　　　　　　　　　　　　　　　　　　　　　　(R.37, p. 17.)

It was found that

> . . . about 62,000 air-miles or 11% of the total travel between base hospital and university hospital could be saved.　　　　　　　　　　　　　　　　　(R.37, p. 20.)

This saving involved both patients (some of whom did not need to be transferred to the southern hospital) and specialists. No reduction in quality of medical care seems to have occurred; indeed, the increased opportunity for consultation between the base hospital and the university teaching hospital was an added benefit.

A similar tele-education project in Newfoundland and Labrador found that, through the provision of audio and video links between the provincial capital and regional centres, "approximately 60% - 75% of travel time can be substituted by the use of telecommunications to deliver continuing medical education" (R.37, p. 24). This is a significant finding for a province where, in 1975-6, a total of 918 students and 51 instructors were involved in such education; of these 240 people had to travel a total of 134,611 miles in the absence of telecommunications facilities.

More experiments of this kind are clearly desirable: on the one hand, the benefits, in terms of convenience, time-saving and energy conservation are potentially very great, but there are also arguments that the increase in communications facilities may themselves generate increased demand for face-to-face contact and therefore lead to increased transport. One of the U.S.A. contributions to the Ottawa Seminar (R.26) concludes that at present the net effects on energy use of telecommunications improvements remain to be determined.

THE LOCATION OF NEW ENERGY FACILITIES

As noted already (p. 38), one of the French papers for the Ottawa Seminar suggested that future energy developments were not likely to affect the distribution of industry and population so profoundly as did the adoption of steam power in the nineteenth century or of electricity, oil and gas in the earlier part of this century. Nevertheless, the same paper pointed out that the location of the energy-generating systems themselves will give rise to significant planning problems. So far as nuclear electricity is concerned, for example:

> En raison des nécessités de refroidissement, les centrales sont en effet demanderesses d'espace dans les vallées des grands fleuves et le long du littoral, c'est-à-dire dans les zones pour lesquelles il existe déjà une très forte demande pour d'autres activités

industrielles ou de grandes infrastructures (installations portuaires notamment),
pour l'urbanisation, pour les loisirs, et qui constituent bien souvent des espaces
naturels sensibles qu'il convient de protéger.*   (R.12, p. 6.)

Such pressures are likely to increase if objections to nuclear or conventional energy
facilities (on safety, pollution or other grounds) force such facilities into remote locations. If centralized energy production (especially of nuclear electricity) was less important there would probably be less difficulty integrating energy facilities into the pattern
of human settlements. It seems likely, however, that the provision of energy facilities
will be a planning issue of growing importance during the remainder of the century in
proportion to growing concern for the quality of life. A Canadian contribution to the
Ottawa Seminar described, for example, the problems involved in selecting the most
appropriate route through the 150 km of the Montreal Laurentians for the 735 kV electricity transmission lines from the James Bay project. Long-distance transmission is
not a new problem for Hydro-Québec, but the detailed analysis required nowadays
meant that over 227 alternatives and sub-alternatives involving a total length of 850 km
were analysed before the route was determined (R.29, p. 11).

---

* *Editor's translation:* "Because of their cooling water requirements, the generating stations are in practice seeking to locate in major river valleys or on coastlines, i.e. in the areas where there already exist many
demands from other industrial activities, major installations (especially port developments), urban growth
and from recreation, although the areas themselves are often significant natural landscapes that should be
preserved."

Chapter 3

"ENERGY CONSCIOUS" HUMAN SETTLEMENTS PLANNING

PLANNING FOR UNCERTAINTY

How are regional planning objectives and policies likely to be affected by future changes in energy supply, including the introduction of new supply and transformation technologies?

What should urban and community planners do differently in future in response to recent and anticipated energy changes? (1/Add.3, Annex IV, para. 2.)

These questions did not receive clear answers at the Seminar. Similarly, relatively few of the fifty specialized papers prepared for the Seminar set out to define the roles and responsibilities of community and regional planners in an energy-expensive and energy-scarce world. Of the four or five papers that were concerned with this issue, two were limited to the lessons learned in relatively small and distinctive new communities (Louvain-la-Neuve, Belgium, and Fermont, Canada); the other three papers all came from a single country, France.

The subject, it seems, is one that is too vast to tackle effectively at the present time, when we have only a very limited understanding of the role of energy in the community. A city, or any other similar human settlement, represents a complex integral of energy use: different purposes, amounts and forms of energy, different periods of energy use, and different priorities. It is evident that some types of human settlement use energy very differently to others of comparable size; for example, the pattern of energy use in Los Angeles must differ greatly from that in New York on grounds of climate and city form alone. To a large extent, indeed, the form and function of cities such as Los Angeles and New York are responses to the influence of energy factors at the time of their growth; such influences can be identified in cities and human settlements of all kinds: pre-Industrial Revolution, nineteenth century, or contemporary. Since these settlements account for a very large proportion of national energy consumption—and presumably also of national energy waste—and since they are the home of millions of people who are vulnerable to a future energy situation very different from those that influenced the growth of these settlements, there seems little doubt that the urban and regional planner has a major role to play in assisting such settlements, and the populations they contain, to adapt to the changed energy situation.

It is easier, however, to show that the planner must have such a role than to define what that role is or to identify the actions that are needed. The first difficulty is our present lack of knowledge. The integral of energy use in a city or similar community is so complex that neither the planner nor anyone else has at present an adequate quantitative understanding of the various elements in this integral or even, in most cases, of

57

the sum total of energy use of all kinds. One of the French papers for the Ottawa Seminar likened the energy exchanges in a city to those in natural systems, but pointed out that urban exchanges are more complex because man today draws heavily on accumulated reserves of energy (coal, oil, gas or nuclear) whereas natural ecosystems depend more directly on solar energy (R.11, pp. 3 - 4). The paper urged that quantitative investigation of the energy fluxes in urban areas should be a first priority for research; at present, however, we are unable to identify opportunities for conservation or for the substitution of one form of energy for another; nor can we establish which forms of energy use are most essential.

Still less can we evaluate reliably the differences in energy balances between cities or over time in the context of other social, economic or environmental characteristics of these cities. There is therefore little basis at present for saying, for example, that a higher level of energy consumption in one city is "worse" than a lower level in another city; the energy consumption may be essential for some characteristic of life in the first city that is valued more highly. At the extreme, it is evident that the *per capita* consumption of energy in Manchester, Lille or any other city that developed during the Industrial Revolution is higher today than it was in the nineteenth century. But few would wish to return to the overcrowding and other social evils that were associated with the absence of adequate transportation systems. This is an extreme example, but in general it is difficult to put a value on energy use in human settlements unless the problem is defined very narrowly.

Thirdly, even if adequate evaluations of energy use and energy waste were available, the planners' ability to alter present patterns is limited by the long life of individual structures, and the even longer life of urban forms. If Paris, or Manchester, or Los Angeles, are inefficient users of energy in terms of their urban form, there is relatively little that can be done in the short and medium term. Cities adapt, but slowly.

The limitations on the planner's role are further increased by the fact that the energy changes come at a period of stabilization of the population of the ECE region. Opportunities for designing and building imaginative energy-conserving new communities will be much more limited in the future. It is, indeed, one of the ironies of the present situation that the relatively brief period of cheap energy coincided in the ECE region with a similarly limited period of rapid population growth and post-war reconstruction, so that an excessive proportion of our present stock of human settlements is modern structures erected with little or no concern for the price or supply of energy to them.

In the face of these major uncertainties, what then should be the planner's role? As one of the French contributions affirms, it is first of all necessary to recognize that no action is "energy neutral":

. . . même si l'on est pas encore en mesure d'affirmer avec certitude ce qu'il faudrait faire, il paraît être de la responsabilité des planificateurs et aménageurs d'intégrer rapidement cette préoccupation dans leur réflexion et sans leur pratique. Il est, en effet, illusoire de penser qu'une politique urbaine quelle qu'elle soit puisse être neutre vis-à-vis de l'énergie.*   (R.11, p. 10.)

* *Editor's translation:* "Even though we are not yet in a position where we are certain what should be done, planners and managers seem to bear some responsibility for integrating this concern into their thought and action as quickly as possible. It is, indeed, an illusion to imagine that urban policy of any kind can be neutral in regard to energy."

A second requirement is that the planner should constantly keep in mind the need to balance energy objectives against other human settlement objectives:

> . . . si l'énergie sous toutes ses formes est un facteur essentiel du bien-être matériel, elle n'en constitue pas l'essence. Il importe donc de savoir l'utiliser de la façon la plus efficace possible de sorte que sa rareté ou son renchérissement ne deviennent pas une contrainte dirimante pour la satisfaction du désir général au mieux être en ville.*
>
> (R.11, p. 10.)

It is also an illusion to think that the planner is master of the situation:

> Il serait illusoire d'espérer réduire "mécaniquement" la consommation d'énergie des villes par un agencement particulier de leur configuration spatiale: la planification n'a pas la maîtrise de cette consommation et, par ailleurs, même si on la considère comme nécessaire, elle ne constitue probablement pas une condition suffisante pour réorienter de façon radicale les processus du développement urbain.†
>
> (R.11, p. 6.)

II.2   In the discussion that took place in Ottawa, several delegations emphasized that, at a time of such uncertainty concerning future energy supply and use patterns, and the price and availability of different fuels, one of the most useful roles of the urban and regional planner may be to ensure that energy options are kept open wherever possible: that buildings or communities do not become tied unnecessarily to a single form of energy for space heating, transportation or other purposes. Decisions affecting such uses tend to be taken at the present time with little regard for the long-term implications or rigidities that they involve. Many of these decisions, further, may be taken in terms of existing energy price and availability considerations, which may be very short-lived indeed. The French paper for the Ottawa Seminar urged that:

> . . . LE CHAMP D'ACTION DE LA PLANIFICATION URBAINE en matière de conservation de l'énergie (qui, parce qu'elle touche aux structures, est plus fondamentale qu'une politique d'économies d'énergie) NE PEUT QUE S'INSERER DANS UN OBJECTIF DE REDUCTION DE L'INELASTICITE STRUCTURELLE DES CONSOMMATIONS URBAINES.‡
>
> (R.11, p. 7.)

The argument that the urban or regional planner has less "responsibility" for reducing energy waste and increasing efficiency in human settlements than might at first appear does not reduce the need for the planner to acquire a much better understanding of the urban energy balance. In the complex human settlements of the present day,

---

* *Editor's translation:* ". . . although energy in all its forms is an essential factor in material well being, it is not the central element. What is important is to know how to use it as efficiently as possible, so that its scarcity or its rising cost shall not be major barriers to the achievement of widespread aspirations for an improved urban lifestyle."

† *Editor's translation:* "It would be foolish to seek to reduce "automatically" the use of energy in urban areas through some specific form of urban layout. Planning is not in control of such energy use and, moreover, even if they were thought to be essential, energy considerations are probably not a sufficient reason for revolutionary changes in the process of urban development."

‡ *Editor's translation:* "THE AREA OF CONCERN FOR URBAN PLANNING SO far as energy conservation is concerned (which, because it affects structures, is more fundamental than an energy saving policy) CAN ONLY FORM PART OF THE OBJECTIVE OF REDUCING THE STRUCTURAL RIGIDITY IN URBAN ENERGY USE."

energy is as central an element as employment, shopping facilities, traffic movement, and other aspects of urban life with which the planner has long been directly concerned.

Quantitative studies of this urban energy balance must be broadly based. One Canadian paper for the Ottawa Seminar, which reviewed existing literature and research on "Energy and Urban Form" (R.48), found a wide diversity of views, and often conflicting conclusions, on such basic matters as the relationship between amount of energy use and the density of urban development, between energy use and the form of development, and the effect of different land-use patterns on energy use. It is very difficult to isolate such influences from other factors such as the size of the city, its physical setting and climate, and the characteristics of residential and other buildings (e.g. age of building, ratio of single family dwellings to apartments, etc.).

Since an overall view of urban energy balances must wait on much more detailed investigation, the planner's role was discussed at the Ottawa Seminar mainly in regard to three specific aspects: urban mobility, heating systems and the role that urban and community planning should have on the form and orientation of individual buildings.

II.6   **MOBILITY**

The functional separation of activities within the city (especially the separation of employment from residential areas) has been a canon of urban planning for a long time, especially after it was set out as a basic principle in the 1933 Charter of Athens. In recent years it has come under increasing criticism, partly on the grounds that such separation is wrong in principle (it assumes too mechanistic a view of urban areas), but also because it is in any case becoming less and less relevant to contemporary conditions. The glue factory, the chemical plant and the tanning works are no longer the threat to the quality of life—or even to basic health—in residential areas that they used to be, because such activities form a much smaller proportion of total employment and economic activity in ECE countries than they did half a century ago, and because the planner's professional concern to reduce such nuisances has been transformed into public concern for the quality of the urban environment.

Functional separation can be criticized on energy as well as social grounds.

> The spatial separation of urban functions reached its peak when the motor car became the dominating mode of transportation transforming the image of the towns through the large amounts of space used for roads, urban freeways, and parking facilities, and through the encouragement of further urban sprawl.*

Functional separation by its nature requires movement of people between functions. This may not merely be socially inconvenient and unnecessary (especially in societies with a more emancipated view of the role of women than in the past); it may be very wasteful of energy in transportation.

Such mobility, as has been noted already (p. 52) is "mobilité obligée": the type of urban movement that those involved would be very willing to avoid if acceptable alternatives were offered, in contrast to the "mobilité souhaitée" that all available evidence

---

* Economic Commission for Europe, *Human Settlements in Europe,* ECE/HBP/18, United Nations, New York, 1976, p. 35.

suggests they value very highly. The problem, of course, is how to reduce this forced mobility in existing cities that have such well-established and durable rigidities. Put another way, since planners have spent half a century encouraging functional separation in cities, the process cannot be rapidly reversed even if it is agreed to be desirable. Nevertheless, several ways of reducing energy consumption do exist. In many cities, for instance, improvements in urban transit, especially those involving metro or light rapid transit construction, have been linked to the development of suburban employment, or to commercial and similar development. This, over time, may appreciably reduce the average length of regular trips. Such developments may also generate other problems, such as inner city decline, underlining the need for a comprehensive understanding of the costs and benefits, throughout the economy and society, of measures to improve energy economy and efficiency.

II.2　　As a substitute for the functionally segregated urban model, one of the French contributions to the Ottawa Seminar offered the concept of the "archipelagic city", which is currently being studied in the French *Centre de Recherche d'urbanisme*. This type of city would be composed of a number of "islands" of activity, each relatively self-contained and limited in area to about 100 ha. These islands would be separated by open spaces that are used by the distribution and transportation systems that link the islands together.

> Dans le domaine des transports, une élévation du prix de l'énergie devrait aller à l'encontre des tendances récentes à la spécialisation des espaces urbains (zones d'habitat, de commerce, d'affaires, de loisirs, d'enseignement, d'industries . . .), à l'extension et à la dédensification des zones suburbaines. Les tendances inverses (quartiers plus complets, plus diversifiés et plus autonomes, développement des transports en commun et des espaces piétonniers, densification de l'habitat et des activités autour de transports collectifs en site propre . . .) correspondent aux options principales de l'urbanisme en archipel.* 　　　　　　(R.11, p. 9.)

Stockholm is suggested as the city that comes nearest at the present time to this archipelagic model.

Some recent investigations in the United States and other countries have attempted to quantify the effect on energy use of different patterns of urban and suburban land use. For example, the counties of Suffolk and Nassau, in the urban fringe of eastern Long Island, are an area where the present population of 2.5 millions is expected to reach 4.0 millions by the year 2000. Two patterns of future land-use planning were compared: a continuation of the present "urban sprawl" and a pattern of "corridors, clusters and centers".† It was estimated that the energy demand by the additional population would be 19.0 per cent less if the expansion took the "corridors, clusters and centers" form. The largest potential savings were in transportation, where energy

---

* *Editor's translation:* "In the transport field, a rise in energy prices should work against recent trends towards specialization of urban land use (residential areas, and similar areas for trade, businesses, recreation, education, industry . . .), towards urban growth and declining densities in suburban areas. The opposite trends (neighbourhoods that are more diversified and self-contained, public transport systems and pedestrian zones, clustering of living activities around transport nodes . . .) correspond to the major opportunities of the archipelagic city."

† *Land Use and Energy Utilization, Interim Report,* BNL 20577, Brookhaven National Laboratory and State University of New York at Stony Brook, 1975, p. 99.

use would be less than half the urban sprawl figure. If this saving were combined with the larger savings that are possible through using more efficient automobiles, the total transportation energy use in the region (including that by the 2.5 millions who already live in urban sprawl conditions) would in the year 2000 be only 65 per cent of the consumption in 1972, although the population would have risen by 65 per cent.[*]

At a time when the "étalement urbain" seems to be over in most ECE countries, the direct relevance of the Long Island study to other areas may be limited. Nevertheless, the methodology used in the study is relevant to the type of quantitative urban energy budget analyses that are needed throughout the ECE region. The study also provided quantitative support for the belief that many of the principles of urban and suburban planning, designed to reduce urban sprawl, that have been developed and implemented in most ECE countries since 1945, have already had a significant effect in restraining the growth of energy demand in human settlements.

An American contribution to the Ottawa Seminar suggested that among the prospects for urban transportation in the U.S.A. are:

> Continued increases in car ownership among non car-owning families of low and moderate income as they rise in the economic scale and are able to purchase the means of personal mobility, with its resulting freedoms of choice and psychological satisfactions. Continuation of the present thrust of U.S. policy to seek energy conservation within this expansionist framework rather than encourage more families to do without a car.   (R.26, para. 20.)

Although there are some who would regard this continuing emphasis on access to individual transportation as misguided, it is likely to be characteristic of most countries in the ECE region. Nor need it conflict with the distinction drawn in the French paper (R.11) between "forced mobility" and "desired mobility". Measures to reduce the amount of forced mobility caused by urban functional separation, etc., are unlikely to reduce the desire of the majority of people to achieve desired mobility. Quantitative studies in the U.S.A. have also shown that a greater return, in terms of energy efficiency, can be obtained by improving car mileage/fuel consumption ratios than by feasible shifts from private to public transit.[†] A Canadian paper, based on an analysis of transportation needs in the province of Quebec, reached a similar conclusion:

> In the short term, the energy saving from a realistic transition to public transportation would be only 2.77 per cent of the energy consumed for transportation in Quebec; 1.73 per cent would be in the Montreal area alone. In the longer term . . . (a transition from 40 per cent to 70 per cent of trips by public transportation) the energy saving would barely be over 10 per cent. On the other hand, it has been shown that by increasing the number of small cars to 50 per cent, and by maximizing the energy efficiency of present engines, the savings would be 8 per cent and 12 per cent respectively.   (R.31, p. 5.)

Measures to improve automobile efficiency are much easier to implement, and are more acceptable, than attempts to divert people from private to public transportation.

---

[*] *Ibid.*, p. 132.

[†] Ford Foundation, Energy Policy Project, *A Time to Choose,* Ballinger Books, 1974, pp. 443 - 4.

In Canada, as in other countries, steps have already been taken to initiate this process:

> Since 1974 new cars sold in Canada have been subject to a graduated excise tax based on automobile weight. . . . Mandatory fuel efficiency (sales-weighted fleet averages) have been announced for the range of automobiles in Canada. These standards are set at a minimum of 8.5 km/1 (24 miles per gallon (mpg)) for 1980 and 12 km/1 (33 mpg) for 1985.*

BUILDING FORM

Although the energy implications of building form are primarily a matter to be considered in Chapter 5, building form is likely to be influenced strongly by decisions taken in the wider context of urban planning. At the present time it seems probable that in most instances such decisions may have undesirable effects, although this is accidental rather than deliberate.

As an American contribution to the Ottawa Seminar pointed out:

> . . . the dimensions, shape and topography of the site, as well as regulations regarding set-back distances and space between structures, may determine much of the building envelope design and seriously impact the energy consumption of the building. The need, therefore, is to consider the conservation of energy when planning the community, the subdivision and the individual site in order to moderate the constraints placed upon the design of the building. . . .

> The shape and size of lots, setback distances, space between buildings and, in turn, the shape and size of buildings are controlled to a great degree by zoning ordinances and restrictive covenants in the United States. The size, location and configuration of streets are determined by traffic engineers or city and county planning commissions. Real estate values are established by appraisers, financial institutions, mortgage insurance agencies and partially informed purchasers.

> The groups responsible for preparing the myriad regulations and procedures governing planning and construction are primarily concerned with maintaining property values, separating conflicting land uses, the efficient movement of traffic and the provision of convenient services. To date they have not expressed a dedication, or an interest, in energy conservation. There is no recognition that as the cost of non-renewable fuel escalates that energy efficient sites may become more valuable than those rigidly conforming to prescribed real estate doctrines. The results of the work of these groups may hinder or enhance later attempts to reduce energy consumption during the building planning process.   (R.4, paras. 4, 30, 31.)

Although the structures of local planning, and the parties involved in the process, differ considerably from one country to another, the energy implications of the shape and orientation of buildings may be largely ignored in most countries in favour of other criteria. This need not necessarily happen, and the American paper described how the problem is being overcome in one community:

---

* Canada, Ministry of State for Urban Affairs, *Habitat and Energy in Canada,* pp. 57, 58.

In the city of Davis, California, a consortium of municipal authorities, planners, academicians and environmentalists is attacking the energy problem with a multidisciplinary approach. . . .

II.2   In this city a comprehensive study designed to promote energy conservation has produced several recommended policy changes. . . . Building standards were examined with the intent of providing improved thermal performance. Neighborhood planning was studied to determine the energy-consuming constraints of planning practices. Finally, commentary was provided for solar heating and cooling design in the city. . . .

The most promising aspect of the Davis program concerns the neighborhood planning proposals. This approach consists of examining the various ordinances that provide obstacles to the utilization of solar energy in neighborhood design and proposing revisions of each. The investigation has ranged from minor concerns such as the placement of fences on lots to major concerns such as street design.

Three-dimensional envelope zoning is proposed in an effort to assure shadow-free solar collector locations and unobstructed windows. Not considered among the Davis proposed regulations is an attempt to regulate air movement. Cold air moves in much the same manner as water moves—seeking the lowest level. Ordinances and covenants now cover the movement of surface water from one site to the next. Sunshine laws are enforced and right-to-light decisions are being rendered by many courts. It may not be too unreasonable to predict similar laws on air movement as more becomes known about the effect on energy consumption.

                                                              (R.4, paras. 35, 36, 38, 39.)

II.5   **HEATING SYSTEMS**

     As noted in Chapter 2, the installation of district heating systems in suitable settings appears to offer major benefits in terms both of increasing energy efficiency and in user convenience and cost. However, it is also apparent that the main barriers to the more widespread adoption of such systems are not technical so much as administrative and institutional; attitudes also play a significant role.
     It is doubtful, for example, whether many urban and regional planners, in regions or countries where such district heating schemes are rare at present, have much knowledge of the technology or economics of such systems, or of the benefits and costs that are involved. Yet, by the nature of the work they do, urban planners are in a particularly good position to identify opportunities for such systems, in projects for redevelopment, rehabilitation, urban extensions, and so on.
     More broadly, it seems reasonable to suggest that urban planners should in future accept a responsibility to take space heating and cooling implications into account in their work, in individual as well as district or centralized systems. Further, the vulnerability of the individual energy user, discussed in Chapter 2, is something that should
I.1   surely be a legitimate concern of the planner. In the past it might have been legitimate to take energy supplies for granted, but it would be difficult to justify this at present and in the future. If, to take one example, large numbers of people occupy modern

high-rise buildings that depend on a single source of energy, or a narrow range of sources all of which are beyond the control of the individual occupants, the community planner surely bears some responsibility for ensuring that such people have reliable energy supplies at reasonable prices.

TWO EXAMPLES OF ENERGY-CONSCIOUS PLANNING

The town of Fermont in subarctic Quebec, described in a Canadian paper for the Ottawa Seminar and visited by seminar participants on the subsequent study tour, illustrates a number of the points made in the American paper on form and orientation quoted earlier in this chapter. The town, completed in 1976, accommodates 5000 people in a compact area of only 190 acres (77 ha)

> In Fermont, a linear five-storey multi-purpose windscreen building was designed to give protection from the cold north-western, northern and north-eastern winds. According to calculations based on tests, the wind shadow of this 50-foot-high windscreen building affects the microclimate of almost two-thirds of the townsite area. . . .
>
> Care must be taken that wind breaks do not obstruct the downhill flow of cold air. . . . In fact, the windscreen building in Fermont is designed to facilitate this flow of cold air and diverts it sideways to a gully at the western section and the lake to the east.
>
> Approximately one-third of all dwelling units in Fermont form part of the windscreen building; one-third are town-houses or semi-detached homes in the windshadow of the windscreen building and one-third are detached single-family dwellings built in enclaves interspersed with belts of trees for wind protection.
>
> (R.33, pp. 6, 7, 9.)

The area of Fermont, it may be noticed, closely approximates the size of one of the "islands" in the archipelagic city described earlier in the chapter. High density combined with low rise has also enabled the city of Louvain-la-Neuve in Belgium to be designed for a maximum population of 50,000 (13,500 by 1980) in an area of 350 ha, and in a radius of 900 m.

One feature that is of particular interest is that, at the time that the master plan for Louvain-la-Neuve was approved in 1970, energy conservation was not a significant factor. Nevertheless, the plan includes a number of elements encouraging energy conservation, indicating again that conservation of energy is often likely to be compatible with good urban planning to meet other objectives. The concentrated nature of the development, for example, reduces journey distances and encourages walking rather than vehicular transport; it has also had a beneficial effect on the microclimate, protecting the town from cold northerly winds blowing across the Plateau of Lauzelle; and has enabled the use of a district heating system serving all buildings in the town (R.24).

In their respective ways, Fermont and Louvain-la-Neuve are both atypical when compared to normal planning problems, which are seldom concerned with the creation of subarctic towns or new university communities. From another perspective, however, they can be regarded as examples of common sense uncommonly applied to planning problems. There is no reason, for example, why the many earlier subarctic mining towns that were built in previous decades should not have incorporated similar energy-saving ideas to those used in Fermont. The microclimatic opportunities have been understood for a long time, and the benefits can be justified in terms of comfort and convenience as well as in terms of energy conservation. Louvain-la-Neuve *was* planned in the form it has mainly for comfort and convenience, but the design also proved to be energy-saving as well. There seems no reason why these examples—or the example provided by Davis, California (p. 64)—should be so rare as they are. Despite all the uncertainties about the present use of energy in human settlements, despite the greater uncertainties of future energy supply, and despite the limited influence of the urban and community planner, there is considerable scope for energy-conscious settlement planning if the opportunities are recognized and taken.

Chapter 4

NATIONAL POLICIES AND STRATEGIES CONCERNING ENERGY USE AND ENERGY CONSERVATION IN BUILDINGS

Although, as previous chapters have indicated, it is difficult to define at the present time clear directions for public policy in regard to the integrated use of energy in human settlements, the problem seems much more manageable at the scale of the individual building. There is a large amount of detailed knowledge and professional opinion, indicating that most existing buildings use excessive and unnecessary amounts of energy for space heating and other purposes. There is a similar consensus that many opportunities and techniques are available to reduce this waste. In particular, new buildings can be designed and constructed that will use much less energy than existing ones. The demand for such action is as strong from those professionally concerned with energy use in buildings (see p. 27) as it is from building users who are acutely aware of the rapid rise in energy prices in recent years. This sense of both the urgency and the practicability of action was reflected in the discussions at the Ottawa Seminar where, in the debate on energy conservation in buildings:

> . . . the majority of delegations expressed a firm conviction of the necessity of urgently developing and implementing an energy-saving policy by enlisting appropriate government agencies in the solution of this problem at all administrative and political levels, national, regional and local.   (CRP.10/Add.2,p.2, see also p. 135.)

The Ottawa Seminar recognized, however, that "reducing energy consumption is a more difficult problem than increasing energy production" (*ibid.*). It may well be more desirable and effective in the long term: as the International Energy Agency pointed out:

> A barrel saved is as useful as a barrel produced—better in many respects. . . . Most careful studies indicate that investments required to achieve energy savings will have a higher return on investment and thus a more positive effect on GDP growth and employment than many of the supply expansion alternatives being considered in IEA countries.*

Increasing energy supply is, however, in many respects a more straightforward problem. To build a new thermal power station, to develop new mines, oil wells or similar facilities is a complex operation, but when constructed they serve the needs of thousands of individual users of energy. If energy use in human settlements is to be reduced, by

---

* *Energy Conservation in the International Energy Agency,*

contrast, this involves concerted and continuing action of all these users. Faced with the enormous difficulties involved in changing the energy *use* patterns of the whole population, it is scarcely surprising that, as the IEA found, many governments have opted, in the short run at least, for the "technological fix", searching for alternative ways of maintaining and increasing energy *supply*.

I.3   **THE NEED FOR BETTER DATA AND ADEQUATE MODELS**

As with energy budgets of communities, there are major gaps in our knowledge of energy use in individual buildings, and these are at present major constraints on policy and programme development. Data on housing conditions and other building characteristics have been collected in all ECE countries for many years; the emphasis in the past, however, has not been on data that are relevant to energy use, but on socioeconomic factors such as the availability of basic facilities, overcrowding, etc. Some of the available data can be used to provide broad estimates of energy use, but there are also many gaps in essential knowledge.

In the United Kingdom, for example, there are major differences in energy consumption—and also in the potential for conservation—between houses that were built with external cavity walls and those that are of "solid" construction. The changeover from solid to cavity construction took place about 1936, and data are regularly collected on the approximate age of the existing housing stock. Nevertheless, there does not appear to exist at present a reliable figure (accurate to ± 10% in a total of about 10 millions) of the actual number of houses in the United Kingdom that lack cavity walls. Similarly, there are great differences in energy use in row housing, depending on whether the individual unit is at the end of a row or in the middle, or in apartments between top-floor apartments and those in the middle of a block. Yet in all countries it is possible only to make broad estimates of the relative proportions involved.

In the past the main way of providing quantitative estimates at the national level, other than by such generalized estimates based on surrogate data, was by making detailed studies of a small number of individual buildings, and then extrapolating the results. Although such detailed studies are essential as a basis for conservation policies based on particular techniques, the dangers of extrapolating individual characteristics to national totals that may be counted in hundreds of thousands or millions are obvious.

The problem is not one merely of obtaining reliable data about the energy characteristics of the main types of building. Knowledge is also required about the modifications that have already been made to such buildings and the behaviour and desires of building occupants. Such data is essential not merely in order to make energy conservation targets more realistic, but also because it is important to know what energy conservation measures can be left to individual initiative, and which require government intervention or assistance if they are to be effective.

Expressed more simply, in order to develop appropriate policies, strategies and programmes for energy conservation in buildings, governments need reliable models of current energy use in buildings. At the present time the models available are inadequate
I.6   because the data base on which satisfactory models can be developed is inadequate. Efforts are under way in the ECE region to remedy this problem. For example, the

Economic Commission for Europe itself is organizing a seminar in 1979 on the use of models in energy conservation. Meanwhile, the paper prepared for the Ottawa Seminar by the International Institute for Environment and Development illustrated the complex problems involved in developing a model that is adequate for national policy-making and programme development. The IIED Energy Project model was initially developed to describe the energy use in the United Kingdom housing stock, but it is designed to be adaptable for use in other countries. The model is a disaggregated one, enabling the elements that are distinctive in one country to be replaced by those of another.

Given any climatic region, energy used for space heating depends on eight factors:

1. internal temperatures to be maintained;
2. hours during the day/night during which this temperature is to be maintained (occupancy);
3. internal floor area and volume of the dwelling to be heated;
4. ventilation rate;
5. built form (intermediate flat, mid-terrace house, detached house, etc.) . . .;
6. type of wall construction (e.g. cavity and non-cavity walls) and the U-values of walls and roofs;
7. window or glazing area as a percentage of total wall area;
8. fortuitous or "free" heat gains from hot water, cooking, appliances, lights, occupants, etc. . . .   (R.39, pp. 3 - 4.)

With a knowledge of climatic conditions, these data can be used to estimate the *useful energy demand* for space heating. These can then be converted to national estimates of *delivered energy* and *primary energy* requirements (see diagram, p.40). As Fig. 2 indicates, this disaggregated approach involves complex calculations; provided that the data problem can be overcome, however, such disaggregated models are likely to be much more reliable than the very generalized estimates that must be used in most countries at present.

THE PROBLEM OF INDIVIDUAL VARIATION

Although models such as that described above will greatly facilitate the development of comprehensive strategies and programmes for improving the efficiency of energy use in buildings, the implementation of such programmes needs to take into account the fact that energy use in an individual building is dependent on the characteristics of that building and the behaviour of its occupants. In the final analysis each building is unique, and most effective national strategies must reconcile this individuality with the necessity for an overall approach.

The residential sector in all countries, for example, consists of an almost infinite variety of housing types, styles and ages. Even when new and unoccupied, houses of identical style may have significant differences in their energy budgets (e.g. different rates of natural air infiltration due to faults in construction). These differences increase enormously over time as the buildings are constantly modified by their occupants: such occupants have at present relatively little knowledge of the energy implications of such

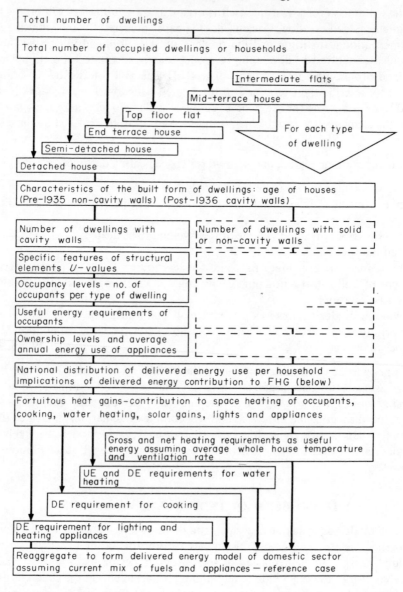

Fig. 2. Methodology for U.K. domestic sector model of energy use. (Source: R.39.)

modifications in comparison to the professional managers of large office or similar premises. To achieve maximum efficiency in the use of energy, each building therefore requires individual assessment and treatment, but this is scarcely practical in a national programme affecting millions of buildings. There does, however, seem to be a need for some intermediate stage between individual building assessments, and generalized advice that necessarily minimizes the importance of individual building characteristics.

II.3
II.4

As one of the Dutch papers (R.21) for the Seminar showed, generalized studies, and advice developed from them, can lead to significant improvements in current practice, but something more is needed.

One attempt to provide such a bridge was described in a Canadian paper for the Ottawa Seminar, and was also described to participants in the study tour.

> . . . a public system of thermal analysis of all relevant components of individual dwellings was first developed in the Province of Prince Edward Island. Run successfully as a pilot program on the island, the computer-based system "Project Enersave" relies on the householder's responses to simple questions, mainly on the dwelling's envelope characteristics. From these, the householder is given an analysis which includes fuel and money savings for the proper upgrade actions, the cost of the actions (and a "payback" period which justifies and ranks their potentials), and commentary on individual points including some problems and possible risks in extensive upgrading of certain houses. . . .   (R.46, p. 20.)

Particular care was taken to keep the questions simple, so that errors would not be introduced by inaccurate responses. No areas, window sizes or similar complex dimensions were to be measured: the most difficult requirement was for a linear measurement of the total perimeter around the liveable floors.

> Other responses are simpler, denoting fitting a "basic shape" (plan), "style" (cross section) and foundation exposure. . . .

> The *perimeter/shape* responses alone are forced into an envelope prognosis of sufficient accuracy for the Enersave purposes. . . . The gross wall area is taken directly from the perimeters. . . . Window area is taken as a typical relationship for house age and "style", but qualified by the owner. Roof area is differentiated into approximate proportions: "accessible attic" and "inaccessible ceiling space" by the householder. Exposed floor, if any (exposed to the outdoors, in effect), must also be noted. The complex house can thus be expressed as envelope components with their areas defined well enough for approximate analysis of savings potential.

> The major difficulty to be overcome concerning the heat saving calculations was the means to express in the analysis results:

> 1. The effect of extensive addition of insulation on the *air leakage* characteristic of a component and thence the *air change* characteristic of the whole house.
> 2. The changing proportional effect of "free" replacement heat in better insulated houses. . . .

> The pilot run of Enersave in Prince Edward Island elicited an encouraging 60% return of mailed questionnaires. This is in itself a startling success. . . .

> Field checks and manual analyses have shown that the Enersave printouts are reasonably accurate and appropriate. . . . Further Canadian Enersave campaigns

will be undertaken in 35 communities during the summer of 1977. . . .

(R.46, pp. 23, 24, 25.)

The Enersave project, as just described, is mainly directed at improving the energy characteristics of residential buildings. It has been supplemented on Prince Edward Island by a similar project for commercial and other larger buildings, using a mobile "energy bus" that visits each premises and enables immediate computer assessment of the major characteristics and conservation opportunities (and also, in appropriate cases, identifies the need for more detailed analysis by energy use consultants).

Of even greater importance, perhaps, are the differences in energy use between one building and another that are caused by variations in individual behaviour. The variation in energy use of 5 to 10 times in buildings of similar type that was cited in the CIB paper for the Ottawa Seminar (see p. 35) was confirmed by other delegations on the basis of their national investigations. In such circumstances, "technical fix" approaches may bring little or no benefit; more insulation, for example, is of little benefit if the main heat losses are caused by excessive ventilation caused by the preferences—or carelessness—of building occupants. Little is known, however, about the willingness or ability of people to modify their habits in order to save energy. National strategies must emphasize information, education and public involvement, and can be expected to yield significant results only over the long term.

I.3

THE DISTINCTION BETWEEN PUBLIC AND INDIVIDUAL BENEFIT

Variations in individual behaviour patterns, and reluctance to alter these patterns, may indicate that public objectives are not easily reconciled with the priorities of individual building users. This has already been touched on in regard to the lack of any general public perception of an existing or impending energy crisis (Chapter 1, pp. 27-8), and the Irish paper prepared for the Ottawa Seminar paid particular attention to the diversity of outlook. Six methods of assessing the effectiveness of energy conservation measures in buildings were examined, and the Irish paper then went on to point out that:

The building user's main concern is whether or not it is worthwhile to invest in a particular energy conservation measure or to choose between a number of conservation measures which may be mutually exclusive. With all its problems and limitations, cost-effectiveness remains the most appropriate technique for this type of decision. . . .

The Government's concern is first of all to establish whether certain energy conservation measures should be supported and, if so, what methods should be used to ensure their implementation. This is a more complex problem. A cost effectiveness assessment of the measure is clearly of interest, but this will not generally be sufficient. . . .

(R.13, pp. 10, 11.)

One of the Finnish papers referred to a similar problem:

In Finland . . . from the national point of view the optimum thickness of insulation is greater than that from the private point of view. That is why we think in Finland that there must be regulations in official building codes for insulation thicknesses. . . .

(R.23, p. 10.)

Similarly, the United Kingdom paper pointed out that:

The evaluation of the benefits of thermal insulation techniques in existing dwellings can in theory be looked at from a number of points of view.

a. Direct energy and cost savings to domestic consumers.
b. National energy savings on a heat supplied basis.
c. National savings of premium fuels, particularly those that can be used for transport and/or chemical feedstock.
d. National energy savings on a primary energy basis.
e. Long run benefits of any savings from investment in conservation measured against investment in supply.
f. Social, health and environmental benefits. . . .

The main difficulty in the household sector is to attempt to relate the short term decisions of 19 million householders—amongst them 10 million owner occupiers— to the longer term national needs. It is unlikely that they will individually decide to use discounted cash flow techniques in looking at investment and so one of the major roles for the British Government will be to devise ways in which they can be encouraged to act in the longer term interest. (R.43, paras. 4.1, 4.12.)

II.3

THE CHOICE OF OBJECTIVES IN NATIONAL STRATEGIES

When governments establish their priorities among the range of opportunities listed in the U.K. paper, such decisions have major implications for the type of national policies, strategies and programmes that are devised. The overall desirability of reducing energy waste and improving the efficiency of energy use in human settlements can be taken for granted, but there are considerable differences in the current and future problems between countries, and between different groups or regions within individual countries, and these are likely to have a major influence on the type of strategy adopted.

Several countries, for example, have found it necessary to seek to reduce energy use in the domestic and other sectors because of the rapid deterioration in their external balance of payments position, arising from the rise in price of imported energy resources since 1973. The papers prepared for the Ottawa Seminar by, for example, Finland (R.22), France (R.12), and Denmark (R.10) refer to this problem. For such countries, the initial and overriding imperative is likely to be a reduction in total energy use, or at least to achieve a substantial reduction in the rate of growth of energy demand as compared to the pre-1973 period. A subsidiary objective may be increased utilization of indigenous fuel and other energy resources, even though these may have been uncompetitive with imported supplies in earlier years.

I.2   Other countries may place more emphasis on the need to assist their populations to minimize the damaging effects of energy price rises on standards of living or quality of life. Here the priority is defined not so much in terms of national energy use as in rela-tion to individual or family situations and budgets. Particular attention may be paid to special groups in the population that are particularly severely affected. In Canada, for example, the overall cost of electric space heating in Nova Scotia or Prince Edward Island was reported to be five times that of gas-fired space heating in the province of Alberta. The poor are also hard hit: the ECE Secretariat recently quoted American studies which showed that:

> . . . a general rise in the relative price level of energy would be socially regressive because energy intensive products comprise a larger proportion of the budgets of low income than of high income families.*

1.1   Yet another type of strategy may be primarily designed to reduce the vulnerability of countries or energy users to sudden changes in the conditions of energy supply. The vulnerability may be felt at the national level, where, for example, it forms a major ele-ment in the United States' National Energy Plan:

> The U.S. has three overriding energy objectives:
>
> — as an immediate objective that will become even more important in the future, to reduce dependence on foreign oil and vulnerability to supply interruptions;
> — in the medium term, to keep U.S. imports sufficiently low to weather the period when world oil production approaches its capacity limitation; and
> — in the long term, to have renewable and essentially inexhaustible sources of energy for sustained economic growth.†

To reduce vulnerability may also be important at the individual level, as in the depen-dence of certain users in eastern Canada on oil-based electric space heating, or more widely in the problems of occupants of multi-occupation blocks who have little control over the means of space heating and other energy uses.

On a long-term view it could be argued that national policies and strategies should be designed less to react to current problems and more to assist energy users in making the transition to the energy supply conditions that are likely to become the long-term norm. The major problem, of course, is that it is very difficult in most cases to forecast what that norm is likely to be unless, as in France, a major policy decision is taken to commit future energy development to the nuclear option. In practically all situations, however, national policies can safely be based on the assumption that the real cost of energy is likely to rise during the remainder of this century as conventional sources become de-pleted. Rather than seeking to raise energy prices within countries towards the inter-national price, therefore, it may be more realistic—if more difficult—to adopt the long-run marginal cost of new energy supplies as the desirable base.

The fact that national energy policies and strategies are likely to be based on an assump-tion of rising energy prices emphasizes the need for reconciliation between energy poli-

---

* Economic Commission for Europe, *Increased Energy Economy and Efficiency in the ECE Region,* E/ECE/883/Rev.1, United Nations, New York, 1976, ch. I, para. 64.

† United States, Executive Office of the President, *The National Energy Plan,* Washington D.C., 1977, p. ix.

cies and human settlement policies designed to meet other objectives. The human settlement planner must be concerned that strategies adopted to reduce energy use and to
facilitate the transition to a different long-term pattern of supply and use should not
unnecessarily damage progress towards other important goals for the quality of life in
human settlements.

As an illustration of the potential conflicts that may arise in regard to specific proposals for energy conservation, one of the Swedish contributions to the Ottawa Seminar
included an evaluation of a possible nationwide programme to install internal insulation
on external walls of dwellings. Over a 15-year period, the costs and benefits were estimated as Table 8.

TABLE 8. *Millions of Swedish Crowns at January 1977*
prices; present value discounted at 2%[a]

1. Investment (private; secondary benefits not included)	+ 3748
2. Restricted competition	−37
3. Unemployment	−226
4. Vocational training	+ 32
5. Costs of removal of labour	−1
6. Workers' compensation for absence from home	+ 77
7. Reduced noise level	−534
8. Premature replacement of wallpaper	+ 66
9. Cleaning job and preparations	+ 262
10. Decrease in apartment area	+ 6327
11. Evacuation of apartment	+ 157

	9871
Energy saved at 0.1 Sw. Cr. per kWh	7709
Net benefit (negative = net cost)	−2162

[a] A discount rate of 2% may seem surprisingly low . . . But remember that it is the real rate. With an inflation rate of 10% the nominal
rate of interest should be 12 - 14%.   (R.17, p. 7.)

It is evident from Table 8 that the dominant factor causing the costs of internal insulation to exceed the benefits is the decrease in apartment area caused by the addition of
internal insulation: ". . . in Sweden we value a reduction of one square metre at about
20 US dollars a year" (R.17, p. 5). Other countries, or other Swedish analyses, may
of course choose to adopt different monetary values for the various costs and benefits
that are difficult to quantify, but the value of the Swedish example in the present context is that it illustrates very clearly the need for careful analysis of the impact of proposed energy-saving measures on the quality of life in human settlements and the need
also for better data and more sophisticated models of energy use in order that such
evaluations can be sufficiently comprehensive. It was against the background of a discussion of problems such as these that the Ottawa Seminar concluded that:

In several countries comprehensive and integrated policy for energy conservation
requires coordination of policies in several sectors such as finance, employment,
research and development, education and training. In these countries it must
furthermore embrace both residential and public buildings and be directed towards

both new and existing buildings. The resulting costs and benefits must be distributed in an equitable and socially acceptable manner. (see p. 154.)

I.5

III.2

THE RESPONSIBILITY OF THE PUBLIC SECTOR

The implementation of national strategies for increased energy efficiency in human settlements is not limited only to the encouragement or compulsion of others to take action; governments have a particular responsibility to take action in their own areas of responsibility. Because of the large elements of energy use in human settlements that are directly under their control, such action will have a major impact in quantitative terms. It is also likely to be important as an example to other energy users of what can be achieved.

The opportunities for direct action by governments include four principal areas of concern. Firstly, large amounts of office and other space in public buildings are owned or leased by governments for the performance of government functions. In the United Kingdom,* for example, buildings directly owned by central government account for almost 2 per cent of all floor space in buildings; in addition much more is leased, and still more is under the control of other levels of government. Energy-saving measures in such buildings act as an example to the thousands of people who work in or visit the premises. For example, the head office of the provincially-owned electricity supply utility in Ontario was visited in the course of the Ottawa Seminar study tour. The modern headquarters of Ontario Hydro in Toronto is unconventional only in the fact that it has no conventional heating plant: space heating is provided through utilization of "free" heat from lighting, office machines, occupants, and by waste heat recovery systems that include thermal storage systems in underground water tanks.

Secondly, and probably of much greater significance, very large amounts of housing in most ECE countries are either directly owned by governments or are financed by governments. As the ECE publication *Human Settlements in Europe* (p. 84) pointed out, "astronomical sums of public money are locked up in these schemes", and it would be unrealistic if governments sought to encourage increased energy conservation by the private sector while lagging in the implementation of similar improvements to the housing stock for which they are directly responsible.

Thirdly, as the Ontario Hydro example reminds us, a large part of the energy supply systems in ECE countries is either owned or closely regulated by governments. In the centrally planned economies, virtually all energy supply is under direct public control; in the market economies there are significant differences between countries, and particularly between different forms of energy supply. Electricity utilities, for example, are generally in public hands except in the U.S.A., but the supply of oil products is normally handled by the private sector. In all countries, however, the regulatory power of governments over all forms of energy supply has been established for a long time because of the quasi-monopoly conditions under which it is usually efficient to supply the energy and because of the central role that energy supply plays in national economies. At the present time, energy utilities almost everywhere remain primarily oriented

---

* Pat Tindale, Energy and statutory controls in buildings, *Building Science,* Supplement, 1974, pp. 67 - 83.

towards meeting the demand for energy. Whether in public or private ownership, they do not perceive their primary role as that of minimizing energy use. Nevertheless, their position in the economy and their immense reservoir of expertise and experience cause energy supply utilities to be, potentially, the best armies for energy conservation that governments possess.

The fourth major area of human settlement energy use that is directly under governmental control is public transport. Here again, many systems are owned and operated by governments, usually at the municipal level; other systems are in the private sector but are again closely regulated by public bodies.

III.4   Much governmental responsibility for energy conservation, it will be noticed, is concentrated not at the national level but at other levels and particularly in municipal governments. Municipalities are generally the principal managers of public housing, and they are often responsible for public transport. In some countries, such as Sweden, they may also be responsible for energy supply systems, and in total they account for a large proportion of the floor-space devoted to public buildings. To a very great extent the success of any *national* strategies aimed at increasing the efficiency of energy use in human settlements depends on the efforts of municipal and other levels of government. Apart from their areas of direct responsibility, they administer building regulations, implement zoning laws and often administer financial and other assistance to housing.

The importance of the municipal level was recognized in energy conservation proposals recently prepared by the National Board of Physical Planning and Building in Sweden, and included in one of the Swedish papers for the Ottawa Seminar. The Board proposed that:

> . . . the Act on Municipal Energy Conservation should be supplemented for the purpose of making the Act directly applicable not only when it is a matter of providing buildings with energy but also in respect of measures to save energy in buildings. The Act should therefore be expanded so that it becomes incumbent upon the municipal authorities to collaborate in producing energy conservation programmes for existing buildings.
>
> The collaboration of the municipal authorities in the planning of energy conservation measures should be stimulated by means of contributions paid in accordance with similar principles as those which apply to support municipal summary planning. The Board preliminarily estimates that a sum of Skr. 10 million per annum should be put at disposal during the next three fiscal years.   (R.18, p. 7.)

The Swedish National Board also proposed that the management of central government loans or grants for energy conservation should be decentralized to the municipalities. This would entail also the creation of an inspection service at the municipal level to ensure that measures for which financial assistance has been provided are in fact implemented. Lastly, it is recognized in Sweden that if the municipal level of government is to fulfil this role effectively, the technical capacity of appropriate municipal departments in regard to energy conservation will need to be increased. A similar situation is likely to exist in most ECE countries, and municipal governments should perhaps become a special target group in programmes of education and information about future energy supply conditions and the opportunities and need for energy conservation in human settlements.

EXAMPLES OF EVOLVING NATIONAL POLICIES
AND STRATEGIES

As already noted, one of the Finnish contributions to the Ottawa Seminar remarked that "Distinct energy policy objectives were lacking until the 1970s . . . (R.22, para. 6), and much the same could be said of the majority of ECE countries, although countries with centrally planned economies have generally integrated energy supply into the framework of national development plans. In the relatively brief period that has elapsed since the 1973 crisis, it is inevitable that new energy policies, and especially energy conservation policies, have tended to be tentative and fragmentary. Nevertheless, virtually all countries in the ECE region have been forced to make major readjustments to their energy supply and use patterns, and many have begun to develop long-term policies. A number of countries reported their progress to the Ottawa Seminar.

Several countries, including Sweden and Canada, have begun by establishing targets for future energy consumption that require a marked reduction in the rate of growth in demand typical of the period up to 1973. In 1975, for example, the Swedish Riksdag (Parliament) established a target for energy growth of only 2 per cent per annum during the 10-year period to 1985. Although this is a marked reduction in growth as compared to the pre-1973 period, it meant particularly severe restrictions in the human settlements sector, since it was anticipated that most of what growth in energy consumption did occur would be used to meet industrial demands. Similarly, in Canada a major objective of the federal government is

> . . . to reduce the average rate of growth of energy use in Canada over the next ten years to less than 3.5 per cent per year. . . .

> All Canadian Government departments and agencies have been directed by the Cabinet to consume 10 per cent less energy in 1976-77 than in 1975-76. This level of consumption is to be held for 10 years, regardless of future increases in building inventory.   (R.49, p. 1.)

Targets of this kind, it is evident, are established through a "top-down" approach; they are based on a perceived need at the national level for overall savings, and there is little attempt to take the social costs and benefits of such targets into account. The ways in which the savings are to be achieved are generally devised after the targets themselves have been established: the target does not emerge as a result of analysis of available options. Such an approach, while it may be justifiable or even essential as a quick response to a sudden and serious crisis, is obviously insufficient as a basis for a long-term policy. Apart from the possibility of inequities and similar problems, it may well be that the targets are too modest or conservative, when compared to what is really possible. The Swedish Riksdag recognized that its initial (1975) targets were only interim ones, and decided to review them in 1978 in the light of experience and research into supply and conservation opportunities. By 1977 it was already clear that changes would be necessary:

> The forecast indicates a total energy consumption for 1977 falling short of the level which would have been permissible according to the averages indicated by the Riksdag resolution of 1975. This shortfall is attributable to the industrial sector. Energy consumption in the transport and communications sectors appears to be rising relatively fast, while in other sectors it seems to be developing more or less at the speed estimated in the documentation underlying the Riksdag resolution. The forecast also indicates an increase in electricity consumption outstripping the average growth of energy consumption.

> The next resolution on energy policy is to be taken by the Riksdag in 1978, but the Riksdag has already proclaimed an urgent need for savings over and above the 1975 resolution. This will demand the reinforcement of existing measures and the addition of new ones.   (R.18, p. 2.)

Other considerations have influenced the responses that have been taken up to now in other countries. One of the Dutch contributions to the Ottawa Seminar mentions that unemployment was a factor:

> In the period from 1974 to 1977 funds were made available on behalf of energy conservation measures in the building industry, with a view to stimulating employment.   (R.20, para. B.2.)

The paper from Czechoslovakia (R.6) suggests a number of principles in design that would make buildings less vulnerable to changes in energy sources in the future. At the present time, however, the most comprehensive approach to future energy needs and supply is probably that contained in the United States' National Energy Plan, published in April 1977. It is intended to be "a practical blend of economic incentives and disincentives as well as some regulatory measures".*

Equity is also a major consideration: ". . . the United States must solve its energy problems in a manner that is equitable to all regions, sectors, and income groups."†

In this Plan (which by late 1977 was still awaiting formal approval by the U.S. Congress), conservation and improved efficiency in energy use are seen as fundamental:

> The cornerstone of the National Energy Plan is conservation, the cleanest and cheapest source of new energy supply. Wasted energy—in cars, homes, commercial buildings and factories—is greater than the total amount of oil imports.‡

The American plan does incorporate evidence collected since 1973 about specific opportunities for energy conservation, and this may account for the importance accorded to conservation. In many respects, however, it is still very largely a "top-down" approach, based as it is on the principal short-term objective of reducing the dependence

---

* *The National Energy Plan, loc. cit.,* p. xiii.

† *Ibid.,* p. 27.

‡ *Ibid.,* p. 35.

of the U.S.A. on external sources of energy. Meanwhile, however, the American and other ECE governments are beginning to receive well-documented advice on the scale of benefits that can be looked for from conservation, at least in technical terms. Much of the evidence relating to human settlements was brought together in the Symposium on Energy Conservation in the Built Environment that was organized by the energy conservation working group (W67) of the International Council for Building Research, Studies and Documentation (CIB), which took place at Garston (U.K.) in 1976. Other similar meetings have been organized on a national basis, for example in Canada* and France.†

On the basis of estimates made in the "Composite Ten" western European and North American countries (see p. 24), the CIB's paper for the Ottawa Seminar noted that:

> A cautious estimate . . . of the aggregate potential for energy conservation is 10 - 15 per cent of the total annual primary energy consumption of the "Composite Ten".   (R.15, para. 11.)

This figure, it should be noted, although it could be achieved from energy savings only in buildings, is expressed in terms of overall national energy consumption, and is therefore even more substantial than it appears at first sight. So far as new buildings are concerned, the prospects are particularly good:

> Judging from research evidence available at this time it appears quite feasible that it is possible to construct houses in the future which use only about one-third of the primary energy typical of today's buildings, without costing significantly more or without being radically different from the kind of housing with which people are familiar.   (R.15, para. 57.)

On the basis of preliminary results from its disaggregated model of energy consumption in existing dwellings in the United Kingdom, the IIED was able to be more specific in its estimates. For example:

> If all dwellings were insulated to a standard that, on a cumulative cost basis, is cost-effective against present gas prices using a 10% discount rate, the total outlay for consumers would be £4,000 - £5,000 million. This works out at £200 - £250 per occupied dwelling, though the actual cost per house varies widely from £32 for an intermediate flat to £670 for some detached houses. . . .

> Reducing heat losses caused by excessive ventilation rates is by far the most cost effective energy saving measure for (UK) dwellings. It is estimated that, for a total capital expenditure of less than 15% of that for insulation, the total UK Primary Energy demand could be reduced by 1.5%.   (R.39, pp. 6, 7.)

It can be anticipated that national plans and strategies will increasingly depend on such quantitative estimates of savings and costs as adequate data become available and the appropriate models for using the data to provide such estimates are developed.

---

* *Proceedings of the First Canadian Building Congress: Energy and Buildings, Toronto, 25 - 27 October 1976*, Ottawa, 1977.

† *La Ville et l'Energie*, Paris, 19 - 20 January 1977.

Meanwhile, the existing policies adopted by governments have begun to yield signifi-cant results, although it is difficult to identify the effect of individual measures, espe-cially as the period has been one in which rapidly rising prices for energy could be expected to be a powerful inducement to economy, independently of any other action. The U.K. Government, for example, reported that:

> In 1975 conservation measures, including the effects of prices and publicity, were estimated on the basis of 1973 trends to have produced energy savings perhaps as high as 6% ± 4%.   (R.43, para. 1.4.)

The degree of uncertainty indicated in the U.K. estimates reflects the fact that reduc-tions in energy use may not simply be the result of higher prices and conservation poli-cies. The period immediately following the 1973 energy crisis, for example, was marked in many ECE countries by relatively low levels of economic activity and mild winters; both these factors are likely to be quantitatively important in restraining the rate of growth of energy demand, but in our present state of knowledge their quantitative sig-nificance is not easy to identify precisely.

Chapter 5

IMPROVED ENERGY BUDGETS IN
NEW BUILDINGS

The discussion of energy conservation measures for new buildings at the Ottawa Seminar was based on an acceptance of the premise that techniques for reducing energy use in new buildings are well known and generally cost-effective. Improving the efficiency of energy use in new buildings is generally recognized to be much simpler than making similar improvements to the existing building stock. Although the ratio of new buildings to existing stock at any particular time is relatively small,

> In the longer term it is new housing which provides the most scope both technically and economically for conservation. (R.15, para.52.)

At some future date, indeed, the effectiveness of our present response to the changing energy conditions is likely to be judged more by the energy efficiency of new construction than by how we adapt the present stock; there is little justification for continuing to build in the energy-wasteful ways that we have adopted up to now.

ENERGY USED IN THE CONSTRUCTION PROCESS

Although this topic was included in the topics for discussion at the Ottawa Seminar, it received little attention, mainly because the two specialized contributions had found it of less significance than other aspects. A Canadian paper on the subject found that for a Canadian-type bungalow of 102 m² floor plan:

> The typical wood frame house appears to require about a third less gross energy than do the main alternatives, steel or concrete. . . . Solid masonry consumes twice the energy in production compared to typical wood frame housing.
> (R.25, paras. 20 - 21.)

Canadian estimates of construction energy use are larger than European calculations, mainly because of the large amount of energy used in constructing the standard full-size Canadian basement, usually with energy-intensive concrete.

Taking all items and services involved in the construction process into account, the Canadian paper concludes that:

> . . . the total typical house now must represent about 350 million BTU (100,000 kWh). That range represents the heat used through 4 Canadian winters.
> (R.25, para.22.)

The Norwegian paper on this subject also noted the energy economy associated with the low-rise wood-frame buildings common in that country. Over a 40-year life it found

83

that energy used in construction was less than 2 per cent of total energy use, and the energy "content" of the building materials (i.e. the energy used to produce them) was less than 6 per cent. Building heating over the 40 years, by contrast, accounted for 92 per cent of energy use, and the Norwegian paper therefore concluded that:

> The main effort should be concentrated on developing constructions with high thermal insulation performance and air tightness to save energy.

> (R.9, para. 6.2.)

It was on these aspects, and the barriers to their implementation, that the Ottawa Seminar did focus its discussion relating to new buildings.

II.7   **TECHNICAL OPPORTUNITIES FOR REDUCING
                                  ENERGY BUDGETS**

1. Insulation

Since 1973 there has been widespread recognition that many countries had, prior to that time, been using large amounts of energy as a substitute for insulation in order to provide adequate thermal standards in new housing and other buildings. This generalization is not valid for Norway and a few other countries, but insulation standards normally were very poor. In the U.S.A., for example:

> Houses built before 1965 were, in general, poorly insulated—typically 1½" insulation in the ceiling, none in the walls, none in the floors, and plain windows. About 50 per cent of single-family homes are backfitted with storm windows. In the 1965-72 period, increasing amounts of insulation have been installed. The present practice appears to be 2" - 3" in the walls, 4" - 6" in the ceilings, with the higher figures generally applying to electrically heated homes. Windows are usually plain, though sometimes fitted with storm windows by owner. . . . Construction practices on doors and windows have probably deteriorated in the past decade and the effect of better insulation may have been partly offset by leaking doors and windows.*

The paper prepared by the European Insulation Manufacturers' Association (EURIMA) for the Ottawa Seminar showed comparisons of standards before and after 1973 in eight European countries (Tables 9 and 10).

There has clearly been a significant improvement in most countries, although it should be noted that by mid-1976 the new standards adopted by countries outside Scandinavia were less rigorous than those prevailing in the Scandinavian countries before 1973. The EURIMA paper suggests that:

> . . . as a round figure, the savings by improved regulations and practice for thermal insulation are about 20%.

But, what is even more important, is the fact that a further improvement of the

---

* Ford Foundation, Energy Policy Project, *A Time to Choose,* Ballinger Books, 1974, Appendix A.

TABLE 9. *Improvement of insulation levels in new buildings, expressed as k-values (W/m². k)* (adapted from a table prepared by the European Insulation Manufacturers' Association (EURIMA))

Structural element	Period	Denmark	France	Federal German Republic	Netherlands	Italy	Norway	Sweden	United Kingdom
Wall	Before Oct. 1973	0.42	1.57	1.57	1.67	1.39	0.58	0.58	1.70
	Mid-1976	0.36	0.70	0.81	0.68	1.39	0.43	0.35	1.00
	Imminent or recommended	0.30	0.41	0.47	0.57	0.36	0.27	0.30	0.55
Window	Before Oct. 1973	3.00	5.23	5.23	5.00	6.05	3.14	3.10	5.68
	Mid-1976	3.00	3.40	3.49	5.00	6.05	2.79	3.10	5.68
	Imminent or recommended	2.50	2.33	3.02	2.86	3.77	2.33	2.00	5.68
Roof	Before Oct. 1973	0.37	2.91	0.81	0.97	2.03	0.47	0.47	1.42
	Mid-1976	0.27	0.55	0.69	0.68	2.03	0.33	0.25	0.60
	Imminent or recommended	0.20	0.30	0.38	0.62[a]	0.32	0.20	0.20	0.35
Floor	Before Oct. 1973	0.55	2.33	1.01	0.97	1.47	0.70	0.47	1.00
	Mid-1976	0.51	0.80	0.83	0.97	1.47	0.35	0.40	1.00
	Imminent or recommended	0.30	0.71	0.47	0.97	0.70	0.24	0.30	0.50

[a] Sloping roof 0.48.

TABLE 10. *Oil consumption (litres) per heating season in different types of new buildings (adapted from a table prepared by EURIMA)*

	Bungalow			1½ Storey		
	Before Oct. 1973	Mid-1976	Imminent or recommended	Before Oct. 1973	Mid-1976	Imminent or recommended
Denmark	3300	3050	1950[a]	2700	2450	1650[a]
France	8750	4700	2300	8950	4700	1650
F.G.R.	7250	5450	3400	6250	4850	2850
Netherlands	6000	4700	3700	5000	3750	2750
Italy	7250	6400	3750	6700	5500	3300
Norway	5100	3650	2700	4100	3000	2200
Sweden	5100	4100	2350[a]	4200	3300	2050[a]
U.K.	6300	4750	3500	5250	3850	2850

	2 Storey			5 Storey		
	Before Oct. 1973	Mid-1976	Imminent or recommended	Before Oct. 1973	Mid-1976	Imminent or recommended
Denmark	7,900	7,250	5,400[a]	34,100	32,500	20,900[a]
France	19,500	14,150	5,350	63,600	34,300	20,650
F.G.R.	18,350	14,300	8,850	80,800	57,350	37,250
Netherlands	14,650	11,050	8,500	58,300	47,300	32,150
Italy	18,400	16,250	10,600	64,200	59,950	38,600
Norway	12,000	8,800	6,450	49,700	39,950	32,000
Sweden	12,250	9,800	6,500[a]	52,600	46,150	23,850[a]
U.K.	15,200	11,400	8,450	59,950	49,850	42,300

[a] Including the effect of limitations on window areas.

same order of magnitude can be achieved by realizing the indicated aims for the future transmission coefficients (k-values).

It must be pointed out that this further increase of savings can be achieved without any new or revolutionary construction or building technique, and can be obtained by relatively small increases in construction costs.   (R.2, p. 13.)

The effect of such improvements, EURIMA estimates, would be to reduce the amount of heating oil or other fuel required for space heating by approximately one-half as compared to the pre-1973 conditions, depending on the type of building and the winter climate.

2. Glazing

There appears to be a wide, and perhaps unjustifiable, divergence of views and practice in regard to the role of windows in energy conservation in buildings. This is partly a result of the multiple functions which windows serve in a building; as the CIB paper for the Ottawa Seminar pointed out:

> Windows, necessary to let daylight into buildings, can be regarded at the same time as both passive solar energy collectors and badly insulated parts of the walls.
>
> (R.15, para. 18.)

Despite the importance of the internal heat loss through single-glazed windows (exemplified in the pre-1973 transmission values for windows in most of the countries in Table 9), and despite the fact that windows continue to act as passive solar collectors even when double- or triple-glazed, the trend towards the installation of multiple glazing as standard practice is by no means universal in the ECE region, even in non-Mediterranean areas. Countries such as the Netherlands, for example, do not believe that multiple glazing is economically justifiable at present, although it may become worthwhile in the future:

> In view of the fact that, with present energy prices and those to be expected in the near future, the high cost involved in the installation of double window panes will not be economically justified, the specifications in this respect have been confined to the requirement that it should be possible in due course to install double window panes or double windows in a simple manner.   (R.20, p. 5.)

Meanwhile, in more severe climates, Sweden, where double-glazing is already the norm, is likely to require triple-glazing in all new buildings that are heated to internal temperatures of 18°C or more. At the Ottawa Seminar a Finnish delegate noted that:

> . . . there is a satisfactory standard of insulation in new housing construction throughout Finland since the standards which have been adopted by the Nordic Committee on Building Regulations are generally applied. But he also noted that in the future it will be necessary to increase the regeneration of heat and further to increase the level of insulation and also to introduce four-pane glazing which would make a 25% reduction in energy consumption possible.   (See p. 137.)

Scandinavian countries such as Sweden and Denmark have also introduced regulations limiting the amount of window area (as a proportion of total wall area) that will be permitted in new buildings, although additional glazing may be permitted if the potential energy loss can be recaptured by other means.

In summary, the climatic differences that certainly exist in the ECE region do not seem sufficient to account for the diversity of view among countries—from single-glazing in many countries to the prospect of quadruple glazing in Finland and perhaps other Scandinavian countries in the foreseeable future. There also does not seem to exist an adequate comprehensive study of the energy role of window areas in building energy budgets, which integrates (a) the role of multiple glazing in reducing losses of long-wave internal heat, (b) the contribution that windows can make to internal heat budgets as passive transmitters of short-wave solar energy (see p. 44),   and (c) the optimum glazing area in buildings.

3. Heating Systems

Although most ECE countries have initiated or extended their regulatory powers in regard to insulation and glazing, there has been generally less attention paid to the regulation of heating systems in new buildings. The principal exception to this generalization arises where district heating schemes are required by the authorities. As one of the Finnish papers for the Ottawa Seminar emphasized (p. 49), the Government of Finland has taken steps to ensure that local government utilizes opportunities for introducing district heating systems whenever possible. The paper prepared by the U.S.S.R. similarly stressed the need to plan heating systems as part of overall development planning:

> The success of the whole system of power-and-heat supply can be achieved only provided all the three links—the combined power-and-heat generating plants, the heat supply network and consumers—are developed in accordance with a single co-ordinated plan. Infringement of this principle leads to losses.   (R.47, p. 4.)

The situation in Denmark is of particular interest:

> In Denmark at present about 10 per cent of all heating is district heating. Independent of which type of fuel will be used in the future, district heating is planned to cover at least 20 - 30 per cent of all heating.   (R.10, para. 17.)

The Danish experience and prospects were discussed in greater detail in Ottawa.

> The implementation of a national heating plan as a part of the overall energy plan was reported on by Denmark. . . . In producing heat, surplus energy from different sources is used and a better energy economy is achieved than burning fuels in individual homes. Still, individual heating will prevail in single homes because of the relatively high investment cost for connections and adaptations to the community-wide system. . . . The repayment period for the heating plan is estimated to lie between 10/15 years. Considerably more experience has to be gained with the implementation of this system and a number of hurdles have still to be overcome . . . . The seminar considered this national heating plan as one of the most advanced in the ECE region. . . .   (See p. 133.)

Similar planning is being undertaken in several other ECE countries, and one of the Canadian papers for the Ottawa Seminar emphasized the importance of early decisions on district heating and similar plans in view of the demographic changes and the slower rates of construction likely in the future:

> . . . it must be concluded that, while district heating is attractive as a means of reducing energy consumption, increasing efficiency of energy use and reducing the expected price impact on consumers, the most opportune time in which to incorporate district heating in urban development is practically upon us. Beyond 1990, as urban growth slows and new community emplacement diminishes, the opportunity to take advantage of district heating savings potentials will wane.

>   (R.50, p. 40.)

Another technical factor in regard to heating systems for new buildings was identified in the CIB paper for the Seminar: the preference that should be given to low-temperature heating systems in buildings.

> There is an important gain in flexibility if provision is made for low temperature space heating systems in order to be compatible with the performance characteristics of heat pumps, solar energy and district heating. Low temperature heating systems mean either larger radiator surfaces or warm air heating. The latter is particularly difficult to install at a later date if the building was constructed for a wet heating system in the first place. Warm air systems may be easier to design for rapid response, which is likely to be more important in future as the incidental gains will amount to a larger proportion of the total space heating requirements.
>
> (R.15, para. 53.)

4. Ventilation Control and Heat Recovery Systems

Increasing attention is now being paid to the conservation opportunities provided by ventilation control and waste heat recovery. As one American paper for the Ottawa Seminar made clear:

> How much ventilation is adequate is a highly controversial question. There are no uniformly accepted ventilation standards, and those that exist assume that an entire building will be ventilated continuously and at a constant rate. The codes also fail to account for air infiltration, which occurs particularly in entrance and windowed areas. Both assumptions contribute to over-designed ventilation systems and hence unnecessary energy consumption. (R.27, para. 56.)

The new interest in ventilation control seems certain to increase as insulation and glazing standards are brought up to levels where further improvements yield rapidly diminishing returns. In well-insulated buildings, as one of the Finnish papers (R.23) for the Ottawa Seminar pointed out, heat losses due to ventilation may amount to 40 per cent of all losses. They are therefore the logical next step in improving energy efficiency in new buildings. Not surprisingly, it is the well-insulated Scandinavian countries that have made the greatest progress in reducing ventilation losses, and regulations issued in 1976 as a supplement to the Swedish Building Regulations (SBN 1975) require that the maximum rate of natural air leakage in new buildings be reduced to 0.5 air changes per hour (ach).*

In several respects this Swedish regulation represents a major new departure in energy conservation in buildings. It is by no means certain that the building industry (in Sweden and other countries) can routinely build to such high standards without significant increases in costs, and there are similar problems in developing routine methods for testing that the required level of performance has in fact been achieved. Without such methods there is the obvious danger that regulations on ventilation control could become a dead letter. If the required levels of airtightness can be achieved, however, other attractive opportunities open up, including the extension to houses and other

---

* National Swedish Board of Physical Planning and Building, *Regulations on Energy Conservation in New Buildings,* Report 1976-10-08, p. 2.

TABLE 11. *Site orientation chart*

Objectives	Cool regions	Temperate regions	Hot humid regions	Hot arid regions
Adaptations	Maximize warming effects of solar radiation. Reduce impact of winter wind. Avoid local climatic cold pockets	Maximize warming effects of sun in winter. Maximize shade in summer. Reduce impact of winter wind but allow air circulation in summer	Maximize shade. Maximize wind	Maximize shade late morning and all afternoon. Maximize humidity. Maximize air movement in summer
Position on slope	Low for wind shelter	Middle-upper for solar radiation exposure	High for wind	Low for cool air flow
Orientation on slope	South to south-east	South to south-east	South	East-south-east for afternoon shade
Relation to water	Near large body of water	Close to water, but avoid coastal fog	Near any water	On lee side of water
Preferred winds	Sheltered from north and west	Avoid continental cold winds	Sheltered from north	Exposed to prevailing winds
Clustering	Around sun pockets	Around a common, sunny terrace	Open to wind	Along east-west axis for shade and wind
Building orientation	South-east	South to south-east	South toward prevailing wind	South
Tree forms	Deciduous trees near building. Evergreens for windbreaks	Deciduous trees nearby on west. No evergreens near on south	High canopy trees. Use deciduous trees near building	Trees overhanging roof if possible
Road orientation	Crosswise to winter wind	Crosswise to winter wind	Broad channel, east-west axis	Narrow, east-west axis
Materials coloration	Medium to dark	Medium	Light, especially for roof	Light on exposed surfaces, dark to avoid reflection

The chart was prepared for the U.S. Department of Housing and Urban Development by the AIA Research Foundation.

small buildings of mechanical ventilation systems and heat recovery techniques.

It may well be both unacceptable and unnecessary to require that building occupants be prevented from opening windows, as is the case in many large office and similar buildings erected in recent years. It may, however, be feasible and economic to install mechanical ventilation systems that, for the vast majority of the time, eliminate any desire by building occupants to open windows or doors and thereby accelerate energy losses. The advantage of such mechanical systems in relatively airtight houses and other buildings is that they can readily be linked to the next stage of energy conservation: systems that extract the heat contained in both waste water and stale air and recirculate it within the building. This is essentially what is done in the Ontario Hydro building in Toronto; as noted on p. 76, this eliminates the need for a conventional heating system, even during the severe winter.

5. Shape and Orientation of Buildings

The importance of incorporating microclimatic considerations in city design and development was exemplified in Fermont and Louvain-la-Neuve, as described on pp. 65 - 66 . An American contribution urged similar attention in design of individual buildings, although until recently this has been a neglected factor.

> Little incentive has been provided for the passive approach . . . the relation of the building to the site in order to utilize the solar heat gain and natural ventilation and to minimize wind chill. . . . Once a building is poorly located or faultily oriented, the opportunity for correction is gone forever, or the cost is prohibitive.
>
> (R.4, para. 1.)

Table 11 is taken from this American paper, to illustrate the broad adaptations to climate that are desirable in the four main climatic regions of the U.S.A.

IMPORTANCE OF THE DESIGN PHASE IN BUILDING CONSTRUCTION

II.5
II.6

Practically all the opportunities for energy conservation in new buildings described above require that major decisions are taken in the design phase of building construction. The crucial importance of good energy design was recognized in several of the papers prepared for the Ottawa Seminar. For example:

> Integrated design systems, where the architect and the engineers can communicate with each other in all design phases, is becoming more common . . . in Finland. That is the only way to find the optimal solutions.
>
> It is also important that the experts are involved in the building project from the very beginning. At the beginning of the project great decisions are made which influence to a great extent . . . the first and operating costs of the building.
>
> (R.23, p. 11.)

A paper that discusses energy conservation design measures in new office and other large buildings for the Government of Canada similarly noted that:

> It is a paradox of the design process that decisions at early stages, which may have
> a significant impact on performance, must be made at a time when the poorest
> estimate of their consequences is available.   (R.32, p. 4.)

The Canadian paper pointed out, however, that energy analysis by computer is now
feasible as a means of testing alternative approaches before key decisions are taken.
Experience in using such techniques up to now has been hindered by the fact that:

> The architectural design is usually quite advanced by detailed design stage, the
> time when energy analysis is performed. . . . Consequently, although ESA [Energy
> Systems Analysis] is often used to show that the architectural concept which has
> been chosen is unattractive from the energy point of view, it is generally too late to
> do anything about it.   (R.32, p. 9.)

The Canadian paper suggested that the process should begin with the development of
a number of architectural concepts, each of which should be analysed in terms of different HVAC (heating, ventilating and air conditioning) concepts. The latter might
include:

> (i)   use of outdoor air for "free cooling";
> (ii) use of heat recovery from condensor water;
> (iii) use of heat pumps for heat recovery;
> (iv) use of thermal storage tanks;
> (v)   use of solar energy.   (R.32, p. 6.)

Only when a satisfactory combination of architectural and HVAC concepts has been
achieved should the project proceed to the stage of detailed design. This may sound
obvious, but it has not been characteristic of building design in the recent past:

> Buildings as we have designed them in the past have been designed essentially by
> four independents: (1) the architect who designs an envelope; (2) the structural
> engineer who designs a frame to support this envelope, with little concern over
> what's in the frame; (3) the mechanical engineer who designs the mechanical system
> which is stuffed into a building; (4) the electrical engineer who designs his electric
> system and usually the illumination. . . . These really are designed as four separate
> entities, pushed all together into a common package.*

COMPONENT STANDARDS OR PERFORMANCE STANDARDS?

If integrated building design is essential for efficient energy use, it seems logical to
suggest that attempts, by governments and others, to establish targets or limits for
energy use in buildings should similarly be holistic: they should be defined in terms of
the overall energy *performance* or budget of the building rather than in terms of the

---

* R. R. Kirkwood, "Energy conservation: ASHRAE's opportunity, in *Energy Utilization and the Design
Professional,* American Society of Heating, Refrigeration and Air-conditioning Engineers (ASHRAE),
1974.

individual *components* of which it is constructed. Instead of specifying, for example, that the *k*-value for a wall should not exceed 0.30 W/m² K (see Table 9), that ventilation should not exceed 0.5 ach or glazing exceed 15 per cent of the surface of external walls, building regulations might require that the energy use of a building should not exceed a specified amount, expressed in gigajoules per square metre of floor area or per cubic metre of building volume.

Such a performance-based standard would have several advantages. It would be more directly related to the objective, which is the economical use of energy, whereas component standards are normally at least one stage removed from this objective. It would also encourage innovation in design and construction to find the most economical and acceptable ways of meeting the required standard, as far as appearance and convenience are concerned. Precise component standards, by contrast, tend to force building design into a straitjacket without necessarily attaining the desired objective.

There are, however, major difficulties in such an approach; the Nordic Committee on Building Regulations, for example, has concluded that it is not feasible to establish regulations based on performance at the present time. The difficulties already discussed concerning the achievement and monitoring of ventilation standards indicate the type of problem that must be overcome before performance standards become feasible. The new Swedish standard on ventilation is, however, a step on the way towards performance standards, since it involves the assessment of the ventilation characteristics of the entire structure in completed form. Another step might be through the gradual introduction of "product labelling" for buildings: the specification by the builder of the expected energy budget of the structure. It has been remarked many times that it is now mandatory for small electrical and other energy-using appliances in ECE countries to be labelled with indications of their energy requirements, yet the largest item normally acquired by most people—their home—does not come with any indication of the overall energy use characteristics.

OTHER BARRIERS TO IMPROVED ENERGY STANDARDS IN NEW BUILDINGS

1. Cost

It is widely recognized* that a long-standing and widespread problem in the provision of adequate housing for all is that of the first cost. Great, and often very successful, efforts have been made in recent decades to reduce this barrier through industrialized building methods, mortgage assistance, etc., but the first cost of housing remains a formidable barrier to improved housing quality in both public and private sectors in practically all ECE countries. Proposals to improve the quality of housing through more efficient use of energy similarly face the problem that, however worthwhile they may be in the long run, they involve additional initial investments. As already noted (p. 33) the Austrian paper (R.3) recognized that one rationalization used in the past to justify energy consumption as a substitute for better insulation was that operating costs

---

* See, for example, Economic Commission for Europe, *Human Settlements in Europe,* ECE/HBP/18, United Nations, New York, 1976, Ch. 8 .

(for houses as well as commercial properties) were less of a barrier than capital costs.

Many of the problems may be due to habits of thought and practice that are in need of change. Mortgage systems, for example, may fail to take into account life-cycle costs; taxation systems may penalize capital expenditures in favour of operating costs (especially in commercial properties). The rising price of energy may soon reverse these biases that encourage the minimization of first costs and the neglect of operating costs. It is also significant that the Danish paper for the Ottawa Seminar suggested that the cost of improved efficiency was likely to be very small when compared with the benefits:

> It is assumed that, compared to the requirements of the earlier [Danish] building regulations, the new provisions will result in an increase in building costs of 2 - 3 per cent in the case of smaller houses and of ½ - 1½ per cent in the case of blocks of flats. The saving obtained is expected to be 40 - 50 per cent in the case of smaller houses and 25 - 35 per cent in the case of blocks of flats.   (R.10, para. 24.)

2. Awareness of energy use characteristics and relative efficiency

Reference was made in Chapter 1 to the difficulty of making the public aware of the impending energy crisis and of the fact that practically all ECE countries are in the midst of major changes in the pattern of energy use. Even where the awareness exists, there may often be the problem of imperfect information concerning the main opportunities for energy conservation. At the very simplest level, for example, people may attempt to save energy by reducing the number of lights burning in their houses, but may neglect similar attention to water-heating or space-heating systems. The use of energy in a light bulb is easily noticed; water heating is not. Often the occupants may have only a vague understanding of the relative orders of magnitude of energy involved: the light bulb may use 100 W and the water heater 2500 W, but the occupant does not perceive that attention to the thermostat or period of use of a water heater may be 25 times more significant than switching off the light. The problem may not be helped much by energy conservation campaigns based on the principle that any energy saving is worthwhile. So, in principle, it is, but there seems to be a greater need for consumers to have a better understanding of the relative magnitudes of different types of energy use and to demand efficient systems in new buildings.

A related problem, already mentioned, is the frequent inability of the consumer to discover the energy implications of his actions, even when he wishes to do so. It is, for example, difficult for the layman to discover where his conservation efforts in his house may be most useful when there exist at present no simple techniques for measuring or estimating the relative losses by transmission, air leakage, etc., and when the potential occupant lacks any quantitative "product label" that will indicate which house is most energy efficient.

3. Institutional Problems

As the representative of the International Union of Architects remarked at the Ottawa Seminar, "architects . . . mirror the society they live in"; the same is true of the builders and other groups involved in defining the energy budget of individual buildings. Although all these groups are responding to the needs of society and the demands of individual consumers to reduce the burden of high energy costs, the long period of cheap energy has left a legacy of ignorance about the energy implications of energy decisions that will not be easily overcome. As one American expert has remarked:

> . . . we really don't know what we are designing for. Do we want 30% relative humidity in the building, 20%, 5%—we don't really know. . . .

> We made all the decisions for the Veterans' Administration [in the U.S.A.] on what conditions should be maintained in hospitals. We couldn't get this kind of information from the medical profession or behavioural scientists. I would estimate that 10% of the energy we waste is to reach this so-called optimum which no one really appreciates.*

The situation is further complicated by the fragmentation of the construction industry itself which, in many ECE countries, is organized in small units, making diffusion of improved standards and techniques difficult. In the U.S.A., for example, the largest single producer of housing was, in 1973, responsible for less than 0.5 per cent of the total market.† This may be contrasted to the situation in the automobile industry in that country, where measures to improve fuel economy involve only about four domestic manufacturers and a number of foreign importers. The construction industry in most countries also has high proportions of unskilled labour and low investment in research, both restricting the introduction of higher standards.

With all these problems, however, great improvements in the energy performance of new buildings are likely to be achieved throughout the ECE region during the next decade.

---

* F. Dubin, in J. R. Wright and Paul R. Achenbach (eds.), *Scientific American Roundtable on Energy Conservation in Buildings,* 1974.

† Richard Schoen and others, *New Energy Technologies for Buildings: Institutional Problems and Solutions,* Cambridge, Mass., Ballinger Books, 1975.

Chapter 6

ENERGY CONSERVATION MEASURES FOR EXISTING BUILDINGS

SOCIAL AND ECONOMIC CONSIDERATIONS

This topic was one of the principal concerns of the Ottawa Seminar and was the issue that produced the largest number of specialized papers. It is not difficult to see why. Existing buildings, especially the residential sector, are the homes, workplaces, etc., of the present population, and it is in these buildings that the effects of the 1973 energy crisis and subsequent price rises have been experienced. Secondly, with the general decrease in new construction typical of recent years, and the anticipated stabilization of the population in many ECE countries in the remainder of this century, existing buildings are likely to represent three-quarters of the building stock at the end of the century. Even in countries like Canada, where new building rates are expected to remain high for some time, 60 per cent of the buildings likely to exist at the end of the century are already built. Thirdly, there is a general recognition that the thermal efficiency of existing housing in most European countries is very poor. In older buildings, this tends to reflect the inability of the first occupants to afford higher standards in construction and facilities; in more modern buildings it is largely the result of the tendency in much of the post-war period to use cheap energy as a substitute for insulation. The thermal quality of such housing directly affects the comfort and budgets of the present occupants, and it is usual to find that the poorest groups in the population occupy the worst buildings.

A striking feature of the Ottawa Seminar was that the concern expressed for the improvement of existing buildings is as evident in countries where standards are already relatively high (such as Scandinavia and Canada) as it is in those countries which have paid relatively little attention to building energy budgets until recently. The Danish paper, for example, reported that:

> about half of the 1.1 million dwellings in one- and two-family houses in Denmark have insufficiently insulated outer walls, unsatisfactory window types and poorly fitting joints. (R.10, para. 28.)

The Danish Government envisages a major effort to improve such conditions, and has calculated that:

> . . . it pays to invest on average around 10,000 d.kr. in 1975 values in insulation for each dwelling constructed before 1965 in the period 1976 - 1985. This investment will be paid back in terms of less expenditure for energy before 1995, and later on the net gains will grow steadily to considerable amounts. (R.10, para. 14.)

97

Although other countries would endorse the general principle that measures to improve the conservation of energy in existing buildings are justifiable and necessary, they may not be willing to go quite so far or so fast as Denmark, if such action has to be justified by the potential energy savings that can be realized. The U.K. paper, for example, points out that:

> A particular problem that faces British policy makers . . . is that quite a large sector of the population uses comparatively little fuel and therefore will save little or no energy through insulation—thus in these cases the social benefit and public health criteria may have to be introduced to justify improvements. . . .
>
> . . . Since the average total expenditure on fuel, light and power in Great Britain by better-off families is considerably less than £5 per week it follows that there is little temptation to undertake all but the most basic improvements irrespective of the prospect of future price increases. If these arguments are true for better off families there is an even greater problem with poorer families, most of whom will not find it easy to borrow money.   (R.43, paras. 4.2, 4.7.)

As the British paper indicates, more powerful arguments for improvements to existing buildings may in some countries be the social and medical benefits of raised comfort levels that better insulation, modern heating systems and other improvements make possible. In Ireland, for example, it has been estimated by the National Institute for Physical Planning and Construction Research that in non-centrally heated houses (which represent up to 80 per cent of all residential accommodation at present) practically all the initial benefits of improved insulation will be taken in the form of higher temperatures rather than as fuel savings. One experiment in New Zealand, in fact, found that energy use in well-insulated buildings tends to be *higher* than in poorly insulated houses, since the occupants were able to heat the whole house efficiently where insulation was good, whereas in poorer-quality houses only certain rooms were heated at any one time. Such findings do not, of course, reduce the importance of such improvements—the social and health benefits may well be found to exceed the costs of the conservation measures—but they do emphasize the importance of defining objectives and estimating probable benefits before such measures are undertaken.

The Ottawa Seminar, indeed, was very much concerned with the social and human implications of improvements to existing buildings. In the specialized papers and in the discussions in Ottawa, it was clearly recognized that such measures tend to be expensive, especially when compared with the costs of making comparable improvements in new buildings. Where should the financial burden fall: mainly on the occupants of the buildings that are improved, or mainly on governments? How are the improvements to be achieved on the necessary scale: by relying on individual initiative, with financial assistance in certain cases, or do national policy considerations require a degree of compulsion, through retroactive legislation if necessary? Answers to questions such as these are complicated by the fact that all but the simplest improvements involve inconvenience to building occupants whilst they are in progress, and may result in permanent losses in amenity (e.g. in reduced living space by the addition of insulation) as well as energy efficiency benefits.

THE TYPES OF IMPROVEMENTS

The United Kingdom and Sweden both included, in their papers for the Ottawa Seminar, classifications of the various types of improvements that are possible for existing buildings. In Sweden:

. . . the National Board of Physical Planning and Building has divided the energy conservation measures into the following four groups:

1. Modified operation and supervision;
2. Adjustments and maintenance;
3. Simple improvements;
4. Extensive improvements.

Modified operation and supervision covers measures which should be taken by the caretakers, e.g. the supervision of boilers and ventilation systems, and by the occupants themselves who should avoid opening windows to air rooms in chilly weather.

Adjustment of heating and ventilation systems is required.

Maintenance measures in buildings comprise, e.g. sealing of windows and doors. . . .

Simple improvements are normally necessary in respect of installations, e.g. automatic control systems, but there are also measures which concern the building, e.g. thermal insulation of lofts.

Extensive improvements often occur on the building structure and principally refer to additional insulation and sealing of external walls and the replacement or conversion of windows. Installation measures can occur, e.g. in the installation of appliances for heat recovery and conversion to district heating.

The measures 1 and 2 are practically always justified . . . from the point of view of building economy. The costs for improved operation and supervision are insignificant. For adjustments and maintenance the investments are as a rule less than Skr 0.5 per saved . . . kWh. Also simple improvements . . . are as a rule also justified in respect of large parts of the existing buildings and cost about Skr 1 per saved kWh. Extensive measures . . . should normally be combined with other measures which are conditioned by regular maintenance and long-term planned rebuilding. Investment costs can often amount to Skr 2 - 3 per saved kWh and the profitability is greatly dependent on whether the measures can be combined with regular maintenance or planned rebuilding.   (R.18, addendum, pp. 1 - 2.)

The classification of measures contained in the U.K. paper for the Ottawa Seminar is summarized in Table 12.

As might be expected, the two classifications have much in common although such classifications are intended to provide only general guidelines at the national scale. The U.K. paper points out that:

Selection of a particular option will depend on a number of factors, of which the most important will be:

Physical characteristics of buildings, e.g. solid or cavity wall.

Microclimate, e.g. exposure to driving rain.

Intended length of life of dwelling.

Occupancy pattern, e.g. is house occupied all day?

Cost of available treatments.

Whether building can be vacated during thermal improvement work.

Benefit to be gained from thermal improvement.

Potential need for change of fuel and/or heating system.   (R.43, para. 2.1.)

Similarly:

> . . . . *the range of costs will vary quite significantly between individual dwelling types* and even between quite minor variations in construction within the same dwelling type. For example the presence of overhanging eaves and simple window cills will have a favourable effect on the practicability and economics of external wall insulation.   (R.43, para.2.2.)

TABLE 12. *Thermal improvement levels*[a]

FIRST AID Cost range per dwelling: £50 - £250 Energy-saving range: 0 - 20% [b]		Roof insulation—50 - 100 mm Tank lagging Draught sealing Non-thermal work—e.g. electric blanket and curtains Basic repair work Simple damp treatments Improved heater (not central heating)	A repair and improvement package particularly for older stock, especially short life stock and that likely to change hands and then undergo more major improvement to *Insulation* or *Matched* standards Capable of do-it-yourself skills
INSULATION Cost range per dwelling: A: £150 - £350 B: £500 - £1200 Energy-saving range: 5 - 25%	A B	Roof insulation—100 mm Tank lagging and draught sealing Selective double glazing and/or curtaining Cavity fill wall insulation Radiator shelves and reflectors Similar but for solid wall house; internal or external wall insulation	A B	For application to sound stock, particu- larly where cavity walls can be filled All do-it-yourself capable except cavity fill Can be done whilst house is occupied Do-it-yourself except for wall insulation—if internal cannot easily be done whilst house is occupied
MATCHED Cost range per dwelling: £500 - £1800 Energy-saving range: 10 - 30%		Roof insulation—100 mm Tank lagging and draught sealing Selective double glazing and curtaining Internal insulated lining or cavity fill Changed heating system and/or improved controls to match building construction Improved window ventilation control	For application when stock undergoing major improvement, assumed with residents rehoused if internal lining taking place Not suitable for do-it-yourself if cavity fill or wall lining used Heating system work needs specialists
INTEGRATED Not readily applicable to existing stock		*Conventional technology* A range of measures more suited to new buildings, and which lays great stress on integrating the design of heating system to building fabric and incidental gains including window sizing and orientation of dwelling	
AMBIENT Cost range per dwelling: £1000 - £2500 [c] Energy-saving range: 25 - 60%	A	*Developing technology* An extension of the *Matched* treatment to include the use of ambient energy devices, particularly solar collectors and heat pumps. Possible use of heat reclaim in either or both ventilation and hot water	A growing factor in home improvement market Solar water heating a potentially large market which is likely to find wide scope in existing housing in the future Much technical development needed in all fields before reliable and cost effective

[a] Energy saving range estimates are for space and water heating and assume no major shift in primary energy use by conversion from electricity.

[b] Potential for *increased* use in some stock.

[c] A conjectural figure based on likely cost of solar water heating.

Source: R.43, tables 1 and 2.

The latter point is also taken up in the paper for the Ottawa Seminar prepared by the Federal Republic of Germany, which also points out that there is seldom only one approach that can be taken in the case of an individual building:

> It is above all the execution of secondary constructional work which causes additional cost. . . .
>
> If, for example, one wishes to improve the exterior thermal insulation of the outer walls of an existing building, it may become necessary, among other things, to set up—and subsequently remove—a scaffolding (possibly including awnings to protect residents and passers-by), to adapt roof overhangs and gutters to the new facade, to remove and refix downpipes (possibly including an alteration of main pipes in the base), to remove and refit sill covers, to remove from and refix on the facade light fittings, switches, signs and nameplates, etc., to adjust balcony slabs, partitions and balustrades and to repair damaged or stained green spaces, footpaths, etc. . . .
>
> . . . in practice, the task is not to find the best solution with respect to a single structural element—a window or an outer wall—but to reduce the energy consumption for heating in an entire building in the most effective way possible and with as little construction work as possible. There are always several alternative ways to do that. (R.19, paras. 4, 5, 23.)

A Canadian paper for the Seminar made the point that the potential for energy savings of different building types does not necessarily follow the same hierarchy as the relative energy efficiency of the different types. Bungalows, for example, are often regarded as less thermally efficient than more compact dwellings, because of their high ratio of surface area to usable space. However:

> . . . a bungalow and two-storey single house of equal living area and construction cost may be about equal in heating cost but may differ in the return on dollars spent on upgrading: the bungalow has much more attic and basement, and is easy to upgrade, while the two-storey house has much more exposed wall, which can be considerably more costly to upgrade and becomes an uneconomical proposition if a small amount of insulation is already in the wall space. (R.46, p. 8.)

ESTABLISHING PRIORITIES FOR IMPROVEMENT

The paper from the Federal Republic of Germany made another point that is easily forgotten:

> When comparing cost and benefit, one must keep in mind that it is easier to produce a relatively great effect in buildings with poor thermal insulation. . . . In other words: the poorer the existing thermal insulation of a building, the more economic the measures to improve it. (R.19, para. 7.)

The importance of this lies in the fact that it is usually the oldest houses or other buildings, with the shortest anticipated future life, that have poor thermal insulation. Nevertheless, they may well justify treatment, especially if the buildings are occupied by the elderly or the poor, on whom the burden of higher energy prices may be particularly onerous.

As noted above, and in Chapter 4, the establishment of priorities for improvement is consequently very difficult. Even in terms of cost, the U.K. paper points out that, in addition to variations caused by the type and style of individual buildings, there are two other significant variables:

> *The second influence on costs is whether the work can be accomplished by "do-it-yourself" or voluntary labour,* or whether the work has to be done by professional labour. . . . Do-it-yourself techniques are suitable for a large part of the privately owned housing sector, but they are not suitable for the majority of the rented sector under present arrangements. . . . Do-it-yourself methods are also not applicable in the case of elderly and infirm people . . . [and] certain kinds of work such as cavity fill are not suitable for DIY application since they need both elaborate equipment and high operative skill before they can be successful.

> *The third influence on costs is the size of the market,* which can be linked to the stage of development of a material or system. This is particularly important in the case of heat pumps and solar collectors, both of which are at present under development in Great Britain. . . .   (R.43, paras. 2.3, 2.4.)

III. 7   Such influences are clearly not constant; do-it-yourself methods can in many cases be developed and introduced where they do not at present exist, governments can also influence the pace of development and the scale of the market for heat pumps and other new techniques, e.g. by action in the large sector of housing which is under public control.

THE COSTS AND BENEFITS OF RETROFITTING

Several papers prepared for the Ottawa Seminar discussed the problems of assessing costs and benefits associated with particular types of improvement—and therefore of setting priorities and of developing and implementing programmes—that arise because of different perceptions of the costs and benefits. At the scale of the individual building it is possible to devise a package of individual improvement measures that, taken together, will provide a maximum of fuel efficiency for a minimum of investment and inconvenience. The nature of that package will depend on the types of factors suggested in the U.K. paper (see p. 100): the thermal characteristics of the building itself, the patterns of behaviour of its occupants, whether the work will be done on a do-it-yourself basis or not, what the assistance or loan terms are, etc. At the national level, however, there is a different perception. The benefits brought from such individual improvements are likely to be generally welcomed as part of the overall concern of governments for the quality of life of the population, but governments are also concerned with evaluating potential costs and benefits in terms of the energy likely to be saved, the implications for external trade balances, and the effects on employment.

There are, of course, close links between these two attitudes, not least because governments will normally be anxious to encourage building occupiers to initiate their own programmes of improvements. Nevertheless, the distinction in outlook is important, and one of the tasks of the Ottawa Seminar was to examine the extent to which they could be reconciled.

Like the paper from the Federal German Republic, the paper prepared by the German Democratic Republic was concerned primarily with the problems and opportunities— the costs and benefits—as determined at the level of the individual building. The paper compared, for example, the comparative advantages of internal versus external insulation of outside walls of residential buildings. It noted that the use of internal insulation means that the thermal storage capacity of the walls themselves can not be utilized effectively, but it found that the cost and other problems associated with external insulation present greater problems in most situations. In general, it was found that:

> Internal insulation is suited best for low-inertia intermittently operated heating systems (e.g. radiators with a small water capacity, electric and gas heating systems. . . .   (R.16, para. 1.1.1.)

Such systems, which permit rapid upward and downward adjustment of temperature, are particularly well-suited for houses that are occupied for only a part of each 24-hour period, because the whole family is at work, education, etc. Conversely:

> External insulation is suited for continuously operated central heating systems as well as slow single heating systems.   (R.16, para. 1.1.2.)

The benefits, with external insulation, from using the walls themselves as thermal stores are also recognized in the paper from the Federal German Republic, which suggests that the problems of inconvenience and space reduction associated with internal insulation are substantial except in the case of single-family homes where such improvements can be undertaken on a do-it-yourself basis as part of redecorating or other improvement programmes.   (R.19, para. 12.)

Several papers for the Ottawa Seminar were particularly concerned wih the development and implementation of large-scale programmes of improvement. These include Project Enersave in Canada (see pp. 71 - 72) and the Swedish attempts to develop cost - benefit analyses of possible improvements that pay adequate attention to broad social and economic factors and effects. As noted already (p. 75), the Swedish analysis has led to the conclusion that internal insulation of external walls is not justifiable because of the high value assigned to the loss of space which it entails. Similar analyses, reported in the same paper (R.17), found that retrofit installation of meters in multi-apartment blocks to enable hot water to be charged to the actual user is also not justifiable. By contrast, the replacement of double glazing by triple glazing was found to be worthwhile, because of the reduced noise levels and reductions in amount of window replacement, cleaning and maintenance that it caused, as well as the energy savings.

The IIED's model of energy use in the present U.K. housing stock has also been described earlier (pp. 69 - 70). It is being used to provide estimates of the possible savings that can be achieved from various types of conservation measure, and then to assess the ways in which residual space-heating demands could be met after such improvements to the existing stock have been carried out. In particular, it enables dependence on fossil-fuel-heating systems to be compared with dependence on electricity-based space-heating systems, using heat pumps for greater efficiency:

In general, the savings in Delivered Energy effected by the utilisation of electric heat pumps are greater than those where improved-efficiency fossil-fuel systems are used, given identical heating demands. However, in terms of Primary Energy savings, fossil-fuel and heat pump systems compare favourably in dwellings which have a large space heating requirement: improved-efficiency fossil-fuel systems have an advantage in dwellings where the space heating demand is lowest.

(R.39, p. 8.)

ENERGY ECONOMY THROUGH IMPROVED OPERATION AND MAINTENANCE

Apart from structural or similar alterations to buildings and the equipment they contain, significant improvements in economy and efficiency can also be obtained, usually at very low cost, by changes in operation and maintenance procedures. Actions of this kind, because they are easy to do and are relatively costless, were particularly important in the immediate responses to the energy crisis of 1973 and to higher prices for energy. It is clear, however, that they also have an important role in long-term programmes of conservation, especially if the new control systems can operate relatively automatically. For example, the paper prepared for the Ottawa Seminar by the Byelorussian SSR noted that:

> The efficiency of central (hot water) heating systems in fully prefabricated residential buildings is improved by the installation of automatic panel heating. Automation of heating and ventilation systems in industrial and residential buildings curtails heat consumption by up to 15 per cent.   (R.5, Summary.)

Similarly, in the discussions in Ottawa, it was recognized that:

> Improving the functioning of heating systems means, apart from anything else, automatic control to maintain the optimum temperature throughout the period in which the living space is occupied; automatic lowering of the room temperature while the living space is not occupied; using only the necessary number of boilers; and also thorough servicing of the heating equipment.   (See p. 139.)

The installation of such automatic controls on a retrofit basis, may, however, be as expensive as the installation of meters, and without automatic systems such control measures may be applied irregularly, especially in private homes. It may be argued, therefore, that the main thrust of retrofit conservation policies for housing should be towards techniques or improvements that do not require constant attention by the occupant, but that can be achieved on a "once-for-all" basis. In the case of large buildings (offices, schools, hospitals, etc.) the situation is different; these are managed by professional staff who are more likely to maintain efficient practices once these have been adopted.

Two Canadian papers for the Ottawa Seminar described the type and scale of benefits that could be achieved by operating improvements in large buildings. It was emphasized that:

> Comfort conditions need not deteriorate, and in some cases will improve, as a result of energy conservation activities.   (R.49, p. 13.)

In one example, a 5-year old, 4-storey air-conditioned building providing nearly 30,000 m² of office and other space in Toronto:

> The initial investigation showed that the lights were operated until midnight for the cleaning staff, fans were running 24 hours a day, outside air was introduced during unoccupied hours and that some temperature controllers of the automatic control system were faulty. In addition the building's cooling capacity seemed inadequate at the peak of summer.
>
> About 20 energy saving ideas were evaluated, covering a wide range of cost-benefit ratios. A number of no-cost or low-cost proposals emerged, providing considerable savings. These were mostly in the area of reducing operating times. At the other end of the scale was an item with negative benefits at high cost: the application of reflective solar film to the double glazed sealed window units. The computer analyses revealed that in this case the solar heating in winter saved more energy than reducing the cooling requirements in summer.
>
> The proposed program of improvements includes six items for immediate implementation at an approximate cost of $10,000. These include the reduction of operating hours for lights and equipment, limiting outside air quantities and a reduction in general lighting capacity by introducing task lighting. The energy consumption rate is predicted to fall from 3050 MJ/m² to 1420 MJ/m². Correspondingly, the estimated savings in energy costs are 39%, or $86,000 at the 1975 energy rates. . . . At the same time . . . the summer cooling problems should be alleviated because of the reduced load on the cooling plant.   (R.49, p. 11.)

A similar programme of conservation instituted by the Government of Alberta established, on an *a priori* basis, a target of 190 kWH/m² per annum for energy utilization in government office buildings. In a survey of twenty existing buildings it was found that, during the 1974-5 fiscal year:

> . . . the annual energy consumption . . . ranged from a low of 549 kWh/m² . . . to a high of 1920 kWh/m². . . .   (R.34, p. 3.)

Among the reasons for this enormous wastage of energy, the Canadian paper emphasized the following:

> Almost consistently, the existing mechanical systems are over-designed by 30% or more. . . .
>
> Generally, lighting systems are 50% over-designed and occupants in existing buildings with high lighting levels are generally reluctant to accept lower lighting levels. . . .
>
> Most of the systems we analyzed were not operating as they were designed to operate. . . . In a lot of cases the systems could not be operated as they were designed to operate. . . . We have also found in a few buildings that the operating personnel do not understand the systems they are responsible to operate. . . .
>
> The greatest percentage savings in energy are obtained through the scheduling of mechanical and electrical systems—specifically the on-off timing and set-up and set-back of operating temperatures.   (R.34, pp. 6 - 8.)

EXPERIENCE IN LARGE-SCALE PROGRAMMES OF
RETROFITTING

Up to the present there have been few large-scale programmes to upgrade the efficiency of energy use in existing buildings, especially in the domestic sector. Considerable progress has been made in larger buildings, of the kind described in the preceding
section, and authorities in most countries appear confident that large and permanent
energy savings can be made in offices and similar buildings at reasonable cost and without significant reduction in comfort or convenience. In regard to the very large proportion of the building stock represented by residential accommodation, however,
less has been done up to now, although many governments expect that large-scale programmes will be initiated shortly. In Britain, for example:

> At a time of high unemployment, and with the recent emphasis by the British
> Government towards further improving the inner areas of cities, it is possible that
> a major house insulation programme could be of widespread benefit, additional
> to any savings in energy that are realised. The British Government is therefore
> considering the implications of a major national house insulation programme.
> (R.43, para. 5.6.)

Apart from the Canadian Enersave programme (R.46), another large pilot project
that was reported to the Ottawa Seminar was an experiment by the French authorities
in improving the external insulation of 831 dwelling units; 533 untreated units were
used as a basis for comparison. All the units had been constructed more than 15 years
ago, and were taken as fairly typical of buildings that would need to be included in any
national programme of energy saving.

Although the project is still under way it has already yielded valuable results that
will no doubt modify the objectives and methods adopted in a larger programme. Use
of external insulation methods, chosen because of technical advantages and because
they reduce disturbance to occupants to a minimum, give uneven results in multi-occupation blocks:

> . . . on ne peut faire varier que le G [coefficient volumique de déperdition] moyen
> de chaque bâtiment et non pas seulement les G des logements les plus défavorisés.*
> (R.7, p. 4.)

Similarly, the addition of storm windows was not completely successful:

> Dans bien des cas un double vitrage aurait été préférable ce qui aurait évité de
> nombreuses plaintes de locataires. Ces derniers non avertis ont tendance à utiliser
> les survitrages comme des fenêtres courantes ce qui nuit à la fixation et à étanchéité.
> Ils ne comprennent pas d'ailleurs l'utilité d'une deuxième vitre.†   (R.7, p. 7.)

---

* *Editor's translation:* "It is only feasible to alter the average value of G [the heat loss per unit volume]
for a whole building and not the actual value of G in the most inefficient units."

† *Editor's translation:* "In many cases double-glazing would have been preferable, and would have avoided
a large number of complaints from tenants. Those who did not understand, tended to use the storm windows
as regular windows, nullifying their installation and protection. The tenants, moreover, did not understand
the value of an extra pane."

Although the evaluation of the project, over a 3-year period, is still in progress, a number of preliminary conclusions can be drawn. Among them are the following:

— l'équilibrage des bâtiments est, sans la plupart des cas, insuffisant, ce qui conduit à surchauffer bon nombre d'appartements;

— le bon équilibrage est une opération délicate, surtout avec des installations anciennes;

— les premières opérations d'équilibrage sont déjà intéressantes car elles permettent une économie sensible d'énergie. . . .* (R.7, p. 9.)

Because experience in other countries is likely to be very different, the desirability of conducting more large-scale experiments of the Enersave or French kind seems undeniable. Such large-scale experiments also provide an excellent opportunity for the type of public participation in energy conservation programmes that the Ottawa Seminar recognized was essential:

. . . large-scale energy programmes for existing buildings . . . directly affect the living conditions of those who live and work in them. . . . Those to be affected should be consulted in advance so that they can understand the need, costs and benefits of proposed measures and make their views and preferences known before major decisions are taken and implemented. (See p. 154.)

---

* *Editor's translation:*
  "— thermal adjustments of buildings are, in the majority of cases, inadequate, so that a substantial number are overheated;
  — careful adjustment is a difficult task, especially with older equipment;
  — the first attempts at modification are already interesting, since they have made possible appreciable savings of energy. . . ."

Chapter 7

PERSPECTIVES FOR THE YEAR 2000*

We know that the cities of the year 2000 already exist for the most part, and that sociological trends evolve very slowly and over very long periods of time. . . . In the case of energy, we can also anticipate the overall tendencies of the evolution of consumption rates for various energies as well as the scarcities which we shall have to face up to in terms of the availability of both urban space and natural resources. We also know that the options selected in the years to come will dictate the "energy life style" that can be expected in 25 years.

And yet incertitude remains, for progress is never made in a linear direction, but by erratic advancement and regression. . . .

. . . it is essential to adopt an essentially pragmatic course of action, to encourage flexible solutions and minimal investments so that programmes remain adaptable to the more or less unforeseeable trends of the future. This, in effect, is a process of continuous evaluation which, in the absence of an overly rigid or ambitious plan, can be adjusted to new tendencies, and for all its modesty may represent one of the most fruitful long range courses of action.   (R.45, pp. 14 - 15.)

Faced with the problems of price, reliability of supply and permanence of energy resources, countries in the ECE region have begun what is recognized will be a long period of adjustment to the new circumstances. This involves fundamental questions such as the feasibility of dependence on fuel imports, the choice between centralized and decentralized energy generation and the future role of electricity. On a slightly smaller scale, it involves policy decisions about district heating schemes, combined generation, solar and other "new" technologies, the allocation of research expenditures, institutional changes (e.g., in regard to the mandates of energy supply utilities) and the introduction of specific legislative and regulatory measures. Similarly, in regard to energy conservation, the adjustment involves decisions about the appropriate amount of retrofitting in the existing building stock, the resolution of potential conflicts between energy conservation and other economic and social objectives, and decisions on the extent to which conservation measures should be enforced rather than encouraged. The transition will certainly involve measures to ensure that individuals as well as governments are much better informed about the energy situation than they have been in the past.

---

* The title of this chapter is taken from the French paper (R.45) which provides the opening quotation. The remainder of the chapter is a shortened version of the final chapters of the Ottawa Seminar theme paper (R.1), and was written by the present editor.

Despite the uncertainties, despite the great differences between countries, and despite the early stage at which the ECE region stands at present in this adjustment, it is possible to identify a limited number of general scenarios that seem to be guiding energy planning in most ECE countries. Some countries may appear at present to be closely identified with a particular scenario; but more often present policies and actions in individual countries may be compatible with more than one scenario. Yet, again, actions may be being taken on an interim basis, since the necessary information and data base, on which broad policy choices can be made, are not yet available. The scenarios are presented here, therefore, not in order to represent the actual nature of energy policy making, but to demonstrate that different energy policies are possible, and to examine the implications for human settlements planning of different policies.

Four possible scenarios are:

(1) minimum disturbance and "good housekeeping";
(2) the nuclear-electric option;
(3) the "soft technology", non-nuclear option;
(4) the two-stage transition.

1. Minimum Disturbance and "Good Housekeeping"

At present this might also be described as the "wait and see" option, since it could be argued that the present energy supply situation is so confused and uncertain that major departures from past patterns cannot be justified at present although they will probably be required in the future. For some years to come countries will be engaged in long-neglected data collection, research, exploration for new energy resources and experiments with new techniques. It is impossible to forecast the results of this activity, especially because of the difficulty of evaluating in advance the advantages of one line of research as compared to another. In terms of energy generation, for example, fast breeder nuclear reactors may seem to offer certain economic and resource advantages when compared to existing forms of electricity generation. Will these advantages still exist if fluid bed combustion of coal can be introduced on a commercial scale? At the point of end-use, similarly, will district heating schemes, especially on a retrofit basis, still be attractive if better heat pumps for domestic premises become available?

The basic assumption in this scenario is that the heavy dependence of most ECE countries on oil and gas will change only slowly over time. It is recognized, of course, that this dependence on oil and gas must ultimately be substantially reduced, since depleting reserves will be high priced and may need to be allocated to uses where substitution is not easy (e.g. the petrochemical industry). But this is seen as a gradual process, reaching a climax in the twenty-first century. Well before then, the opportunities for new energy supplies and more efficient energy use will be much clearer. For example, current problems in nuclear fission technology, including nuclear waste disposal, may have been solved. The prospects for nuclear fusion will be better understood, and similarly the viability of "soft" technologies using renewable resources (solar energy, wind, biomass, wastes, waves, etc.) should be much clearer than it is now.

The energy-related activities of governments, in this scenario, would therefore probably have four principal objectives during the next 10 to 15 years:

(1) Develop known resources of conventional energy and ensure that exploration for new resources is maintained at a high level.
(2) Adjust energy pricing policies to reflect (a) general world price levels for different fuels; (b) calorific content rather than cost of supply; and (c) relative scarcity of different fuels. The overall impact of such considerations is likely to be a rise in energy prices, but the relative importance attached to these and other factors in determining price is likely to vary from country to country.
(3) Provide substantial encouragement for research, development and demonstration of new energy supply technologies, and for more efficient techniques of energy use. This involves support across a broad range of activities including both "hard" and "soft" technology. In particular it would encourage the evaluation of alternative energy supply and demand strategies so that when, later in the century, major policy choices have to be made, governments are well-equipped to make them.
(4) Recognize that present energy consumption patterns involve considerable waste of resources, and take firm steps to ensure conservation. Since estimates of the life of present resources are based on a continuation of past very high rates of growth in energy consumption, the life of present resources can be extended considerably by effective measures to reduce that growth.

So far as the impact on human settlements planning is concerned, it is the last of these objectives that is of greatest importance during the present century. Overall, this option probably contains the fewest shocks to the present system; consumption patterns change only gradually. Changes will take place in energy pricing, in fuel substitution, and in conservation measures. Over a period of a decade or so, new construction standards and retrofitting programmes bring recognizable benefits to individual energy users, and make a substantial contribution to reducing the rate of growth in energy demand. The process, aided by programmes of education and information about energy issues, is self-reinforcing, and efficiency in energy use is demanded as a matter of course in buildings, transport and other elements of human settlements.

Price changes and other actions by governments will encourage the use of more efficient transportation systems, probably including the widespread use of electric vehicles for special purposes. Although much higher standards will be required in new buildings, economic factors will still play a major role in determining these standards. Performance standards gradually replace component standards, but general adoption of energy consumption limits is achieved through pricing rather than by enforcement. Energy issues influence the form and type of new building development, but the great savings possible in all types of development mean that the choice between high-rise or low-rise, etc., can be made primarily in terms of other human settlements criteria. Similarly, district heating schemes overcome economic and institutional barriers but do not force new developments into particular layouts.

This scenario envisages a continuation of the present trend toward the transport of fuel and energy over long distances. Planning conflicts are likely to arise at the sites of major production facilities such as strip mining areas, and the number of these may be increased by the emphasis on the development of indigenous resources within ECE countries. The transport of fuel and energy will bring similar problems (pipeline routes, tanker terminals, high-voltage transmission lines, etc.). Social issues will arise, including the impact of large energy projects on remote communities, and the creation of energy-resource communities which have only a limited life expectancy.

2. The Nuclear-electric Option

This scenario rejects the "wait and see" approach, or indeed any approach based on a gradual change of energy supply patterns spread over several decades. This, it can be argued, merely delays the inevitable. The prospect of continuing rises in energy prices and the eventual exhaustion of non-renewable resources is already clear enough, and the time to make the necessary adjustment is now. Indeed, the faster that conventional, non-renewable energy resources such as oil and gas can be replaced by other forms of energy, the longer we can continue to use oil and gas for those purposes for which substitution is difficult. Such arguments are, of course, especially convincing in those countries which have few conventional energy resources within their borders, and which, therefore, are particularly concerned about the reliability of future energy supplies.

This option rests on the belief that nuclear power generation has proved its feasibility and reliability, and that uranium supplies are adequate for the foreseeable future. It assumes the fast breeder reactor will be introduced commercially during the 1980s, and also that current problems of nuclear technology, such as high capital cost and nuclear waste disposal, are sufficiently close to solution to justify a major policy and programme commitment to nuclear energy. It is recognized that fission technology may be replaced in the next century by nuclear fusion, but it is argued this transition will be relatively easy to accomplish since the main form of energy from both fission and fusion generation systems will be electricity. Adjustment by the consumer will therefore be negligible. In broader economic terms, the adoption of a nuclear-electric policy may be justified on the grounds that electricity is a much more appropriate form of energy for a post-industrial economy and society than oil and gas. The latter should be used as raw materials rather than as substances to be burned for energy purposes.

The implications of this option for human settlements planning are very different from those in the previous scenario. On the energy supply side, human settlements planners are likely to be closely concerned with such matters as the location of nuclear power stations, fuel reprocessing and nuclear waste disposal facilities, electricity transmission and distribution facilities, and sometimes with uranium extraction. Since nuclear energy development is a controversial issue in several countries, the human settlements planner may find himself involved in a dispute between nuclear planners, on the one hand, and those who object to nuclear development for environmental, safety and similar reasons, on the other.

In regard to energy use, the nuclear-electric scenario offers a number of advantages. In the planning of urban communities, for example, recent attempts to achieve a closer integration of housing, places of employment and recreation, and services are assisted by a greater emphasis on electricity as the main form of energy. While it facilitates such integrated development, the nuclear-electric option places relatively few constraints on the form and character of communities, since the energy is supplied through a flexible distribution system already in place. The exception to this is in transportation systems, where public transit may gradually return to tramway and trolley-bus systems at the expense of diesel buses.

Battery-powered vehicles will similarly become widespread, especially for local delivery and similar purposes. Such battery-operated vehicles will take advantage of off-peak discounts for electricity, and similar discounts will influence water heating, space heating, etc., because of the economic advantages of maintaining a constant load on nuclear generating facilities.

If nuclear generation stations are located within or close to major population centres (e.g. Pickering, Canada; Hartlepool and Heysham, England), the overall efficiency of such stations may be improved by linking them to district heating schemes. This may include connection of existing building complexes and communities to such schemes in order to reduce the consumption of oil and gas. Thermal storage systems are likely to be incorporated in such schemes, so that the electricity and heat output ratio can be adjusted efficiently during peaks and troughs of demand.

A fundamental requirement in the nuclear-electric scenario is high standards of energy performance in both new buildings and the existing stock. These standards will ensure the most efficient use of electricity, which will become the main form of space heating in buildings. The standards, in addition to improving insulation levels, will seek to minimize the residual energy needs of a building by utilizing heat from lighting and similar sources through heat recovery systems, and through the use of heat pumps, which are a more efficient method of using electricity than resistance-heating appliances.

Since it is much more difficult to retrofit the existing building stock to high standards, the nuclear-electric scenario may accelerate the replacement rate by increasing obsolescence. It may also encourage high-density row housing and apartment complexes, which have a lower residual demand for energy than one- or two-family houses.

3. The "Soft" Technology, Non-nuclear Option

Like the nuclear-electric option, this scenario requires an early decision on the main thrust of future policy. It rejects, however, the nuclear-electric option for a number of reasons. The most important of these are the high cost of nuclear-electric and similar advanced technological solutions; environmental and safety objections to current methods of nuclear generation and waste disposal; stronger objections on similar grounds to the introduction of fast breeder reactors; and more fundamental physical objections to the centralized generation and distribution of electricity on grounds of inefficiency.

This option therefore requires a reversal of the trend established in recent decades towards large and expensive systems of energy generation (not just in nuclear power stations) and instead returns to simpler, localized systems based mainly on renewable resources. These systems would be cheaper because they can avoid the expensive technology of centralized systems.

In practical terms this scenario encounters—indeed challenges—major institutional barriers, since the trend towards high-technology, centralized systems of energy supply is well established and highly institutionalized in both market and centrally planned economies. It would require energy supply utilities to be transformed from agencies designed to meet rising consumer demands for energy into organizations seeking to reduce substantially the dependence of the economy, society and individuals on such centralized supplies.

It is relatively easy to identify those energy supply technologies which would be rejected by the scenario, but it is more difficult at present to identify clearly the route which should be followed. This is partly because the keynotes of the "soft" decentralized approach are variety and flexibility, so that the appropriate technologies may vary with location. Solar systems may be widespread; wind power may be feasible in a number of locations; refuse-burning district heating schemes may serve larger communities; and so on. The uncertainty is, however, due more to the novelty of the approach and the lack of attention paid to it until very recently. Although energy generation remained essentially decentralized until the twentieth century, throughout the present century the emphasis has been on increasing centralization of energy production or conversion. An alternative approach, compatible with contemporary needs and standards, was scarcely contemplated until a few years ago.

The general outline of decentralized energy technologies can be identified, the economic and technological barriers do not seem insuperable and prototypes (e.g. solar-heated houses) are being tested, but soft technology energy generation is some time away as far as general adoption is concerned. Research and other funds which might otherwise have gone into expensive hard-technology programmes can be diverted to accelerating the development of soft technologies, but it will be a decade or more before these technologies are introduced widely.

Meanwhile, it is vital that community demands on conventional centralized supply systems should be reduced to a minimum. New building regulations and retrofitting may therefore be required to standards as high as those in the nuclear-electric option. There is no reason why this overall reduction in consumption should be accompanied by reductions in human comfort or aspirations.

This scenario differs considerably from the others in that soft technologies do not at present appear capable of providing a significant contribution to transportation energy needs. This may change in the future, but at present the soft technology scenario implies that solar, wind and other systems will be used in human settlements mainly to meet the energy requirements of buildings—especially for space and water heating. This would enable oil and other non-renewable resources (including coal used to generate electricity) to be conserved for transportation, etc. Such resources could have a greatly extended life if, as is usually assumed, the soft technology scenario forms a major element in a broader conservation-based approach to socioeconomic organization and the use of resources. In such a setting, careful land-use planning and other measures designed to reduce the need for transport will play a significant role in making the approach successful.

In terms of urban design, and even more of building characteristics, the "soft" technologies may impose more complex demands than those of other scenarios. The demands will also differ considerably from one soft technique to another. If decentralized solar systems are to be widespread, for example, individual houses may require appropriate collection and heat storage systems to be incorporated in the design. A district heating system based on refuse incineration is likely to involve forms of density and development very different from that where solar heating of houses on an individual basis is the main mode. These design requirements, it is sometimes suggested, may conflict with other planning objectives. The prospect has been raised of serried rows of uniform low-rise housing, all units aligned in the same direction to meet the requirements of the solar collector. Such fears seem premature. It is the task of human settlements planning to accommodate such requirements within an overall framework of good urban design, and the task seems *prima facie* easier than the planners' more familiar problem of accommodating the automobile in cities never designed for it.

In earlier chapters, emphasis was laid on the obstacle to close integration of energy planning and human settlements planning caused by the fact that the basic decisions about energy supply tend to be taken at a national level, whereas many key planning issues involve conditions in, and decisions by, local communities. This problem is much reduced in the soft technology scenario. To a large extent the energy used in a community will be generated or converted in that community, and there is much less dependence on external decisions or on long-distance energy supply and transport systems. It seems likely and desirable, therefore, that the planning and development of community energy needs will become an integral part of overall community planning and development.

4. The Two-stage Transition

For most countries in the ECE region, the 1970s have been a period of growing dependence on imported energy resources, or of growing concern for the price and reliability of supplies. For some countries, however, especially those situated around the North Sea, heavy previous dependence on imported energy is declining as indigenous off-shore supplies of oil and gas are developed. These resources are high-priced when compared to conditions during the 1960s, but are now fully competitive with alternative supplies on the world market, and are making a major contribution to the economies of the countries concerned (principally Norway, the Netherlands and the United Kingdom).

Even for these countries, however, the same long-term prospect lies ahead: depletion of resources and the need to transfer to alternative energy sources. For these countries, therefore, the main problem is that of finding ways to utilize the relatively brief period of energy abundance in order to prepare for the necessary transition to other sources early in the twenty-first century.

For different reasons, some of the countries in eastern Europe also face a two-stage transition. At present, a number of them are in the midst of a shift from dependence on solid fuel to greater use of oil and natural gas. As noted earlier (p. 21), this is to some extent a delayed version of the shift accomplished in western Europe and North America in the 1950s and 1960s. It has, however, the significant difference that it is taking place in a situation of rapidly rising world energy prices, when the gradual depletion and ultimate exhaustion of non-renewable resources is increasingly a factor in energy planning. Like the North Sea countries, therefore, eastern European nations must devise policies that will enable them to capture the benefits of the immediate future without causing human settlements and other consuming sectors to become over-dependent on energy sources with only a limited life.

During the last few years some of the most significant and contentious planning problems in countries bordering the North Sea have involved the creation of large energy transport and delivery facilities: construction sites for off-shore drilling and production rigs; pipelines from the North Sea or Siberia; and port facilities for liquefied petroleum gas, etc. These novel problems have generated novel planning solutions (e.g. in the Shetland Isles). For better or worse, however, the majority of such problems have by now been solved. More important at present are major policy decisions about the uses to which these fuels should be put. For example, should North Sea gas be burned in power stations to generate electricity? From one perspective the answer might be clearly negative: the "energy overhead", or loss involved in generating electricity as compared to direct end-use of natural gas is very great, and natural gas is a precious fuel (and raw material) that should be conserved as much as possible. From another viewpoint, however, the decision involves a longer-term judgment on the role of centralized versus decentralized energy conversion. If, when indigenous oil and gas resources decline at the end of the century, the second stage involves greater dependence on centralized electricity generation (from coal, nuclear or other sources), then the use of natural gas in generating stations now may be justified as part of a long-term adaptation to an electricity-based energy economy. If, however, decentralized systems are envisaged there may be much less justification for the use of natural gas in this way.

Once again, a further important factor is the time dimension, in relation to rates of replacement of unfit or obsolescent buildings. If it is anticipated that the vast majority of existing buildings will be replaced by the time oil and gas supplies diminish, the strategy of fuel use is likely to be different from that required if we assume that much of the existing stock will have to be adapted to conditions of declining oil and gas supplies. For example, on the former assumption, the trend may continue towards the installation of improved heating systems (burning oil and gas directly) in existing housing which is difficult or expensive to retrofit with insulation. On the latter assumption, much greater emphasis will need to be paid to retrofitting, despite the problems. Overall, there is perhaps rather less incentive to adopt very high performance standards for buildings or transportation in this scenario. For new buildings the guiding principle may be to achieve a steadily rising standard compatible with other objectives such as keeping the price of housing at a reasonable level. For existing buildings, especially those with an expected life of no more than 25 - 30 years, insulation and similar upgrading must be justified on economic or similar criteria.

In this scenario, therefore, emphasis on rising standards of comfort and convenience in human settlements is maintained, though rising energy prices and other actions encourage the steady growth in the efficiency and economy of energy use. As in the first scenario, the key long-term decision about future energy supply, and the consequences for human settlements, may not be taken for a decade or more.

The four scenarios, it is clear, have different impacts on human settlements; consequently they generate quite different problems and priorities for settlement planning and development. Tables 13 and 14 indicate some of these differences, viewed from the perspectives of the energy planner and the human settlements planner respectively. There are also some general conclusions which are common to, or independent of, all the scenarios, and which therefore cannot adequately be represented in the tables.

(1) Whatever the scenario adopted, energy conservation and the elimination of energy waste in human settlements are of great importance. If the rapid rate of growth of world energy demand, typical of earlier years, can be significantly reduced, this will enable the life of non-renewable resources to be extended and will provide the time necessary to discover, evaluate and implement long-term solutions. Since the ECE region accounts for three-quarters of world energy demand, ECE countries bear the main responsibility for action to reduce that demand; if expansion of energy supply systems can be reduced or avoided by energy conservation programmes, there are obvious environmental benefits: less strip-mining, less risk of air and water pollution, smaller land requirements for generation and distribution facilities, etc.

The importance of energy conservation in human settlements is particularly strong in the "nuclear-electric" and "soft technology" approaches, going well beyond the elimination of waste in the direction of human settlements that make only very small demands on purchased energy supplies. In the nuclear-electric case, the main justification for conservation is economic: for example, electricity is an economically efficient means of space heating, etc., only if buildings are well-insulated. In the soft technology approach, other considerations play a larger role: energy demands should be reduced to a minimum as a matter of principle rather than because of price or similar considerations. Such non-economic arguments for maximum energy conservation can, however, be applied to all four options.

(2) In all the options it is evident that significant changes in energy supply and consumption patterns will take place during the lifetime of communities and buildings which already exist or are now being created. Since the human settlements planner has a responsibility to the future as well as to the present, it is desirable that he should recognize the certainty of these changes and plan for them. Paradoxically, however, it is clear that this mainly involves, at present, allowing for uncertainty. Only in the nuclear-electric option does the planner have a reasonably clear idea of the principal types of energy likely to be available in individual human settlements more than a few decades from now. A choice in favour of soft technologies at present is more a rejection of hard technology than a clear identification of what alternative method is best in a specific community. The minimum disturbance and two-stage options similarly accept that long-term decisions about future supply will not be made in our present state of uncertainty. This again is an argument for maximum conservation, since the most effective way of planning for uncertainty is probably one in which purchased energy demands, from whatever sources, are reduced to a minimum.

(3) The two-way relationship between energy and human settlements is of fundamental importance whatever energy decisions are taken. The latter depend very much on forecasts of future demand as well as on expectations of future supply. Consequently, if substantial changes are likely in the pattern of future demand (e.g. if a significant reduction in the current ECE forecasts of 3.6 per cent annual growth in the period 1974-85 can be achieved), then energy policies are likely to be modified also.

As the Ottawa Seminar clearly demonstrated, there is a great variety of influences and constraints on energy planning in human settlements: economic, financial, environmental and institutional. Perhaps the greatest constraints of all are those represented by the massive existing infrastructure of human settlements and energy systems them-

TABLE 13. *Summary of the characteristics of different energy supply scenarios of relevance to human settlements*

	Availability	Location	Price and cost	Convenience
Minimum disturbance Good housekeeping: use of pricing and other energy conservation measures. Defer other major energy policy decisions for 10 to 15 years to get clear view of options	Continued use of oil and gas based on well-established pattern of international supply and national distribution throughout ECE region. Gas and solid fuel supplies more restricted than oil and electricity	ECE region meets more of its energy needs than had been anticipated before 1973 but still depends on intra-region and inter-national trade in energy resources	Considerable uncertainty re future price levels, but general expectation of continued rises in oil and gas prices, and to less extent, of other fuels	Depends on continuity of supply: if this is assured, no abrupt changes in methods of energy use, but growing range of options, e.g. for space heating
Nuclear-electric Based on immediate or early decision that future energy needs can best be met through nuclear generation of electricity	Virtually all households etc., in ECE region already connected to electricity supply. Nuclear supply systems available throughout region	Apart from uranium supplies, energy planning largely in national control	Price dependent on three main factors: (a) cost of capital for generating stations; (b) price of uranium; (c) availability of fuel from fast breeder reactors	Electricity the most convenient form of energy for many purposes, though less so in transportation (e.g. air)
Soft technology Based on immediate or early decision to avoid nuclear energy and to promote use of renewable energy resources	Some techniques already available. Past neglect of R&D means that mass market systems unlikely for several years	Solar, wind geothermal and other resources un-evenly distributed in ECE region, but at present seem to be adequate as potential resources in most places	Some systems already competitive (e.g. solar water heating). But option likely to depend on reductions in unit costs of devices as they achieve mass-market distribution	Much greater reliance on individual end-user to maintain supply systems. Acceptability may rest on development of trouble-free systems
Two-stage transition Increasing use of oil and gas in this century. Nature of subsequent shift in energy dependence to be defined when options clearer	Option rests on assumption that oil and gas supplies relatively abundant for rest of the twentieth century	Option limited to countries with newly available sources of oil and gas	Prices depend on pricing policies adopted, but should reflect the rising costs of oil and gas development. Consumer price is key instrument in making smooth adjustment at second stage of transition	Convenience increases as oil and gas replace other fuels

Reliability	Flexibility	Environmental problems	Permanence
1. Heavy dependence on imports in most of ECE region 2. Long intercontinental and international supply lines 3. Large-scale centralized distribution systems	Overall, great flexibility except for transport needs, but individual consumer in multi-occupation blocks is more constrained than was normal in the past	Some potential negative effects as energy supplies come increasingly from indigenous, remote, or marginal resources, (e.g. strip mining, pipelines, oil and gas terminals, refineries	Assumed that present supplies of conventional energy will last until, say, 2025; meanwhile, planning for long-range alternatives
Reliability a critical factor, as dependence on nuclear energy as the prime energy source increases	Increasing inflexibility both overall and at level of individual consumer	1. Major controversies on nuclear safety, waste disposal, etc. 2. More conventional problems of heat dissipation, location of transmission lines, etc.	Permanence depends on feasibility and economic performance of fast breeder reactors
Overall, high degree of reliability of supply, due to diversity of sources and known characteristics of sun, wind, etc. Much greater chance of temporary failure at individual level	Expectation that decentralized or individual systems will always be supplemented by centralized electricity supply (at higher price)	Potential problems at present (e.g. location of windmills, siting and orientation of solar panels), but should be soluble relatively easily. Avoids problems caused by concentration of energy facilities	Systems based mainly on use of renewable resources. consequently no problems
Reliability mainly a function of oil and gas technology, but storage ability provides extra safeguards	Wider use of oil and gas increases flexibility, at least during present century	Normal problems of energy development and distribution, for which practical solutions generally exist, even if they are not always adopted	Existing resources recognized to have finite life. Second stage of transition largely determined by long-term prospects for non-depleting energy sources

Human Settlements and Energy

TABLE 14. *Summary of the impact of different energy supply scenarios on human settlements planning and development*

	Land use and settlement form	Buildings	Transportation
Minimum disturbance Good housekeeping: use of pricing and other energy conservation measures. Defer other major energy policy decisions for 10 to 15 years to get clear view of options	More development of indigenous energy resources with consequent land use and settlement impacts. Strengthened efforts to avoid urban sprawl and reduce need to travel. Some shifts to higher densities to utilize district heating and other integrated energy use opportunities	1. Greater use of district heating, combined generation and similar systems in response to rising energy prices 2. Marked rise in standards of insulation, etc. with adoption of 'performance' standards as soon as feasible 3. Widespread retrofitting of existing buildings, mainly to economic limits	More emphasis on public transit and on integration of transit planning and settlement planning. Improved economy in fuel consumption. More use of electric vehicles for special purposes. Rising cost of transport leads to substitution of electronic communication systems
Nuclear-electric Based on immediate or early decision that future energy needs can best be met through nuclear generation of electricity	Reduced need for functional separation within cities, and stress on efficiency in electricity use, encourage higher densities and closer integration of community functions. Location problems for nuclear generating plants, transmission lines and associated industrial or other users linked to combined generation facilities	Enforcement of high standards of insulation, etc., in new buildings and major efforts also in existing stock. Object is to reduce sharply the needs for purchased energy of each building, to offset high electricity costs	Oil supplies conserved for transport needs. Electric vehicles increase, especially in transit and goods distribution. Settlement planning utilises opportunities for electric transit systems
Soft technology Based on immediate or early decision to avoid nuclear energy dependency and to promote use of renewable energy resources	Maximum use of natural features in site planning of buildings and energy generating systems (solar, wind); development of new land-use planning guidelines for soft technologies; effects on density and settlement form difficult to assess but are likely to be minimal	Attempt to minimize building energy needs, both in construction and operation. Requirements for solar collectors, etc. lead to significant design changes in new buildings	Little direct application of soft systems in transport. Oil supplies conserved for transport with strong encouragement of transit development rather than individual car use
Two-stage transition Increasing use of oil and gas in this century. Nature of subsequent shift in energy dependence to be defined when options clearer	Energy changes play a subordinate role in land-use planning, until character of future energy transition is defined. Ease of oil and, where available, gas distribution means that fundamental changes unlikely in present century	Improvement in standards of new construction, but less attention to existing stock. No reduction in installation of heating systems based on oil or gas, since in older buildings these more economic than full insulation retrofit	Improvements in economy and efficiency, but little change in present circulation patterns, despite rising prices for fuel

Human consequences	Institutional considerations	Research and development
1. No sudden changes in behaviour patterns, but growing awareness of, and response to, energy factors 2. Help required by some groups to make adjustments, e.g. poor people in old houses 3. Special problems of communities at sites of major energy developments	1. Closer integration of energy and other aspects of planning 2. Gradual shift of energy supply utilities towards promotion of conservation rather than meeting demand 3. Removal of institutional, legal and other barriers to district heating, combined generation, etc. 4. Revision of tax and pricing systems to encourage conservation	Long-term support for wide variety of energy supply and use alternatives, involving both "hard" and "soft" technologies. Similar support for conservation techniques
"Flick of a switch" society from consumer's viewpoint. If safe, economical and continuous supply is assured, supply systems of little direct concern to individual. But continuing individual and community concern for nuclear safety	1. Growing dependence of economy on single energy system increases governmental responsibility for energy supply 2. Strong controls (e.g. through capital allocation) to favour nuclear growth and restrict fossil fuels to transportation, petrochemicals, etc. 3. Strong agencies created to retrofit existing building stock	Concentration of R&D effort on nuclear fission and nuclear fusion problems. Strong support for low-cost retrofit innovations, and for more efficient devices to use electricity (e.g. heat pumps, heat recovery systems)
Reversal of long-established trend: a greater role for individual in meeting his energy needs. Requires acquisition of expertise, perhaps in several methods. Gradual adoption of "conserver society" attitudes	1. Basic decision by government to minimize reliance on nuclear and other high-technology centralized systems 2. Conversion of existing energy utilities into agencies for energy conservation and supply of soft technologies	Reallocation of research funds and expertise from nuclear and other "hard" technologies towards solar and other "soft" systems. Support for full-scale experiments well before economic feasibility is established
General rise in comfort and convenience as oil and gas systems are introduced. Long-term preparation for second stage of transition	Steadily expanding role of government in energy field, though existing structure generally continues	Long-term support for energy supply systems likely to be appropriate for introduction at end of twentieth century. Moderate support for low-cost retrofitting innovations

selves. Nevertheless, there are good grounds for optimism about the future of human settlements in the new energy situation. The initial "negative" reactions at the time of the 1973 energy crisis are giving way to a recognition that a reappraisal of the pattern of energy use and misuse was in any case overdue, and to a belief that the basic objectives of human settlements planning are consistent with rational energy planning. Raising the level of efficiency in energy use is "morally right and economically profitable",* and the quality of life in human settlements in the ECE region is likely to benefit rather than deteriorate as a result of the adjustments required.

* Quoted from the address by Mr. J. Stanovnik, Executive Secretary of ECE, to the *ad hoc* Meeting on Energy Economy and Efficiency in the ECE region, March 1977.

PART III

ANALYTICAL SUMMARY OF THE
SEMINAR DISCUSSIONS*

I. GENERAL DEBATE: OVERALL POLICIES AND STRATEGIES RELATING TO ENERGY USE IN HUMAN SETTLEMENTS

1. In their opening statements, most delegations agreed that developments in world energy markets during the last few years have served to confirm political and public recognition of resource scarcities. Previous habits were based on relatively cheap and freely available energy resources, particularly non-renewable fossil fuels. The future can be expected to require adaptation to rising costs of energy and to increasingly inflexible conditions of supply for depleting fuels. In these circumstances, energy conservation often presents an attractive alternative to, or supplement for, programmes to increase energy supplies. It was generally recognized that the most common goals of conservation policy are: reduction of energy use as such; reduction of imports; and seeking an economic optimum of energy uses.

2. Concerning fuel substitution, it was noted that the fossil hydrocarbons, currently being used largely as fuels, are also highly useful for synthesizing other products. Policy in the Netherlands, for example, aims at reserving natural gas for premium uses. In Hungary it is intended to use oil products only where they are not replaceable, or required to protect standards of living and environment. The representative of the International Union of Architects, suggesting that dependence on renewable resources has gone "beyond the bounds of common sense", said that there is a real question as to whether energy abundance has in fact increased welfare.

3. A major theme of several interventions was the special role of human settlements in the relationships between energy use and economic growth and distribution, both within nations and internationally. The Swedish delegate emphasized that the energy issue is a global one, a question of the wise management of the earth's resources. Its resolution is indeed important for national well-being, but will have to take account of the equity of international distribution. If this were not done, he warned, not only the poor would suffer but the consequences "sooner or later will strike us all". Similarly, the United States expressed the hope that out of the present deliberations could emerge a better forum for the less-developed world to share in the benefits of economic advancement. The delegate of the Netherlands recalled a reference made by the ECE Executive

---

* As the final report of the Seminar had not been issued when this volume went to press, this summary is based on the draft circulated in Ottawa (HBP/SEM.17/CRP.10 and addenda), with minor corrections by the editor (but see note, p. 140).

125

Secretary* to John Maynard Keynes, who said that any economic system, to be viable, must be economically efficient, socially just and promote individual freedom. In the context of domestic energy conservation, the delegate proposed that this implies allowing the individual a range of choice among the means of energy savings. The Netherlands' consciousness of international responsibility is reflected in its natural gas production plans, which take account of the import needs of its EEC trading partners.

4. The phenomenon of economic growth is particularly tangible in human settlements, where improvements in welfare take lasting and visible form. However, the long life of buildings and other components in itself sets some conditions on the incorporation of energy considerations into settlements and buildings. At the rates of building and obsolescence prevailing over much of the ECE region, over half of the building stock for the year 2000 is already in place, which implies a stress on energy conservation measures for existing buildings in the near to medium term. In the opinion of one delegation, a building renewal period of 20 years is too long to permit effective action through measures aimed at new buildings. Another delegation noted that, although in principle buildings are to be written off as investments only when obsolete, in fact there may well be a tendency in markets for units of lesser efficiency to lose value more rapidly. The OECD delegate stressed the need to consider very carefully investment decisions, such as many in human settlements, which are practically irreversible and which may foreclose other possibilities. His organization expects that energy use in the residential sector will grow more slowly than aggregate energy demand for the remainder of this century.

5. Varying conditions of growth in different parts of the ECE region create special energy considerations for human settlements. In Hungary, which is engaged in transition from a rural economy, development of infrastructure is a key feature of the development process, and there are attendant opportunities for alleviating interregional inequalities through planning. Emphasis is being placed on national concentration of industry and promoting population movements to more favourable regions through construction of state dwellings and other incentives. In Greece, at the end of a decade of rapid growth, *per capita* energy consumption is still only one-third of the ECE average, but the infrastructure has been based largely on imported oil. Energy consumption in the residential and commercial sector is comparatively low, due in part to a low level of amenities in housing. Therefore, the goal is still to secure increased energy supplies while avoiding all waste and lowering the energy/GDP ratio. In Ireland, although economic development has been comparatively slow, the population is now rising for the first time in a century, and the high proportion of the population under 25 years of age leads to expectations of a substantial urban expansion. Here also, a study of heating equipment and standards has made it clear that any improvement in energy performance of dwellings is most likely to go into betterment of comfort standards. Similar problems may be encountered within mature economies as well: in the United Kingdom it is believed that potential energy savings are extremely limited for households in the lowest quarter of family incomes.

6. Virtually all delegations found a need to reconcile energy and human settlements objectives with protection of environmental values, and, by the same token, certain

* See p. 14.

elements of the physical environment may considerably influence energy demand and supply considerations. The climates of Finland and Greece very nearly typify the temperature extremes for the ECE region, and the specific requirements for energy in settlements are weighted accordingly. The pattern of cloud cover is decisive for solar power potential. Even the pattern of settlements within a country may be affected: two-thirds of the population of Canada is concentrated in a band within 250 kilometres of its southern border, largely because of the temperature climate favourable to agriculture and living conditions. The delegate of the World Meteorological Organization called attention to the fact that the period of rapid growth in the recent past was also "one of the most extraordinary periods in history when climate has been at, or near, optimum in terms of food production and temperature-sensitive energy consumption". He cautioned that "though we cannot be certain if the climate over the next few decades will be warmer, or colder, we can state that the odds are that climatic conditions will become much more variable—thus complicating energy-demand planning because we can no longer afford to design around all climatic conditions by expending massive amounts of energy". On the other hand, "much of our planned efforts at influencing the climate to any significant degree have been a dismal failure, but we have found that we have extraordinary success at inadvertent modification of climate, especially in and near human settlements. Proper attention to planning in the design and construction of our homes and settlements can create environmentally sound, energy-efficient systems."

7. The discussion of several national energy plans brought out the importance of carrying supply or conservation measures into effect promptly: delays could significantly restrict the range of future options. For example, France had hoped that it would not be necessary to increase oil imports after 1985, but when certain elements of the plan fell behind schedule it became necessary to forecast a deficit of 10 million tons of oil or equivalent. Planners will have to deal with uncertainties of two kinds: deficiencies of data concerning previous developments and the present situation, as well as unpredictable future events.

8. Statistics on energy use in human settlements are typically either highly aggregated or fragmentary, relying on extrapolations from small samples. Much of the large-scale direct collection of information which has been done was undertaken by and for the purposes of energy suppliers. Consequently, data on demand is weak, particularly concerning specific end-uses. There was general assent to the need for agreement on standards, definitions and methods of measurement. In the meantime, some deficiencies can be compensated by imaginative use of data collected for other purposes, to generate information needed for energy policy decisions in human settlements. Agencies of the United States Government have had some success in doing this for municipal studies, and suggested a good starting-point would be an inventory of existing data. In Denmark a building register, which is being established primarily for tax purposes, could also yield information on heating equipment directly, and on insulation standards indirectly by matching the ages of buildings with construction standards that were in force at different periods.

9. Several delegations proposed that, in spite of the scarcity of precise factual data and knowledge, policy decisions will have to be taken and measures implemented with-

out delay. The time required to adapt the building stock and other long-lived infra-structure components argues for an early start. Furthermore, the effects of initial measures can be observed, once they are in force, to obtain valuable information for policy modification. Sweden has had some success with such an approach. Starting with an overall annual energy growth of 4.5 per cent, a 1975 energy plan set the target of 2 per cent annual growth of total consumption to 1985, with industrial energy use to be allowed to grow by 3 per cent each year over the same period to support employment. It was hoped to achieve zero energy growth after 1990. Subsequent experience has shown that the possibilities for increased efficiency in industry might have been over-estimated. On the other hand, the potential for energy savings in human settlements has been found to be even greater than expected. The approach has been to take a long-term planning perspective, while retaining the capacity to adapt to new conditions. The Swedish delegate declared that ''action has to be taken now—but we must be pre-pared to make swift changes when circumstances call on us to do so''. The delegate of Switzerland agreed that the onus is on governments to act, and then wait public response for guidance in modifying early decisions. Canada proposed that the areas of highest priority for action are those with the greatest potential for disruption from supply uncertainties, such as use of oil-based fuels in transport. Also attractive are those areas where savings can be effected quickly and with little cost; things which can be done by expending ''a few hundred dollars and a weekend of effort''. In principle, first action should be directed to changes at the margin, which can be made at any time and which open new options. Last in order of preference are those major changes which are costly and foreclose other options.

10. Closely linked to the need for retaining flexibility in the face of uncertainty is the issue of centralization and concentration of energy supply facilities, and the corre-sponding human settlements structures. Several governments, notably those of Finland, Poland, the Netherlands and Ireland, look to district heating of government buildings, apartments and other premises as a means of utilizing waste heat of industry and power stations, and geothermal resources. Other delegations pointed out that, attractive as those potentials are, district heating is an example of an inflexible system which can foreclose other alternatives, particularly when connected with nuclear power stations. In Norway, the policy direction has been much more toward small-scale solutions suit-able for single-family dwellings, including some which require a high degree of indivi-dual responsibility, such as stove heating. The delegate of Yugoslavia added that care should be taken to match the quality of energy supplied to the requirements of parti-cular end-uses. Finland made a specific effort to ensure that boilers could accept several alternative fuels. Canada stressed the importance, not only of energy conservation measures as such, but especially of utilizing non-conventional renewable energy resources to insure flexibility of human settlements to changing energy conditions.

11. Because the budgetary and other resources of governments, industry and indivi-duals are limited, choices must be made among alternative investments at different levels of generalization: among different energy conservation measures, between con-servation and supply measures, and between energy measures in general and those which contribute in other ways to individual well-being. Several different kinds of criteria may be brought to bear in the decision process, and there was detailed discus-

sion of the usefulness of cost-benefit or cost-effectiveness analysis. As applied to energy conservation, for example, this would imply comparing the cost of an investment with the discounted value of the stream of savings in energy costs expected from it. The method is in rather common use in government planning and budgeting in a number of countries, making it easier to place the energy considerations of human settlements into a pre-existing planning framework. Some governments have in fact made this evaluation technique obligatory for energy conservation investments, but the consequence has sometimes been that only a rather restricted range of investments in new buildings have been found to be profitable. The representative of the International Council for Building Research, Studies and Documentation (CIB) interjected that cost-benefit analysis may be rendered a "fool's paradise" because the fuel cost information that is most often used is based on current average market prices. These energy prices may depend as much upon the relative bargaining power of the agents, as upon underlying economic conditions. There is reason to believe that the long-run marginal costs of replacing the energy resources currently being depleted will actually be much higher than the current prices. Using unrealistically low energy prices in cost-benefit comparisons can have the effect of failing to justify investments in energy conservation or non-conventional supply in human settlements, which would in fact be very profitable in terms of the actual life-cycle savings to be attained. One delegation called for energy producers to make available to governments such information as they have concerning long-run marginal cost functions. In a larger context the delegation of Denmark recognized a political obligation to give the public an understanding of what would happen if nothing were done to meet energy difficulties. This was related to the pricing question through the intervention of another delegate: "there will always be as much energy as we can afford". In other words, the development of energy costs must, in the long run, balance supply and demand, but this might well be by reducing the amounts of energy that consumers can afford, rather than by stimulating increased production. From this reality arises the need to try to take account of resource replacement costs in current planning.

12. Even when cost-benefit analysis is applied with full and accurate cost information, other decision criteria and policy measures have to be brought to bear to ensure distributive equity. Several delegations noted that the burden of higher energy costs had fallen disproportionately on those segments of their populations which were already economically disadvantaged. On the other hand, it was difficult to justify investments, such as retrofitting of houses, purely on energy grounds, in cases where the energy consumption was already small, even though this might be due to low comfort standards. Many delegations reported that the application of cost-benefit principles was modified by redistributive fiscal measures, loan guarantees and the like. Norway had found the response to a programme of public loans for insulation "tremendous", to the extent that the authorities faced serious difficulties to cope with the applications both administratively or financially.

13. A number of interventions stressed the necessity of active participation of all concerned—government, energy producers and enterprises, experts and individuals, to ensure co-ordinated and effective energy policies for human settlements. Very little can be achieved except by the active participation of those most directly concerned:

the residents whose habits, needs and aspirations make up the pattern of life in settlements. The practical significance of life-styles for the outcome of energy measures was
sharply illustrated by interventions of the United Kingdom and Norway, saying that
they found the energy consumption in buildings virtually identical with respect to their
physical characteristics could vary by a factor of 1 to 5, depending on "who lived there".
On the other hand, governments in many cases have a substantial direct role as owners
of buildings, including some residences, and thus have an opportunity not only to control their own energy characteristics, but also to serve as an example and market leader
by assuming the risks of innovations. Several non-governmental organizations took an
active part in this portion of the debate: for example, the representative of the International Real Estate Federation (FIABCI) offered the services of his members both to
gather information and to play an educative role. The importance of active involvement of the private sector in energy conservation programmes was stressed by the delegation of the United States.

II. IMPACT OF ENERGY CONSIDERATIONS ON COMMUNITY PLANNING AND DEVELOPMENT

1. When introducing the discussion of this item, the general rapporteurs, Mr. F.
Parfait (France) and Mr. J. Brenner (Hungary), stressed the importance of energy considerations in urban planning and development. An important aspect in dealing with
this interrelationship is the institutional arrangement for urban planning. In order to
ensure a close co-ordination of the two subject areas, it is necessary to plan the use of
energy along with the use of space and to make these two processes complementary.
Urban planning is being carried out at the national, regional and local level and, consequently, a similar institutional set-up needs to be developed for energy planning. So
far, energy planning is mostly undertaken on the national level. At the municipal and
community level, however, physical plans are implemented and it is here where the real
co-ordination with energy plans has to take place.

2. Local authorities are faced with a number of very practical energy questions, such
as the sources of energy available to them, the location of energy extraction and conversion plants and, of course, the distribution of energy from those plants to their communities and the distribution within the community itself. The long-range security of
energy supply from classical or conventional energy sources has become an issue and
decisionmakers are faced with the problem of adapting both the physical structure and
layout and the maintenance and functioning of their communities to changing forms
and prices of energy. This is a difficult task considering that buildings, and streets,
plazas and open places will last for a long time and may outlive the particular mixture
of energy sources and the related price structure in force today.

3. A number of particular questions arise as a result of these facts. First, there is the
question of what role energy has played and will play in the future in human settlements
planning and development. This seems to be a question of what priority is attached to
the energy issue, while at the same time taking into consideration all other urban planning issues such as economics, employment, education, recreation, housing, social
health and welfare, transportation, etc. In this respect, it is of interest to know whether
the physical structure of our cities allows for the necessary changes without losing the

mix of style, appearance and arrangement of buildings which contribute considerably
to the liveliness and charm of a town. It is, furthermore, a question of technical possibilities, of reducing energy consumption in heating and cooling of buildings, services in
and around the buildings and in the transport system. Finally, it is a question of consumer behaviour and preference, the individual citizen's understanding of the energy
issue and his willingness to make sacrifices in his energy consumption habits in order to
preserve precious resources without, at the same time, modifying his style of life in an
undesirable direction.

4. In the ensuing discussion, many delegations pointed out the close interrelationship of energy and settlements planning. The longevity of the physical structure of the
city was stressed and concern was expressed that energy sources as they are used today
to enable life to function in these cities may in the long run have to be replaced by other
sources of energy. In addition to the structures and the space created by them, the
infrastructure serving our cities is rigid in nature and cannot easily adapt to a change in
energy source. Therefore, attention should be given to the flexibility of the infrastructure in new developments and in urban renewal areas.

5. Population density and the corresponding types of dwellings have a great impact
on energy used. Many governments are making efforts to increase residential density
in the outskirts of towns and in sprawl developments in order, among other objectives,
to improve efficiency in energy heating, urban services and transportation. It was
reported that in some countries government programmes have been enacted to provide
incentives for the construction of multi-family homes instead of single-family units and
that a comprehensive approach is taken to the allocation of urban land for different
functions such as residential, production, commercial, recreation, education, etc., and
to the effects of this on energy conservation.

6. In most European countries energy is considered as an important aspect of human
settlements planning and development. Governments, therefore, are taking steps to
include such aspects in their planning processes and in the relevant assessment procedures. In North American countries, even though they are very much concerned with
energy conservation, the energy issue is at this time only of secondary importance in the
development of urban policies.

7. The next issue stressed by a number of delegations was the necessary co-ordination
of the local, regional and national levels in developing energy policies. Some countries
reported on recent legislation enacted to ensure that national energy policies are not
just transformed to the local level but also that a feedback process from the local level
to the national government takes place. It was well recognized that, at this time, energy
policies are generally set by the national government and thereby become externalities
to the local communities. The need was stressed to make the energy planning process
more compatible with the land-use planning process in order to improve co-ordination
and integration of different policies and their implementation at the municipal level.

8. In a number of examples the importance of the community level for carrying out
physical planning and energy policies was demonstrated. Scenarios for a mixture of different energy sources and their implications to the structure of the community are being
studied in an experimental project carried out jointly by the United States of America
and Greece. In cases where community governments exercise great decision-making

power, such as in Sweden, the necessity for integrating the national and local energy policies becomes even more obvious.

9. Another issue of concern to many countries is the potential sources of energy once fossil fuels are no longer available at their present price and quantity. The concern is about what form of energy should replace the diminishing fossil fuel resources, in particular, oil, gas and their subsidiary products, and what measures need to be taken in the transitional period to adapt to the new energy form. The increased production of electricity from hydroelectric, fossil fuel and waste-burning power plants and also from nuclear reactors has been discussed as well as its use for heating and transport purposes. Besides this, the question of the location of these energy extraction and conversion plants is becoming an issue of public debate in a number of countries, most notably seen in the recent controversy over the location of nuclear power plants.

10. After consideration of these basic questions on the interrelationship between energy and human settlements planning, locational and technical aspects of energy sources, and the institutional structure within which governments are handling such matters, the discussion concentrated on the areas in which most of the energy in human settlements is consumed. The first is heating. The great advantages of district heating were reported by a number of delegations, particularly if the population density is high and if different forms of energy can be burned in central-heating plants. It was mentioned that the basic calorific requirement could be supplied by waste heat from power conversion plants or industry, from the burning of waste material or from geothermal heating. Peak loads could best be covered by conventional sources such as fossil fuels and electricity. The use of non-depletable sources such as wind and solar energy in centralized heating plants is still in the experimental stage, and little practical experience has been gained as yet. Several efforts were reported to experiment with the use of different heat sources.

11. The size of central heating plants and systems was discussed intensively. Even though opinions differ on a number of aspects, it was generally felt that large district heating plants are economically most advantageous for very high residential densities and central business districts. In medium-density residential areas, which are common around the cores of most cities in the ECE region, medium or small central-heating plants have been found to be most suitable. It was reported that, even in rural areas, district heating schemes have been installed and work to full satisfaction. Furthermore, district heating systems can be operated in such a way as to be less polluting than the heating of individual houses, and also the storage and transport of the required heating fuel can be done in a manner that has minimal negative impact on the environment and is, at the same time, safe. As concerns central heating for apartment buildings and individual houses, it was pointed out that progress had been made in the technology of transporting heat to apartment houses. It was generally agreed that in order to maintain a desirable level of comfort, central heating should be provided for apartment houses. For individual homes the idea was put forward to install individual room heating rather than central heating as this could result in a substantial reduction of energy consumption.

12. The setting up of municipal heating districts as a means to advance the concept of district heating in a community was reported. Little experience has yet been gained

with such districts, and the full potential of related legislation has not yet been utilized. The implementation of a national heating plan as a part of the overall energy plan was reported on by Denmark. In the past it has been cheaper to transport energy rather than heat to the dwelling. The transport technology for heat has since improved and, consequently, heat distribution has become economically feasible and thereby an important aspect of physical planning. In producing heat, surplus energy from different sources is used and a better energy economy is achieved than burning fuels in individual homes. Still, individual heating will prevail in single homes because of the relatively high investment cost for connections and adaptations to the community-wide system; home owners are at this time still expected to pay a substantial part of these costs. The repayment period for the heating plan is estimated to lie between 10 and 15 years. Considerably more experience has to be gained with the implementation of this system, and a number of hurdles have still to be overcome. It is thought that making the plan mandatory and establishing price rates would be one way of fostering its implementation. The seminar considered this national heating plan as one of the most advanced in the ECE region, even though a number of other countries are in the process of enacting measures that are a part of the plan. The experience of those countries in respect to the economic and practical feasibility of the district heating system is very similar to that reported by the Danish delegation.

13. The second major consumer of energy in our cities is transportation. The high dependability of North American cities on automobile transportation is well known as well as the consequences for energy consumption. Despite a number of programmes and actions at different levels of government to increase investment in public transportation, which is, of course, more energy conserving than individual transportation, no real change in transportation habits has been observed. Attempts to reduce the necessity for trip making and to reduce the length of trips through planning measures such as locating places to work, live, recreate, etc., closer to each other or through new communication means such as videophones, etc., were discussed some 20 years ago, although at that time the major aim was to reduce traffic volume and traffic congestion. Then, as now, it was well recognized that the land-use structure of a town can change only very slowly and over a long period of time and that a multitude of forces are at work of which energy is only one. Also, new communication technology and its use has not developed to the extent that it has had an impact on travel behaviour. Efforts are now underway to increase the use of electricity as a power source in transportation. In this respect, some progress is being made in terms of urban transportation, e.g. electric railways, trolley buses, etc., but no practical alternative to the gasoline-powered car is yet in sight.

14. The situation in European cities is not too different from that of North America, even though ridership on mass transit is higher and more transit vehicles are powered by electricity, e.g. subways, street cars and trolley buses. Efforts are underway to study alternative fuels for gasoline-powered automobiles, but it appears that the prices for such fuels would be considerably higher than today's gasoline prices. Whether these higher prices will make an impact on car use will still have to be seen.

15. Another approach being seriously considered in a number of countries is to employ urban planning measures in new settlement developments and urban planning

measures in new settlement developments and urban renewal areas, so as to create higher densities, provide more and better public transportation and possibly even scrap plans for urban motorways. This last measure is still a very controversial one and uncertainty exists among planners and decision-makers about the direction in which to move. Other planning measures underway include the increasing provision of bikeways and the creation of pedestrian zones in connection with parking areas. Most of these measures are rather recent, and an evaluation of their impact on energy conservation still has to be made.

16. Some unexpected results were reported from the Bay Area Rapid Transit system operating in San Francisco, U.S.A. It was expected that, as a result of the construction of this mass transit system, densities on the outlying stations would increase and the process of urban sprawl would slow down. Contrary observations have, however, been made at several stations: a down zoning from high density commercial to lower density residential areas has taken place. Also, because of the extensive feeder bus system bringing people from dispersed areas to the stations, urban sprawl has continued or even increased. The full impact of such most recent developments and trends on energy conservation still has to be assessed.

17. A further aspect discussed is the increasing necessity for informing, educating and re-educating the general public, professionals and policy-makers. It was found in a number of instances, in particular in smaller communities that are in the process of experiencing urban growth, that local decision-makers were ignorant about energy issues because of lack of knowledge of the implications of traditional planning decisions on energy conservation. Also, the general public, in order to participate effectively in the debate on urban planning matters, needs to be informed and educated about the comprehensiveness of the problems and, in particular, the energy issues. This affects not only their participation in the planning process but also, what is equally or more important, their consumer behaviour in relation to the use of energy. Furthermore, professionals need to team up with colleagues from other relevant disciplines in order to develop and assess viable alternatives.

18. Finally, some social implications of energy planning in human settlements were pointed out. Among these is the need for employees in energy plants to work overtime in order to supply peak demands for heat and power. This overtime often requires night work which upsets family and social routine and proves to be physically strenuous.

19. In summary it was found that the two major areas of energy consumption, and therefore areas of concern in this context, are the question of heating, together with a number of services in and around the buildings (lighting, hot water, etc.), and that of urban transportation. A number of attempts are being made by ECE governments to cope with the energy issue in human settlements. The most common approaches include:

(a) technical measures to prepare for a shift of energy source and to improve the energy efficiency of transportation and heating systems;
(b) physical planning measures to increase the density of outlying and sprawling residential developments, and efforts to reduce the necessity for travelling and the length of travel by locating places of residence, employment, recreation, education, etc., closer to each other;
(c) means of influencing the public's energy consumption behaviour.

III. IMPACT OF ENERGY CONSIDERATIONS ON THE DESIGN, CONSTRUCTION, IMPROVEMENT AND UTILIZATION OF BUILDINGS

National Policies and Strategies Concerning Energy Saving in Buildings

1. Mrs. I. Årlin (Sweden), general rapporteur, presented a series of issues, referring to the seminar programme (HBP/SEM.17/1/Add.3) and to several specialized papers submitted by governments and international organizations.

2. In the discussion which followed, the majority of the delegations emphasized that the solution of any problem of economic or technological development is unthinkable without the utilization of energy resources. Recently, the problem of energy saving and the rational use of energy resources has been more and more frequently examined, both in connection with population growth forecasts for the next 50 to 100 years and in relation to the problem of protecting the environment. The problem is a serious one since statistics show that the construction and use of buildings and public works account for 30 to 40 per cent of total energy use in the ECE countries.

Some delegations lamented the lack of information and practical experience and, so far, of a systematic and scientific approach to the solution of the problem of energy conservation. However, the majority of delegations expressed a firm conviction of the necessity of urgently developing and implementing an energy-saving policy by enlisting appropriate government agencies in the solution of this problem at all administrative and political levels, national, regional and local. The delegations stressed that energy-saving policy should be tied in with the general economic development policy of the country and, in particular, with the problem of full employment. At the same time, the delegations pointed out the necessity of developing short- and long-term political and practical measures for energy saving and the need to evaluate energy demand from residential buildings in relation to social needs. It was also emphasized that efforts should be made to make more efficient utilization of existing energy sources and to develop renewable energy resources, such as solar energy, geothermal heat and wind power. At the same time, practical means of supplying these new forms of energy to the consumer should be studied.

3. A number of delegations remarked that reducing energy consumption is a more difficult problem than increasing energy production. Energy saving and energy supply should be regarded as two sides of the same coin. The continual reduction of energy consumption is, as a rule, more economic than further increasing energy supply especially in the long-term perspective. A preliminary estimate of possibilities for reducing energy consumption in residential buildings through suitable location and orientation (maximal natural illumination, thermal insulation of walls, double or triple glazing, etc.) shows a possible saving of 10 to 30 per cent of total energy consumption in the building stock as a whole. Very important in this regard are energy price policies and the application of reduced tariffs to take advantage of daily and seasonal variations in total power consumption.

4. The delegations discussed ways and means of saving energy, dividing them into restraining measures (including norms and rules for the design and construction of new buildings taking into account climatic conditions and exposure, increased requirements for wall insulation, etc.) and stimulating measures such as subsidies and credits for the improvement of the thermal performance of existing buildings and the launching of information campaigns to increase the awareness of the public at large of the importance of saving energy. Delegations noted that existing residential dwellings present more difficult problems of energy saving than newly designed ones, but nevertheless such possibilities exist, e.g. by educating the public on better operation of buildings (control of adjustable heating systems, ventilation and power supply, etc.) and by retrofitting measures (additional heat insulation of walls and roofs, triple glazing, etc.). As for new buildings, the delegations noted that the introduction of new building regulations, providing for measures to save energy through better insulation and tightness, by limiting the ratio of window space to floor space (e.g. maximum 15 per cent), by reduced ventilation, etc., will result in energy savings of the order of magnitude of 40 to 50 per cent for small houses and 25 to 35 per cent for multi-family buildings.

5. In seeking to reduce the growth of energy consumption, careful attention has to be paid to how this could be achieved in existing buildings as distinct from new buildings. The basic principle should be that reduction in consumption should not be accomplished by reducing comfort standards or sacrificing other objectives of housing policy. Some delegations reported that special programmes had been developed to reduce energy demand by offering assistance and advice to government institutes and managers of residential buildings and public works, commercial companies and proprietors of private homes. Other delegations pointed out the necessity of implementing a similar programme to evaluate the energy requirements of homes and apartments with a description of the requirements of each home, taking into account the needs and behaviour of residents.

6. A number of delegations stressed that energy consumption in buildings is determined to a considerable extent, not only by the physical characteristics of the structure itself, improvement of its thermal insulation and the development of new kinds of equipment, but also by the behaviour of those who use the buildings. Thus, a considerable part of total energy consumption is a reflection of the individual decisions of consumers. For this reason, a policy directed at achieving more efficient energy use in buildings must attempt to change the attitudes of consumers and to encourage their active participation in the improvement of the thermal performance of the buildings in which they live. The majority of people, lacking information, have a poor idea of how to reduce energy consumption and how to save the energy they use. For this reason it is imperative that consumers obtain more information on different forms of energy consumption and methods of saving energy.

7. In establishing an energy saving policy, one must take into account the effect on the low-income strata of a new energy price structure and measures to save energy. In this connection, the necessity was pointed out of providing subsidies for the construction of new energy-efficient houses and for the stimulation of improvements of existing buildings as part of overall government policy.

Energy Saving in New Buildings

8. Mr. K. Mrázek (Czechoslovakia), general rapporteur, reviewed a number of specialized papers on this subject and presented a series of issues for discussion (HBP/SEM.17/1/Add.3).

9. The majority of delegations remarked that since most of the energy in settlements is used for the heating of premises, the increase in energy consumption in this area can be slowed down considerably by designing new buildings with a view to efficient energy use. However, there was a considerable difference of opinion as to how this could best be achieved. Some delegations felt that the most effective approach to energy conservation is the development and enforcement of laws, regulations and standards which must be adhered to in the construction of buildings, taking their purpose into account. These rules should be disseminated by the ECE and the International Organization for Standardization (ISO) and be reviewed on an annual basis. The new rules would make it possible to optimize the amount of insulating material used, window surfaces, level of illumination, rate of ventilation, type of air-conditioning system, etc. Regulations of this type would promote the design of energy-saving buildings, taking into consideration the climatic zones of the country. It was also mentioned that there is a need to prepare a dictionary of energy conservation terms, which would facilitate the mutual understanding of specialists in different countries. Also mentioned was the need for experimental testing of the new norms and standards in practice. Some apprehension was voiced that a great number of standards and rules would be a heavy burden on low-income groups when buying and using buildings. Therefore those standards may need to be combined with subsidies where lower-income groups are involved.

10. A number of delegations noted that national policies in the energy field should include the adoption of energy conservation requirements in the design of new buildings, expressed in functional or performance terms, relating to interior design and aesthetic requirements, solid construction, ventilation, comfort, etc. The key to better design is a more accurate estimation of the final performance of the building throughout all stages of design, ensuring that comfort and other relevant environmental conditions are maintained or improved.

11. Some delegations reported on their achievements and anticipated results in the field of energy conservation, resulting from the introduction of new standards of insulation, glazing and ventilation. For example, in Denmark over a period of 10 to 15 years, as a result of the introduction of new standards, energy savings of 40 per cent in low-rise building construction and up to 20 to 25 per cent in high-rise housing are expected to be achieved. The Finnish delegate noted that there is a satisfactory standard of insulation in new housing construction throughout Finland since the standards which have been adopted by the Nordic Committee on Building Regulations are generally applied. But he also noted that in the future it will be necessary to increase the regeneration of heat and further to increase the level of insulation and also to introduce four-pane glazing which would make a 25 per cent reduction in energy consumption possible. However, it was pointed out that savings in energy consumption, as applied to ventilation systems, must not affect adversely the health of the occupants. In Sweden, for

example, a regulation is being introduced banning smoking in rooms in order to reduce ventilation costs. By the same token, any reduction in window area should not affect health and comfort. Therefore any reduction should be agreed upon by the architects in consultation with building inspection authorities in each separate case.

12. Many delegations noted the necessity for automatic control of the heating system of buildings and for monitoring of energy consumption through the use of infrared ray devices. All these measures allow for an optimum heat distribution in accordance with the time of day and the need, which is very important when the building is being occupied.

13. All delegations stressed that the architects and engineers, who should work in close contact with one another, must not underestimate the importance of energy conservation since they can in fact make a very important contribution in this field. Energy consumption during the construction and occupancy of the buildings is determined at the design stage. The final result of the architectural process is space where people can live, work and enjoy themselves. These spaces are a part of man's life and environment. If the architects and engineers are recognized as being the creators of life-environment systems, then it is absolutely necessary that they take into account the necessity to conserve energy and that they recognize that energy conservation affects our way of life. Therefore the question of energy conservation and its long-term consequences should be one of the criteria applied to the planning of new architectural endeavours. The training of a new generation of specialists in the universities with a special emphasis on energy conservation in buildings will undoubtedly affect the next wave of building construction. It would seem that the time has come to compare primary outlay and life-cycle costs. The architect must evaluate the profitability of housing or building projects which are cheap to build as compared to those which are cheap to maintain. Any building design which ignores the effect of the environment (the sun, the wind, the geographical position, etc.) almost always uses energy as a mechanical intervention to compensate for the inconveniences which arise. Therefore the architect should understand and foresee the effect of an adverse site or climate on the energy flow in the building.

14. Along with a proposal to regulate heating sources and to monitor them, some countries proposed that architects should also take into account the intensity, the direction and the duration of the light provided by the sun and the effect of its direct penetration into a building or structure, combined with a simultaneous study on the utilization of the sun's energy as a source of heat by storing it in special units. This will make it possible to achieve a maximum saving of energy in a building. In this connection a proposal was put forward for the staging of international competitions for developing a better method of conserving energy in buildings and also for the creation of high-efficiency heating systems based on solar energy.

Energy Saving in Existing Buildings

15. The discussion was introduced by Mrs. I. Årlin (Sweden), general rapporteur.

16. Most of the delegations noted that existing housing represents the greatest potential for saving energy. Using legal, technical, economic, psychological and educational measures, it will be possible to save energy now being expended on heating by 30 to 50

per cent without lowering room temperatures. Among the technical measures which facilitate the saving of energy are practices aimed at improving thermal insulation in buildings, and practices aimed at improving and regulating heating systems, which in turn result in the regulation of room temperatures. Thermal insulation of a whole building can be increased through the improvement of the existing insulation of the entire outside surface of heated areas. This mainly concerns outside walls, windows, top-floor ceilings and ground floors. Improving the functioning of heating systems means, apart from anything else, automatic control to maintain the optimum temperature throughout the period in which the living space is occupied; automatic lowering of the room temperature while the living space is not occupied; using only the necessary number of boilers; and also thorough servicing of the heating equipment.

17. It was stressed that improving the thermal insulation in existing buildings is a rather expensive undertaking. Therefore improving the thermal insulation of existing buildings should only be carried out on an extensive, statewide scale given the relevant state financial assistance and a programme of incentives. This was also noted by the representative of France who said that in his country financial incentives are being offered for energy saving through supplementary insulation in connection with the modernization of buildings. Thus, at the present time, there has been a 15 per cent reduction in energy consumption while, at the same time, there has been an increase in the number of dwellings constructed. From 1973 to 1977 the consumption of insulating materials almost doubled.

18. The representatives of the German Democratic Republic and of Poland noted that in their countries extensive programmes of energy-saving measures relating to existing housing are under way. Above all this entails a great volume of construction and installation as applied to the reconstruction of existing buildings, using low energy-consuming building materials, thermal insulating measures in construction and glazing, a wide range of prefabricated construction units and also a reduction in volume through lowering room ceilings. As a result of these measures a considerable reduction in the use of energy in buildings has been achieved. As regards energy saving related to heat supply, adjustable 24-hour room temperatures (day—20°C, night—14°C, morning—16°C), adjustable heating units, heat regeneration (heat pumps, hot water), and servicing of the heating system all make it possible to reduce energy consumption even further. If the government and the general public take an active part in the extensive modernization of existing buildings it will be possible to cut energy consumption by 30 per cent.

19. A number of delegations noted that about half of all the energy used in their countries goes to heating which in some countries has led to a reduction from 45 to 30 per cent in the construction of one-storey houses, which are high energy consumers. The Swedish delegation pointed out three groups of energy-saving measures which can be applied to existing buildings. All these measures can be adopted when the building is occupied (plugging gaps in door and window frames, constant servicing of boilers and heating and ventilation systems). These measures are not complicated and not expensive and do not disturb the occupants. To the next group belong simple measures such as the thermal insulation of attic ceilings, the installation of thermostats on radiators and electricity consumption meters for each unit. These measures are also relatively cheap and quickly carried out. More radical measures include insulation of walls,

air-circulation equipment, and so on. These measures involve a fundamental reconstruction of the building. However, it has been noted that even after such measures
have been adopted for improving the thermal insulation (a saving of 20 cents per kilowatt a year), energy consumption will be higher than in new buildings. Therefore,
attention was drawn to the importance of educational programmes for professionals
and for the general public which are, however, difficult to organize owing to the lack of
teachers and specialists in the field.

20. The representative of Canada pointed out that an energy conservation programme
had been successfully carried out in Prince Edward Island, where advice had been provided to the inhabitants of that province on ways of conserving energy with a programme of financial incentives on energy saving and related measures on additional
insulation of buildings. A detailed estimate of local energy consumption needs is being
drawn up and, finally, the quality of insulating material and equipment is supervised.

21. A number of delegations pointed out the importance of collecting data and making estimates of the demand for electric energy, the necessity for additional measures
relating to thermal insulation and the subsequent accurate evaluation of the volume of
energy used and saved. Thus, the representative of Finland noted that in his country
the consumption of energy could be cut back by 15 per cent by 1985 and by 20 per cent
by 1990 if consumer services were well organized. Energy-saving work on existing
buildings will make it possible at one and the same time to lower the unemployment
rate in a number of western countries in the ECE region.

22. The delegations of several countries pointed out the effectiveness of the work
which is being done by the International Council for Building Research, Studies and
Documentation (CIB) in the field of energy conservation in existing buildings and the
use of solar energy, and also stressed the necessity of processing meteorological data
from the World Meteorological Organization and the utilization of the material which
is already in existence. Note was made of the necessity of taking into account the interests of the inhabitants in drawing up programmes for saving energy in existing buildings and, in particular, the interests of special groups of people such as invalids, the
handicapped, the aged and others.

NOTE ADDED IN PROOF

The analytical summary of the general debate which appears in the Report of the
Seminar (HBP/SEM.17/2) contains an extra paragraph that would appear here as
para. 14 on p. 130. This contains the text of an additional recommendation proposed
by the delegation of Canada, with the title "Economic Analysis of Conservation
Measures". The operative paragraph is as follows:

"(b) THE ENERGY COST MEASURE WHICH SHOULD APPLY IN ASSESSING THE
COST-EFFECTIVENESS OF ENERGY CONSERVATION MEASURES IS THE RE-
PLACEMENT COST OF ENERGY FROM THE SOURCES WHICH THEY DISPLACE."

The full text of the Canadian proposal will be found in Annex III of the Report of
the Seminar.

CONCLUSIONS AND RECOMMENDATIONS*

I. OVERALL POLICIES AND STRATEGIES RELATING TO ENERGY USE IN HUMAN SETTLEMENTS

Preamble

1. Policies and strategies related to the planning, design, construction and use of human settlements influence, directly or indirectly, the consumption of energy resources in all the three main sectors of "industry", "transport" and "other uses". In the ECE region it may be estimated that around 50 per cent of total energy use is affected by decisions in the human settlements field. Since the ECE region accounts for approximately 75 per cent of the world consumption of purchased energy, activities related to the development and use of human settlements in this region use up nearly 40 per cent of world energy supplies, partly as a result of wasteful consumption habits. Efforts to achieve improved energy economy and efficiency in human settlements are, therefore, not only essential in order to safeguard the interests of present and future generations in the ECE region, but should also be seen as a moral obligation towards the less-privileged countries and peoples in the world and as a subject for global international action and co-operation.

2. In the last decades, the supply of cheap energy was generally taken for granted, and a substantial shift took place from the direct burning of solid fuel in human settlements towards the use of oil, gas and electricity. In recent years the easy dependence on large and ever-growing use of energy resources has in many countries been checked by substantial rises in the prices of all major energy sources and by interruptions in supply. Environmental problems have arisen in connection with the extraction, conversion, transmission and consumption of energy. There are prospects that the principal fossil fuel resources on which most ECE countries depend are being rapidly depleted. In a number of countries, these prospects constitute a particular challenge to decision-makers in the human settlements field because of the long life of building and transportation infrastructure facilities, the need for sufficient amounts of energy to reach and maintain adequate health and comfort standards and the inequitable effects of changes in energy prices on low-income groups and other vulnerable sections of the community.

---

* Following normal practice, the final version of these Conclusions and Recommendations was prepared by the ECE Secretariat after the Ottawa Seminar so as to take account of changes to the revised drafts (HBP/SEM.17/CRP.9/Rev.1 and addenda) that were adopted during the last session of the Seminar.

3. Conversely, human settlements decisions have an important impact on future demand for energy and on the way in which different forms of energy will be used. The great and immediate influence of changes in the energy situation on human settlements has tended to hide the equal importance of this reciprocal relationship. Decisions by settlements planners and developers relating to the choice of heating fuel, to the heat budget of buildings and to energy conservation programmes, profoundly affect energy demand projections and should consequently be taken fully into account in the drawing up of national energy policies and strategies. Such decisions are also of critical importance as a means of reducing the vulnerability of consumers to energy supply interruptions or depletion and of accelerating the rate at which novel forms of energy are utilized.

4. While there are many potential areas of conflict, there is also evidence that human settlements objectives and energy conservation objectives are often and to a great extent compatible. Therefore, long-standing human settlement objectives must not be sacrificed to respond to the urgent need, in many countries, to reduce growth in energy use, especially of scarce and expensive depleting resources. Many opportunities exist to improve the quality of life in human settlements in parallel or in combination with determined efforts to reduce energy demand in such settlements. What is necessary, however, is that these objectives be reconciled through careful consideration and co-ordination of energy and human settlements policies within the context of national economic and social development policies. Thus, in several countries, "energy-conscious" human settlements policies are likely to involve changes in the energy-wasting lifestyle to which people have become accustomed, and will certainly affect employment, capital allocation and other major sectors of national economies.

5. Energy-related problems in human settlements are very diverse throughout the ECE region because of the great differences in climate, geography, population, human behaviour, urbanization, socioeconomic systems and resource endowment. However, there are also many similarities and many common problems. All countries, for example, face the complex problems caused by the long-life expectancy of buildings and settlements, in contrast to the speed with which changes may occur in energy supply conditions. It is therefore important further to develop international co-operation on problems and policies relating to energy and human settlements. The seminar represents an important step in this direction. It constitutes a significant contribution to the implementation in the ECE region of the recommendations adopted at the UN Habitat Conference, held in Vancouver in 1976, and represents a major element in the current work programme of the ECE in energy matters. In particular, the Seminar responds to the provisions of the Final Act of the Conference on Security and Co-operation in Europe relating to co-operation in the fields of science and technology and of environment.

Recommendations

Recommendation I.1

Need for action in a situation of uncertainty

(a) In several countries there are great uncertainties with regard to the future availability and price of different forms of energy. The gravity of the energy problem is, however, so great that we cannot wait until all experiments and investigations are completed.

(b) IN VIEW OF THE PRESENT UNCERTAINTIES IN SEVERAL COUNTRIES WITH REGARD TO THE ENERGY OUTLOOK, AND DESPITE THE SCARCITY OF DATA AND KNOWLEDGE, GOVERNMENTS SHOULD INITIATE IMMEDIATE ACTION TO ENSURE PROTECTION FOR CITIZENS AND HUMAN SETTLEMENTS AGAINST SHORTAGE OF ENERGY FOR CRITICAL PURPOSES AND, TO THE EXTENT POSSIBLE, AGAINST INFLATIONARY PRICE INCREASES FOR ENERGY.

(c) *Such action should include:*
   (i)   Energy conservation measures and the development of new and renewable sources of energy.
   (ii) The planning of buildings and settlements in such a way that they can be easily modified as better data and knowledge become available.
   (iii) Persuasive methods and, where necessary, regulations to ensure optimum energy economy and efficiency in new and redeveloped settlements.
   (iv) The promotion of energy saving by adequate management and maintenance of existing buildings and settlements.
   (v)   The planning and design of buildings and settlements so as to reduce their vulnerability to interruptions in energy supplies, and to increase the use of renewable energy resources.
   (vi) The incorporation, as central elements in such conservation and renewable resources programmes of action, of monitoring and review mechanisms, which ensure that the programmes can be regularly revised to take account of new information and changing conditions.

Recommendation I.2

Co-ordinated policy development

(a) In many countries, rising energy costs and uncertainty of supply challenge long-standing human settlement objectives. Conversely, human settlement development and management decisions influence projections of future energy demand. In many countries, in the recent past, planning in the fields of energy and human settlements was separated and often followed divergent paths. There is a need to promote settlements planning, which will achieve multiple objectives that include energy conservation as well as conservation of other scarce resources, such as land, water and the natural environment.

(b) EXISTING OPPORTUNITIES TO ACCOMMODATE THE ENERGY REQUIREMENTS OF HUMAN SETTLEMENTS WITH EMPHASIS ON APPROPRIATE SUPPLY OPTIONS, EFFICIENCY AND CONSERVATION, SHOULD BE UTILIZED AGGRESSIVELY. TO REALIZE THESE OPPORTUNITIES, ENERGY AND HUMAN SETTLEMENTS PLANNING POLICIES AND STRATEGIES FOR BOTH CURRENT OPERATIONS AND SHORT- AND LONG-TERM PLANNING SHOULD BE CO-ORDINATED.

(c) *Co-ordinated planning requires:*
   (i)   Joint policy development in energy and settlements planning.
   (ii) Mechanisms to ensure the co-ordination and integration of decision making in

the energy and human settlements fields at all levels.

(iii) Priority for energy supply systems that offer opportunities to improve, on a sustainable basis, the quality of life in human settlements and to maintain or enhance environmental quality.

(iv) Priority for community planning, designs and renovations that attain satisfactory living standards at reduced levels of energy consumption.

(v) Thorough consideration of criteria to be used in reconciling energy costs and benefits with those for human settlements, recognizing that the appropriate solution will vary according to individual situations.

(vi) Compensatory measures to counteract important and undesirable results of policy compromises.

Recommendation I.3

Data and research needs

(a) Effective policy planning requires adequate knowledge of the ways in which human settlements utilize energy, especially in view of the great variation in the energy characteristics of different settlements and the large number and diversity of energy-consuming units they contain.

(b) GOVERNMENTS SHOULD ENSURE THAT APPROPRIATE INFORMATION ON ENERGY USE IN HUMAN SETTLEMENTS IS COLLECTED, ANALYSED AND USED IN DEVELOPING ACTION PROGRAMMES. THEY SHOULD ALSO PROMOTE THE DEVELOPMENT OF DATA SYSTEMS AND MODELS TO ASSIST TECHNICAL POLICY AND PROGRAMME DECISION MAKING.

(c) *Action in this field should include:*

(i) Collection of statistics on the use of various forms of energy for different purposes and types of buildings and community designs, including data on the energy implications of alternative transport patterns and systems.

(ii) Addition of the energy performance characteristics of buildings to data regularly collected, e.g. in conjunction with housing and population censuses.

(iii) Regular and comprehensive collection of data on actual energy use in buildings from energy suppliers and/or owners and managers of buildings.

(iv) Collection of appropriate data on energy flow in different types of buildings through sample surveys of adequate coverage.

(v) Determination, in qualitative terms, based on physiological, psychological and similar scientific investigations, of real needs for energy in relation to human health and comfort.

(vi) Analysis of data on energy utilization in relation to meteorological data and on the influence of cultural attitudes towards energy use.

(vii) Research into energy needs and design implications for infrastructure networks in the framework of extended future development including energy conservation concepts.

(viii) The promotion of research and development work aiming at the establishment of realistic models of energy use, especially suitable for the identification of conservation opportunities.

(ix) According greater priority, and greater allocation of resources, to research and development leading to the use of renewable energy resources.

(x) Investigation of the impact of energy conservation and related policies on infrastructure networks in human settlements.

Recommendation I.4

Participation and co-operation of all concerned

(a) The consumption of energy resources in human settlements is a function of the daily behaviour of millions of individuals which, in turn, is affected by decision making at the national, regional and local levels. Energy conservation involves the activities of business and industry and calls for contributions from a variety of experts. If energy conservation is to be achieved on a large scale in human settlements, the full co-operation of all concerned has to be ensured.

(b) GOVERNMENTS SHOULD ENSURE OR PROMOTE CO-ORDINATED AND SUSTAINED ACTION BY ALL CONCERNED AND AT ALL LEVELS OF DECISION MAKING WITH A VIEW TO ACHIEVING OPTIMUM ENERGY CONSERVATION IN HUMAN SETTLEMENTS. THE PARTICIPATION OF NON-GOVERNMENTAL ORGANIZATIONS, THE PRIVATE SECTOR AND INDIVIDUALS SHOULD BE ENCOURAGED BOTH IN THE FORMULATION AND IMPLEMENTATION OF ENERGY CONSERVATION PROGRAMMES.

(c) *Particular attention should be paid to:*

(i) Identification of the roles of public authorities at the national, regional and local levels, of industry and business, of non-governmental organizations, of experts and of individuals in the implementation of energy conservation programmes in human settlements.

(ii) Education and training of experts able to analyse and test the energy performance of buildings and to undertake measures necessary to achieve energy efficiency and economy in buildings and settlements.

(iii) Dissemination of information emphasizing the great and unnecessary waste of heat and power that are presently common in human settlements.

(iv) Encouragement of competent non-governmental organizations to play an active and innovative role in modifying community behaviour, attitudes and motivation with regard to energy conservation and the use of renewable energy resources.

(v) Promotion of conservation measures on a do-it-yourself basis, especially for alterations that would not be cost-effective if undertaken on a commercial basis. Information, advice and assistance should be provided to enable each group and citizen to contribute to the conservation programme.

(vi) Promotion of understanding and co-operation among the various groups and individuals and the provision of a mechanism for members of the community to indicate their knowledge and experience related to energy conservation in human settlements.

Recommendation I.5

Special responsibilities of public agencies

(a) Governments and public agencies of different kinds have a major influence on energy use in human settlements, e.g. through the housing and other buildings that they own, manage, lease or subsidize, the transport systems that they operate, and the energy supply systems that are publicly controlled. The policies and actions of such public bodies are decisive.

(b) GOVERNMENTS AND PUBLIC AGENCIES SHOULD UTILIZE THE SPECIAL OPPORTUNITIES FOR IMPROVING THE EFFICIENCY OF ENERGY USE IN HUMAN SETTLEMENTS IN THE EXERCISE OF THEIR OWN POWERS AND RESPONSIBILITIES, BOTH BECAUSE OF THEIR QUANTITATIVE IMPORTANCE AND BECAUSE OF THEIR VALUE AS EXAMPLES TO THE REST OF THE COMMUNITY. THEY SHOULD ALSO, THROUGH ENERGY PRICING AND TAXING POLICY, STIMULATE MORE EFFICIENT USE OF ENERGY, WHILE HOLDING INFLATIONARY EFFECTS TO A MINIMUM.

(c) *Special opportunities for public action include:*

   (i) Acceptance of an explicit responsibility for energy conservation and the introduction of appropriate supply technologies by governments and public agencies at all levels.

   (ii) Improvement of the energy characteristics of residential and non-residential accommodation that is directly owned, managed, leased or subsidized by public bodies at a national or local level.

   (ii) Improvement of energy efficiency in national and local transport systems controlled by public agencies.

   (iv) Definition or revision of the mandates, objectives and programmes of energy supply utilities so as to use them as instruments to promote energy conservation rather than as bodies primarily concerned with meeting demands for conventional energy.

   (v) In several countries, implementation of selective and equitable pricing policies for energy supplies, especially those that take into account the long-run marginal cost of the supplies, and thereby enable accurate assessment of conservation or alternative energy opportunities.

   (vi) In several countries the replacement of measures that tend to promote undesirable growth of demand for non-renewable energy resources by measures designed positively to encourage shifts to renewable resources.

Recommendation I.6

International co-operation

(a) Despite wide variations in the various determinants of energy consumption, the countries of the ECE region are faced at the present time with problems of energy use in human settlements that have many common features. Progress towards the solution of these problems will be greatly facilitated by further development of international co-operation in this field.

(b) INFORMATION AND EXPERIENCE ON THE PROBLEMS AND OPPORTUNITIES FOR IM-PROVING ENERGY ECONOMY AND EFFICIENCY AND FOR INTRODUCING NEW FORMS OF RENEWABLE ENERGY IN HUMAN SETTLEMENTS SHOULD BE WIDELY SHARED ON AN INTERNATIONAL BASIS THROUGH THE ECONOMIC COMMISSION FOR EUROPE, IN PARTICULAR ITS COMMITTEE ON HOUSING, BUILDING AND PLANNING, AND THROUGH NON-GOVERNMENTAL INTERNATIONAL ORGANIZATIONS COMPETENT IN THIS FIELD.

(c) *Such international co-operation should include:*

(i) Collection and publication on a regular basis of data and other relevant information and experience on energy use in human settlements in a form which will assist the utilization of this material in the development and implementation of energy conservation policies and programmes.

(ii) Further development of joint and co-operative work on regulations and standards for energy economy and efficiency in buildings, based on requirements expressed in functional or performance terms.

(iii) Establishment and maintenance by the ECE secretariat of a register of pilot projects, designated by governments, demonstrating how energy conservation can be achieved and renewable energy resources utilized in settlements and individual buildings in ECE countries.

(iv) Organization, in co-operation with the ECE secretariat, of national and international colloquia to discuss, within the framework and constraints of different situations, the feasibility and implications of implementing "energy-conscious" human settlements policies along the lines outlined at the present seminar.

(v) Regular review and analysis by the ECE Committee on Housing, Building and planning of progress in the implementation of the recommendations adopted at the present seminar, starting with the planned in-depth discussion of the results of the seminar at the annual session of the Committee in September 1978.

(vi) Exchange of data and other relevant information and experience between the ECE and other international organizations, including the Committees on Human Settlements of other regional commissions.

(vii) Convening, by the ECE secretariat, of inter-secretariat meetings, with participation of representatives of the specialized agencies, intergovernmental and non-governmental organizations concerned, to discuss and co-ordinate programmes of international action relating to the promotion of energy conservation and the use of renewable energy resources in human settlements.

(viii) Organization of a second ECE seminar on energy and human settlements in order to evaluate the results of action taken in the meantime, in particular in quantitative terms.

(ix) Promotion of public participation and of technical studies, research, and documentation exchange by the World Health Organization (WHO) and by recognized non-governmental international organizations.

(x) Collection and publication on a regular basis of data on overall energy utilization in different countries.

(xi) Development of concepts for and the collection and exchange of data on energy consumption in communities as a means to identify land-use measures, to improve energy efficiency and on which the assessment of technological measures to reduce energy consumption in urban transport could be based.

II. IMPACT OF ENERGY CONSIDERATIONS ON COMMUNITY PLANNING AND DEVELOPMENT

Preamble

1. The availability and use of different forms of energy have always influenced the location, structure and development of human settlements and the quality and character of daily life and work within them. In ancient times, networks and structures of human settlements were strongly affected by the limited capacities of natural (water, wood and coal) and biological (human and animal) energy sources. Settlements were characterized by: relatively small, uniformly distributed settlement units; concentrated overall structure and close proximity of buildings; close proximity of functions, places of work, services and living. Careful attention was being given to natural conditions and resources, such as topography, climate, fertility of soil, availability of water and natural sources of energy. In those days, a close relationship between the development of settlements and energy existed because of the necessity of a self-supporting energy system.

2. With the rapid expansion of means of production in the nineteenth century, energy development went beyond the limits of the former self-supporting systems by exploiting new manufacturing and transportation facilities. This led to fundamental changes in settlement patterns and the structure of individual settlements. A characteristic feature of this process was a separation of places of energy extraction and places of energy use. This separation, along with new methods of transporting energy, became an important factor in determining the location and structure of human settlements. At the same time there was a separation of basic urban functions as well as their spatial concentration, requiring more and longer trips between places of work, living, recreation and other social and service functions.

3. In recent years the problem of location of energy extraction and conversion plants and relevant distribution systems unquestionably became an important aspect in the spatial distribution and design of human settlements. First of all, there is a general economic and technical problem with far-reaching implications on the spatial location and layout of production facilities, residential areas and other urban functions.

4. Undoubtedly the search for better planning and economy in the production and use of energy coincides with a number of short- and long-term urban and regional planning goals and objectives. However, there are also those instances where aspects of energy economy conflict with physical planning, social and environmental aims.

5. History has shown that the general development of cities causes increasing diffi-

culties, necessitating general study and a new planning strategy. The impact of energy considerations on the planning of human settlements should not, therefore, be seen as an isolated problem but as an integral part of the future development of the city, as the most sophisticated and most efficient form of human settlement.

Recommendations

Recommendation II.1

Energy problems and human settlements

(a) Economic and social progress is not possible unless it is based on the sensible utilization of available energy and on the planned use of the natural environment. It is therefore necessary to plan the use of energy along with that of space. Energy planning must be carried out at all appropriate levels. It is important to co-ordinate energy planning with physical planning, particularly at the regional and local levels.

(b) IT IS THE RESPONSIBILITY OF GOVERNMENTS TO PARTICIPATE IN MEETING ENERGY NEEDS, WITHOUT NEGLECTING OTHER NEEDS AND CONSIDERATIONS RELATED TO THE QUALITY OF THE LIFE OF THE INDIVIDUAL AND OF SOCIETY AND THE RESPECT FOR THE ENVIRONMENT. IN THIS CONNECTION, REGIONAL AND LOCAL AUTHORITIES MUST PLAY AN ESSENTIAL PART BY MEANS OF TERRITORIAL PLANNING IN SUPPORT OF NATIONAL PLANNING TO LESSEN ENERGY REQUIREMENTS.

(c) *The following measures are especially important:*

   (i) A *bona fide* energy code for energy consumers should be established.

   (ii) Energy planning should be undertaken in such a way as to promote the use of polyvalent facilities adaptable to many sources or forms of energy.

   (iii) Regional and local authorities should ensure an equitable distribution of diminishing resources, reduce energy waste, promote recovery of wasted energy and the use of local energy resources, and improve the energy efficiency of public buildings and services.

   (iv) When it is technically possible to recover heat from national or regional energy conversion facilities, measures for doing so should be systematically planned, following agreement by the local planning authorities.

   (v) In order to evaluate trends in consumption, systems to gather information on energy flow should be established; decentralized (municipal or regional) statistical data should be used for this purpose.

Recommendation II.2

Energy conscious physical planning

(a) Because of the great uncertainty of energy supply, which will apply for most of the lifetime of human settlements now in existence or being built, it is urgent to take into account energy considerations in the planning of human settlements. The size, arrangement and density of buildings and settlements have a considerable impact on the energy requirements both for them and for the urban area as a whole. It is also important to allow for a mix of style, appearance and arrangements of buildings, which contribute considerably to the charm of a town.

(b) PLANNERS SHOULD TAKE ENERGY ASPECTS INTO CONSIDERATION IN THE PLANNING OF SPATIAL RELATIONSHIPS AMONG LAND USES AND BUILDINGS AND IN THE DESIGN AND LAYOUT OF BUILDINGS AND HUMAN SETTLEMENTS. IN REVITALIZING EXISTING AND DEVELOPING NEW SETTLEMENTS THE AMOUNT OF ENERGY REQUIRED TO OPERATE THIS URBAN FABRIC SHOULD BE EXPLICITLY CONSIDERED IN THE EVALUATION OF ALTERNATIVE DESIGN SOLUTIONS.

(c) *This will imply:*
   (i) Research on the energy efficiency of different forms of settlements and designs of buildings, and on their adaptability to the use of non-conventional energy sources.
   (ii) Development of planning guidelines and evaluation methods to assess possible changes in future urban pattern, building design and energy supply.
   (iii) Decision-making aimed at keeping the energy consumption of operating the settlement at the lowest level compatible with other regional planning objectives.
   (iv) Education and information of the general public so that it may understand the implications of energy considerations on planning alternatives.

Recommendation II.3

Production and conversion of energy

(a) Increasing demand for energy in the world requires optimum utilization of local sources of energy, such as solar energy or the use of waste. Despite this, a growing number of primary energy extraction and processing facilities will be required. In order to achieve greater yield and economies of scale, there is a tendency for the size of these centres to increase. This creates new problems for planners regarding territorial development and the protection of the environment.

(b) NOT ONLY GENERAL ECONOMIC CRITERIA, BUT ALSO CERTAIN CONDITIONS SHOULD BE TAKEN INTO ACCOUNT IN DETERMINING THE CHARACTERISTICS AND SIZE OF AND NEED FOR ENERGY CONVERSION AND EXTRACTION FACILITIES, SUCH AS THE LOCAL ECONOMY, THE ECOLOGICAL ABSORPTION CAPACITY OF THE NATURAL ENVIRONMENT, THE APPEARANCE OF SITES AND THE VULNERABILITY OF ADJACENT HUMAN SETTLEMENTS TO POLLUTION AND ACCIDENT HAZARDS. IMPLEMENTATION OF THIS PROVISION MUST BE ENSURED BY THE PUBLIC AUTHORITIES.

(c) *Specific measures could include:*
   (i) A search for alternatives based on smaller plants in order to ascertain whether they offer decisive advantages as regards pollution, appearance and safety. These studies should also be used to assess conservation measures which might be taken if substantial changes were to occur in the type or availability of energy supplies.
   (ii) Consideration, as soon as any decision has been made, on the location of energy plants, and of re-deployment of the redundant work force once the facilities have been completed, to maintain the economic potential of the area concerned, or at least to avoid a sudden drop in that potential.

(iii) Before being authorized, every project aimed at exploiting a deposit should be accompanied by a redevelopment plan.

(iv) Development and application of dry refrigeration techniques in order to cool waste water from electric power plants when that water is not recovered.

(v) Collection of waste resulting from various kinds of energy conversion in areas delimited according to the nature of the waste, the location of its production, transportation costs, and the possible incineration of wastes possible in multi-purpose conversion centres. These wastes can thus become new sources of energy.

(vi) Examination of the effect of the implementation of any plan for energy production or transportation facilities with participation of the public concerned.

Recommendation II.4

Energy distribution in human settlements

(a) The planning of human settlements has an important effect on national consumption of energy resources, with regard to its nature as well as its volume. In many countries, urban or regional energy planning is affected by two main factors: physical factors related to the resistance to change of spatial structures, and organizational factors related to differences in levels of decision making.

(b) JUST AS THE AUTHORITY RESPONSIBLE FOR URBAN AND REGIONAL PLANNING HAS A POLICY FOR LAND DEVELOPMENT AND MANAGEMENT, IT MUST ALSO HAVE AN ENERGY POLICY. THIS WILL ENABLE IT NOT ONLY TO SEEK OUT MEANS OF AFFECTING ENERGY SAVINGS BUT ALSO TO BECOME INVOLVED IN DETERMINING SOLUTIONS TO PROBLEMS OF THE NATURE OF ENERGY SOURCES, ITS DISTRIBUTION AND INTERRUPTIONS IN SUPPLY.

(c) *Actions in this area could include the following:*
   (i) Co-operation among communities in energy planning to ensure co-ordination of various municipal activities.

   (ii) Development of techniques for planning of residential areas which can reduce the energy transmission grid, including heat supply within the area. It is advisable to develop and improve methods of laying pipes and cables with and without protective ducts while trying to cut down on energy losses during transmission.

   (iii) Adaptation of urban structures for the appropriate use of coal and the improvement of anti-pollution measures related to coal.

   (iv) Application of techniques to raise the temperature of waste heat (heat pumps) and to store energy (reservoirs above or below ground).

   (v) Use of conventional energy sources (electricity, gas, coal, oil) to provide for peak calorific requirements and new kinds of energy or recovered energy to provide basic heating.

Recommendation II.5

Energy-economy in heating and services

(a) Energy economy depends both on efficient production and effective use of heat. The most efficient heat production is when the community utilizes industrial waste heat or cooling waters of power plants. General experience shows that small boilers have lower efficiency than large heating plants. When producing electricity in condensing power plants, for heating purposes, the efficiency use is low, only 30 to 40 per cent. The economy of heat use in buildings depends on the control possibilities of the system. In systems with individual room control, electrical heating, central water heating and warm air heating, the efficiency of use is relatively good. On the other hand, with simple stoves the individual selection of temperature level is most easily achieved.

(b) IN DECIDING ON METHODS OF HEAT SUPPLY TO BUILDINGS IN A SETTLEMENT (DISTRICT HEATING, CENTRAL HEATING, RECAPTURE AND REDISTRIBUTION OF INTERNAL HEAT OR INDIVIDUAL ROOM HEATING) THE AUTHORITIES AND BUILDING OWNERS CONCERNED SHOULD CONSIDER THE DENSITY AND FORM OF THE SETTLE-MENT AS WELL AS THE ENERGY EFFICIENCY OF DIFFERENT FORMS OF HEAT SUPPLY AND THEIR TENDENCY TO CREATE AIR POLLUTION.

(c) *Attention should be paid to the following considerations:*

    (i) If central heating is used, there are strong arguments in favour of a building density and a layout permitting heat supply by district heating.

    (ii) Electricity produced in thermoelectric plants should normally not be used for space heating unless good use could be made of the waste heat from the cooling water of the plant.

    (iii) Great efforts should be made to plan combined heat and power production facilities and to introduce total energy systems.

    (iv) Possibility of energy savings in low-rise building by appropriate heating systems.

    (v) Recapture and redistribution of internal heat, whenever feasible.

Recommendation II.6

Transportation

(a) Transportation within and between human settlements accounts for a major share of their energy requirements. Various means of transportation have different characteristics in terms of consumption of power: high consumption for private cars and for air transport, low consumption for buses, trams and particularly railways and ships, although there are also other factors to take into account, for example, travel time. Moreover, physical layout and mixture of urban functions can strongly influence the amount of transport required.

(b) IN PLANNING THE STRUCTURE OF HUMAN SETTLEMENTS, DUE REGARD SHOULD BE PAID TO THE AMOUNT AND ENERGY EFFICIENCY OF TRANSPORT REQUIRED. MEANS

OF TRANSPORT REQUIRING A LIMITED AMOUNT OF ENERGY PER TRANSPORT UNIT
AND REDUCING DEPENDENCE ON OIL SHOULD BE FAVOURED.

(c) *This could be achieved by:*

    (i) Avoiding too low densities of urban settlements.

    (ii) Clustering of development.

    (iii) Mixing residential premises with places for work, education and recreation to reduce trip lengths.

    (iv) Favouring energy efficient transport through the physical layout of settlements and through traffic rules, parking rules, speed limits, incentives for car and van pooling, and other transportation system management measures.

    (v) Searching for technological solutions to the problems associated with private vehicles using alternative fuels, e.g. electricity and gas.

    (vi) Favouring railway transport over air transport where the value of time saved does not override energy efficiency considerations.

    (vii) Promotion of and facilitation of bicycle and pedestrian traffic.

    (viii) Exploring and implementing the increased use of alternative communication means, such as telephone, closed circuit television and videophone.

III. IMPACT OF ENERGY CONSIDERATIONS ON THE DESIGN, CONSTRUCTION, IMPROVEMENT AND UTILIZATION OF BUILDINGS

Preamble

1. Buildings form the frame of human life. We spend most of our lifetime in and around buildings. The quality of our buildings and of the built environment is of the utmost importance and in need of improvement in many parts of the ECE region. At the same time, the heating, cooling, ventilation and lighting systems of buildings consume extensive energy and thus represent the greatest potential for energy saving. The two goals of safeguarding or improving the quality of life in buildings and of saving energy therein can be combined in a single and sensitive building policy.

2. In the past, when cheap energy was available in sufficient quantities, there were very weak incentives for public authorities, designers and builders to take energy considerations into account or to pay attention to the total volume and cost of the energy used over the entire life-span of a building. This situation has now radically changed, and all governments in the ECE region are taking a variety of measures to limit the consumption of non-renewable energy in new and existing buildings, e.g. through building legislation and regulations, and loans and grants for retrofitting. Thus, building designers are now compelled to take energy considerations into account as a new constraint on their work. This constraint represents a challenge to the profession in that it provides a means not only of achieving energy conservation but also of improving the quality of buildings, both new and existing ones. Similarly, building owners and managers are faced with a new challenge of ensuring reduced energy consumption without sacrificing comfort standards or increasing the rents charged to the inhabitants of the buildings.

3. In most countries, policies relating to energy conservation in buildings have so far been drawn up and implemented on a piecemeal basis to cope with emergency problems. If the great potential for energy conservation in buildings is to be realized, comprehensive national, regional and local policies and programmes must be established. In many countries, a comprehensive and integrated policy for energy conservation requires co-ordination of policies in several sectors such as finance, employment, research and development, education and training. In these countries it must furthermore embrace both residential and public buildings and be directed towards both new and existing buildings. The resulting costs and benefits must be distributed in an equitable and socially acceptable manner.

4. The consumption of energy in buildings results to a large measure from the habits and behaviour of the individual. The success of any conservation policy therefore depends in the last instance on the motivation of individuals. Consequently, extensive information programmes and advice to individuals constitute important elements in a comprehensive policy for energy saving in buildings.

5. There are wide differences with respect to energy saving opportunities and to problems of implementing conservation programmes in new buildings and in the existing building stock. It is relatively easy and cheap to achieve improved energy efficiency in new buildings, and many ECE countries have already introduced energy-saving stipulations in their building regulations for such buildings. On the other hand, improved energy efficiency in new buildings will have a major impact on total energy consumption only in the long-term perspective. It is nevertheless important to take immediate action in order to halt the construction of buildings with low energy efficiency and thus reduce the growth of energy demand resulting from additions to the existing building stock. Since new knowledge and technology for energy conservation in new buildings is continuously becoming available, it is important to design the regulations in such a way that they provide for and encourage the use of new techniques.

6. In order to achieve an absolute decrease in energy use in buildings, rules for energy conservation in new buildings are not enough. By far the greatest potential saving opportunities exist in the present building stock. However, large-scale energy conservation programmes for existing buildings are more complicated in technical and economic terms and will directly affect the living conditions of those who live and work in them. It is a great responsibility and challenge to devise policies to overcome these problems. Those to be affected should be consulted in advance so that they can understand the need, costs and benefits of proposed measures and make their views and preferences known before major decisions are taken and implemented. Public participation should be encouraged at all levels of planning and decision making by governments and the private sector.

Recommendations

Recommendation III.1

Energy saving and the quality of life
(a) The construction, operation and use of buildings entails the consumption of large amounts of energy and therefore represents the greatest potential for energy con-

servation. At the same time, buildings form the frame of human life and constitute prerequisites for human health, comfort and well-being. It is of fundamental importance therefore to ensure that the quality of life in buildings be maintained or improved when considering ways and means of implementing energy conservation programmes.

(b) GOVERNMENTS SHOULD ENSURE OR PROMOTE THE SAVING OF EXHAUSTIBLE ENERGY RESOURCES AND THE BEST POSSIBLE USE OF INEXHAUSTIBLE ENERGY RESOURCES IN BUILDINGS WHILE, AT THE SAME TIME, PURSUING THE AIM OF IMPROVING THE QUALITY OF LIFE IN BUILDINGS.

(c) *These objectives can be achieved by:*
  (i) Policies which combine the need to improve housing and workplace conditions with the need to conserve energy in buildings.
  (ii) Making the best possible use of sun, wind, geothermal heat and other renewable resources for producing energy.
  (iii) An integrated design of buildings that takes into account functional, aesthetic, cultural and energy-saving aspects.

Recommendations III.2

Need for a national policy for energy conservation in buildings

(a) If substantial energy savings in buildings are to be obtained, there is a need for an explicit policy and effective planning for the rational use and conservation of energy.

(b) POLICIES SHOULD BE ESTABLISHED AND IMPLEMENTED, AT ALL APPROPRIATE LEVELS, TO ACHIEVE ENERGY ECONOMY AND EFFICIENCY IN BUILDINGS IN COUNTRIES. TARGETS SHOULD BE SET FOR SHORT-, MEDIUM- AND LONG-TERM IMPLEMENTATION.

(c) *Special attention should be given to:*
  (i) The need to establish such policies at all levels of government.
  (ii) Defining specific goals and targets for energy saving in the building sector.
  (iii) Defining energy-savings goals for new and for existing buildings based on assessment of the optimal balance between these two sets of goals.
  (iv) Defining ways and means of achieving these goals.
  (v) The need for integrated housing, building and energy-saving policies.
  (vi) The need for continuous review of national, regional and local policies, and the development of methods and techniques for evaluating their effectiveness.

Recommendation III.3

Ways and Means

(a) In many countries there are a variety of alternative ways and means for implementing a national energy conservation policy for buildings. The choice among those alternatives should be based on economic and technical criteria but should also take social criteria and time considerations fully into account. While the economic and technical objectives may be to obtain maximum feasible savings and efficiency, the various measures for doing so will have different effects on the personal lives and budgets of people in different economic and social groups.

(b) IN THOSE COUNTRIES WHICH FACE PROBLEMS IN THIS AREA, GOVERNMENTS SHOULD
USE WAYS AND MEANS FOR IMPLEMENTING ENERGY CONSERVATION POLICIES, AT
ALL LEVELS, WHICH ARE EFFECTIVE AND EFFICIENT BUT WHICH ALSO ENSURE THAT
THE COSTS AND BENEFITS ARE DISTRIBUTED IN A WAY THAT IS EQUITABLE TO ALL
GROUPS IN SOCIETY.

(c) *Special attention should be given to:*

(i) The urgency of achieving rapid implementation of governmental energy-saving
programmes through different ways and means, and of encouraging individual
citizen responsibility in energy conservation.

(ii) The need to make the implementation of governmental energy-saving programmes possible through a review and strengthening of existing building legislation, building regulations and standards, and to develop new programmes,
to achieve energy saving in buildings.

(iii) The encouragement of private initiatives through changes in existing taxation
and pricing policies and the provision of special loans and grants under government programmes for energy savings in buildings.

(iv) The effect of new ways and means on different economic and social groups,
and the responsibility of governments, where applicable, to ensure that the
action taken does not adversely affect the most disadvantaged groups of society
either in the short or the long term.

(v) In countries where this has not already been done, the development of adequate
institutional and administrative arrangements.

Recommendation III.4

Resources for implementing the energy-saving goals

(a) Natural, but also human and financial, resources are limited in most countries.
At the same time, many ECE countries suffer from unemployment and the building industry is not always working at full capacity. Therefore, energy saving in
buildings should be seen as an integral and positive part of economic development
and employment policies.

(b) GOVERNMENTS SHOULD ENSURE THAT ENERGY-SAVING POLICIES FOR BUILDINGS
AND THE BUILT ENVIRONMENT ARE INCORPORATED AS AN INTEGRAL AND POSITIVE
PART OF ECONOMIC AND SOCIAL DEVELOPMENT POLICIES SO THAT THE BEST
POSSIBLE USE IS MADE OF SCARCE NATURAL, HUMAN AND FINANCIAL RESOURCES.

(c) *Special attention should be given to:*

(i) The need for an integrated economic, employment and energy-saving policy
on the national, regional, and local levels, taking fully into account the positive effects of energy-saving programmes on the balance of payments in many
countries.

(ii) The need for education and training programmes to develop new expertise and
skilled labour and to supplement education and training for those already
working in this field.

(iii) The need to bring together existing knowledge on national and international levels for operational application and to encourage effective research on gaps in that knowledge.

(iv) The need for technical information and advice to the owners of buildings and others that can contribute to energy-saving programmes.

(v) The encouragement, through adequate public information, of understanding and motivation for energy savings in buildings.

Recommendation III.5

Design of new buildings

(a) By taking rational measures, energy consumption in new buildings and building systems can be reduced by 20 to 50 per cent. In the long-term perspective, the design of new buildings can therefore appreciably influence total energy consumption in buildings. At the same time, the degree of vulnerability of buildings and building systems to changes in the type of energy can be reduced.

(b) NEW BUILDINGS MUST BE DESIGNED WITH PARTICULAR EMPHASIS ON OPTIMUM ENERGY CONSERVATION, TAKING DUE ACCOUNT OF THE FUNCTION OF THE BUILD-ING AND ITS QUALITY, THE ENERGY REQUIRED TO MANUFACTURE THE VARIOUS COMPONENTS AND THE BUILDING MATERIALS.

(c) *Special attention should be given to:*

(i) Consideration of the total cost of a building during its entire lifetime, including the initial investment and the expected cost of maintenance and energy supply.

(ii) Influence of the shape, form, orientation and heat accumulation capacity on the energy consumption in buildings.

(iii) Application of adequate standards for insulation and air tightness so as to minimize thermal losses, and also for lighting and mechanical equipment in buildings. This should include identification of appropriate and comparable characteristics of a building as regards the energy consumption required for comfort and the optimization of investments required, the building system, the operating expenses for energy as well as energy required for the production of the building materials.

(iv) Comparison and evaluation of several design alternatives with regard to: proper location, orientation of buildings and landscaping of the immediate surroundings; and the relation between the area of the building envelope, the volume of heated space and the area of glazed surfaces.

Recommendation III.6

Existing techniques

(a) The construction of the building has a major influence on heat losses and, consequently, on energy consumption. The use of all current knowledge and existing techniques can contribute greatly to energy conservation in the short term.

(b) GOVERNMENTS MUST RECOGNIZE THAT THE MOST IMPORTANT FACTORS IN ENERGY-

SAVING PROGRAMMES FOR BUILDINGS ARE THE DESIGN OF THE BUILDING, THE PHY-
SICS OF THE BUILDING, ITS OPERATION AND MAINTENANCE, THE EFFICIENCY OF ITS
FACILITIES, AS WELL AS THE AVAILABILITY OF DEVICES FOR REDUCING THE USE OF
ENERGY ACCORDING TO THE PREVAILING ENERGY SITUATION. THE INTERACTION
OF ALL THOSE FACTORS MUST ALSO BE OPTIMIZED.

(c) *Special attention should be given to:*

(i) Analysis of the energy flow in buildings by dividing the structure of the
building into individual components with their respective heat losses.

(ii) The impact of climatic conditions and other major climatic factors, such as
site and building orientation, sunshine, frequency, direction and the speed of
winds; and micro-climatic modifications due to landscaping.

(iii) Design of a building and its installations in such a way that it allows regulation
of the energy needed in different situations. A building should, for instance,
be able to take advantage of the free heat provided by the sun as well as
internal heat from various sources in the rooms.

(iv) Evaluation of the total efficiency of mechanical and water heating systems.

Recommendation III.7

New techniques

(a) Installation plans and the use of new types of energy can have a considerable impact
on the amount of energy necessary for the heating, ventilating, air conditioning
and other mechanical systems of new and existing buildings. The behaviour of
users is one of the main factors determining energy consumption in buildings. The
energy changes planned for communities should be directly related to the application of certain new heating methods.

(b) GOVERNMENTS SHOULD PROMOTE THE DEVELOPMENT AND USE OF NEW TECHNIQUES
WHICH, ALTHOUGH NOT ALWAYS ECONOMICAL IN THE SHORT TERM, TAKE INTO AC-
COUNT THE USE OF NEW KINDS OF ENERGY, THE BEHAVIOUR OF USERS, DEVELOP-
MENTS IN THE CONSTRUCTION OF NEW BUILDINGS AND IN THE ADAPTATION OF EXIST-
ING BUILDINGS.

(c) *Special attention should be given to:*

(i) Development and application of new types of installations which are re-
sponsive to energy conservation requirements and adaptable to changes in the
type of energy used.

(ii) Development and application of new techniques, such as the utilization of
solar and geothermal energy, industrial waste, and cooling water from nuclear
power stations for heating of buildings.

(iii) Development and application of integrated heating systems.

Recommendation III.8

Measures to save energy in existing buildings

(a) In most countries, construction rates exceed demolition rates. Consequently, even if new buildings have excellent thermal performance characteristics, an absolute decrease in energy consumption in buildings can only be achieved by energy conservation measures affecting the existing building stock.

(b) IN ORDER TO ACHIEVE AN ABSOLUTE DECREASE IN THE TOTAL ENERGY CONSUMPTION IN BUILDINGS IN THE SHORT TERM, GOVERNMENTS SHOULD PLAN AND IMPLEMENT EXTENSIVE ENERGY-SAVING PROGRAMMES IN EXISTING BUILDINGS.

(c) *Special attention should be given to:*

  (i) Measures such as insulation, tightening of windows and doors, changing or improving windows, regulation of heating, adjustment of the heating system, change or improvements in heating systems or furnaces, introduction of running times, reduced airflow, recirculation of air or water, heat recovery and improved operations and maintenance, as these measures can be based on existing know-how and can be undertaken with appropriate incentives or disincentives. The possibility of using sensing devices such as thermographic cameras should be recognized.

  (ii) The need to explore further the introduction of new space heating and water heating techniques in existing buildings, such as heat pumps, solar collectors, etc.

  (iii) The preservation of architectural and environmental values. Measures in existing buildings must be chosen not only with regard to their energy savings efficiency but also with regard to the impact they have on the character of the building and its surroundings.

Recommendation III.9

Priorities in energy savings in existing buildings

(a) The implementation of large-scale energy-savings programmes in existing buildings will not only affect the buildings but also the living and working conditions of the occupants. The impact of energy savings in their buildings may be both positive and negative. It is important that measures be undertaken not only with regard to the capital and operations costs but also with regard to the effects they will have on their users. Present-day calculations on the costs of energy-saving investments often underestimate the long-term benefits and overemphasize the short-term costs of these measures.

(b) DECISIONS ON ENERGY SAVING IN EXISTING BUILDINGS MUST BE TAKEN IN ACCORDANCE WITH CLEARLY DEFINED PRIORITIES, BASED ON SOCIAL, ECONOMIC, TECHNICAL AND OTHER CONSIDERATIONS.

(c) *Special attention should be given to:*

  (i) The urgency of extensive energy savings in existing buildings within a limited time in view of the fact that these buildings represent the largest energy-saving potential in the short term.

  (ii) Energy-saving measures that are least costly. The cost, however, must be related to a long-term analysis of energy supply and to the investment, operating and maintenance costs of these saving measures.

(iii) Energy-saving measures that cause the least disruption in the lives of the occupants.

(iv) The desirability that extensive energy-saving measures are undertaken when buildings are also to be rehabilitated for other reasons.

LIST OF DOCUMENTS

Editor's Note

All the items listed below were prepared in limited quantities for the use of participants in the Ottawa Seminar. The present volume is the only item directly relating to the Seminar that is published for wide distribution.

Limited quantities of some of the items listed may still be available on request from the ECE Press Officer, Palais des Nations, CH-1211, Geneva, or from the government or organization that produced the paper. Items that are reproduced in entirety or near-entirety in the present volume are indicated by an asterisk.

The documentation, all items of which carry the prefix HBP/SEM.17 to identify them as part of the Ottawa Seminar, falls into three main groups. Material listed only by a number (e.g. HBP/SEM.17/1) was issued by the ECE Secretariat; the items mainly concern the organizational and other preparations for the Seminar, but the final report of the Seminar (including the conclusions and recommendations adopted by the Seminar) is also in this group. All items were prepared in the three ECE languages: English, French and Russian.

The second group of documents contains the Seminar theme paper and specialized substantive papers prepared by ECE member-countries and international organizations, including the ECE Secretariat itself. These are identified by the letter R (e.g. HBP/SEM.17/R.1) and are available in one or more languages, at the discretion of the country or organization which prepared the paper and undertook its translation. One-page summaries were prepared in the remaining languages if full versions were not available.

Finally, documents circulated during the Ottawa Seminar itself are identified by the letters CRP (e.g. HBP/SEM.17/CRP.1). The majority of these are interim documents (e.g. preliminary drafts of the conclusions and recommendations) which have been superseded by the final report of the seminar. Most, but not all, were prepared in all three languages.

The following list indicates which documents were circulated in full in different languages (E/F/R) and, in the case of the second group of items, the names of the authors or responsible agencies, where these were identified in the paper submitted to the ECE Secretariat. Titles of papers are those used in the English-language summary where no English version of the full paper exists.

During 1978 the following specialized papers will be published in a slightly condensed form in a special issue of the journal *Habitat International,* published by Pergamon Press. The papers will appear in English except where noted below.

HBP/SEM.17/R.2	R.13
R.4	R.14 (French)
R.9	R.15
R.12 (French)	R.16

R.19	R.38
HBP/SEM.17/R.23	R.39
R.24	R.41
R.28	R.47
R.37	R.51

In the following list of documents it is understood that the prefix HBP/SEM.17/ is to be added to the printed reference; e.g. 1 becomes HBP/SEM.17/1; 1/Add.1 becomes HBP/SEM/.17/1/Add.1; etc.

1	Programme and organization (E/F/R)	
1/Add.1	Programme and organization—addendum (E/F/R)	
1/Add.2	Programme and organization—study tour (E/F/R)	
1/Add.3	Programme et organization—addendum (E/F/R)	
2	Report (E/F/R)	
R.1	Human settlements and energy (E/F/R)	Canada (C. I. Jackson)
R.2	Evolution of regulations and practice of thermal insulation in buildings (E/F)	European Insulation Manufacturers' Association (EURIMA)
R.3	Improved thermal performance of existing buildings (E)	Austria
R.4	Designing new buildings of optimum shape and orientation (E)	U.S.A. (D. Keplinger)
R.5	Improved thermal efficiency in new buildings (R)	Byelorussian SSR (Institute of Construction and Architecture of the State Committee for Construction and the 'Belgosproekt' Institute of the State Committee for Construction)
R.6	Design of buildings which are less vulnerable to changes in energy source (E/F/R)	Czechoslovakia (K. Mrázek)
R.7	Increased energy efficiency in existing buildings (F)	France
R.8	Use of unconventional natural energy sources for heating (F)	France
R.9	Energy consumption: Manufacture of building materials and building construction (E)	Norway (A. Hallquist)
R.10	Assessment of methods and techniques	Denmark

	for energy conservation in buildings (E)	(E. Christophersen and D. Pedersen)
R.11	The energy question and urban development: Some lines of research (F)	France (H. Mathieu)
R.12	Regional planning aspects (F)	France
R.13	Assessment methods and techniques for energy conservation in buildings	Ireland (P. Minogue)
R.14	The energy problem in the planning and development of human cities (F)	Poland (B. Kontowicz and W. Suchorzewski)
R.15	Design, construction, improvement and utilization of buildings (E/F)	International Council for Building Research, Studies and Documentation (CIB) (P. Bakke and S. Lundby)
R.16	Structural measures to economize energy in the reconstruction and modernization of residential buildings (E/R)	German Democratic Republic
R.17	Energy saving in residential buildings: a cost-effectiveness analysis (E)	Sweden (B. Mattsson)
R.18	Improved thermal performance of existing buildings (E)	Sweden (U. Thunberg)
R.19	Increased efficiency in existing buildings (E)	Federal Republic of Germany (A. Prömmel)
R.20	Improved thermal performance of new buildings (E)	Netherlands
R.21	Assessment methods and techniques (E)	Netherlands
R.22	District heating in Finland's energy supply (E)	Finland
R.23	Design and construction of buildings with good thermal performance in Finland (E)	Finland
R.24	Energy consumption implications of physical layout: the case of Louvain-la-Neuve, Belgium (E)	World Environment and Resources Council (P. Laconte)
R.25	Choice of materials energy into production and delivery of woodbased and other housing materials and systems (E)	Canada (Scanada Consultants Ltd.)
R.26	Planning urban transportation systems (E)	U.S.A. (O. Sutermeister)
R.27	Improved thermal performance of new buildings (E/F/R)	U.S.A. (J. McCullough)

R.28	Environmental aspects of the combined production of heat and electricity (E/F/R)	ECE Secretariat
R.29	Routing of transmission lines from James Bay through the Montreal Laurentians (E/F/R)	Canada (G. Galibois)
R.30	District energy options and urban impacts (E/F/R)	Canada (E. L. Morofsky)
R.31	Energy considerations in Quebec public transportation policy (E/F/R)	Canada (M.-C. Levesque-Fortin)
R.32	Designing to energy performance criteria (E/F/R)	Canada (R. C. Biggs and D. M. Sander)
R.33	Design for energy conservation in the Subarctic with special reference to Fermont (E/F/R)	Canada (N. Schoenauer)
R.34	Energy utilization and conservation programme—provincial government buildings—Government of Alberta (E/F/R)	Canada (W. A. B. Saunders and R. B. Smith)
R.35	This paper was re-issued as HBP/SEM.17/R.49	
R.36	Planning and evaluation methods and techniques (E)	Hungary (Hungarian Institute for Town and Regional Planning)
R.37	Communications - transportation substitution in the reduction of energy requirements: an exploration of the social and economic impact on human settlements (E/F/R)	Canada (A. Kumar, J. Langlois and K. Watson)
R.38	Research program on wind turbines (E/F/R)	Canada (L. Boulet)
R.39	Energy conservation in United Kingdom dwellings: a national assessment (E/F)	International Institute for Environment and Development (IIED) (F. Romig and D. Runnalls)
R.40	Renewable energy in remote communities (E/F/R)	Canada (M. Glover)
R.41	Planning the utilization of alternative energy and conversion methods (E)	Turkey
R.42	Energy consumption by households and other small consumers in the ECE region in 1974 (E/F/R)	ECE Secretariat

R.43	The thermal improvement of existing housing stock in the United Kingdom and its evaluation in the light of national energy policies (E/F/R)	United Kingdom (N. T. Rees)
R.44	Long-term energy perspectives, and human settlements (E/F/R)	ECE Secretariat
R.45	The city and energy (E/F/R)	France (F. Parfait)
R.46	Upgrading the thermal efficiency of residential buildings in Canada (E/F/R)	Canada (J. Connolly and R. Platts)
R.47	The development of centralized heat supply in the cities of the USSR (E/F/R)	U.S.S.R.
R.48	Energy and urban form (E/F/R)	Canada (J. H. Chibuk)
R.49	Energy conservation in public buildings (E/F/R)	Canada (R. C. Biggs and G. Laszlo)
R.50	The nuclear district heating option— an Ontario perspective (E/F/R)	Canada (Ontario Ministry of Energy)
R.51	Energy from solid waste in human settlements (E/F/R)	Canada (T. E. Rattray)
R.52	Energy processing and environmental protection requirements (F)	Canada (J. Saucier and J. Gagnon)
CRP.1*	Opening statement by the Parliamentary Secretary to the Minister of State for Urban Affairs, Canada, Mr. J.-R. Gauthier, MP (E/F/R)	
CRP.2*	Opening statement by the Executive Secretary of the ECE, Mr. J. Stanovnik (E/F/R) (No documents were issued bearing the numbers HBP/SEM.17/CRP.3 or HBP/SEM.17/CRP.4)	
CRP.5*	List of participants (E)	
CRP.5/Add.1*	List of participants—addendum (E)	
CRP.5/Corr.1*	List of participants—corrigendum (E)	
CRP.6*	List of documents (E/F/R)	
CRP.7	Note concerning the concept of thermal insulation standards, comparisons which may be made between them, and	

	future standards, by O. Barde, Geneva (E/F)
CRP.8*	Draft report (E/F/R)
CRP.9*	Draft conclusions and recommendations (E/F/R)
CRP.9/Add.1*	Draft conclusions and recommendations—addendum (E/F/R)
CRP.9/Add.2*	Draft conclusions and recommendations—addendum (E/F/R)
CRP.9/Rev.1*	Revised draft conclusions and recommendations (E/F/R)
CRP.9/Add.1/Rev.1*	Revised draft conclusions and recommendations—addendum (E/F/R)
CRP.9/Add.2/Rev.1*	Revised draft conclusions and recommendations—addendum (E/F/R)
CRP.10*	Draft analytical summary of the debates (E/F/R)
CRP.10/Add.1*	Draft analytical summary of the debates—addendum (E/F/R)
CRP.10/Add.2*	Draft analytical summary of the debates—addendum (E/F/R)

LIST OF PARTICIPANTS

Chairman: Mr. M. STRONG (Canada)
Chairman, Petro-Canada
P.O. Box 2844
4th Avenue South West,
Calgary, Alberta T2P 2M7
Vice-chairmen: Mr. A. IAKIMTCHOUK (Byelorussian SSR)
Mr. J. SEIP (Norway)

Belgium
Mr. Willy J. BOGAERT
Inspecteur Général
Régie des Bâtiments
Ministère des Travaux Publics
155 rue de la Loi
1040 Bruxelles

Byelorussian SSR
Mr. A. IAKIMTCHOUK
Deputy Chairman of the Municipality of Minsk

Canada
Mr. J.-P. ARSENAULT
Directeur Général
Direction générale de l'urbanisme
   et de l'aménagement du territoire
Ministère des Affaires municipales
680 rue Saint-Amable
Québec, Que. G1R 4Z3

Mr. Pierre L. BOURGAULT
Assistant Deputy Minister
Planning and Evaluation
Department of Energy, Mines and Resources
580 Booth Street
Ottawa, Ont. K1A OE4

Mr. M. S. EVERS
Mayor
City of New Westminster
Federation of Canadian Municipalities
City Hall
511 Royal Avenue
New Westminster, B.C. V3L IH9

Mr. C. Ian JACKSON
Ministry of State for Urban Affairs
Ottawa, Ont. K1A 0P6

Mr. W. A. B. SAUNDERS
Deputy Minister
Housing and Public Works
207 Legislative Building
Edmonton, Alberta

Mr. Lorenz SCHMIDT
Assistant Secretary
Priorities and Operations Branch
Ministry of State for Urban Affairs
Ottawa, Ont. K1A 0P6

Mr. Maurice F. STRONG
Chairman
Petro-Canada
P.O. Box 2844
Calgary, Alberta T2P 2M7

Mr. William TERON
Secretary of the Ministry of State for
   Urban Affairs
Chairman of the Board of Central
Mortgage and Housing Corporation
Ottawa, Ont. K1A 0P6

Mr. Andrew Bruce WELLS
Executive Director
Institute of Man and Resources
50 Water Street
P.O. Box 2008
Charlottetown, P.E.I. CIA 1A4

Mr. Douglas G. WELLS
Executive Director
Technical Services
Ministry of Housing
101 Bloor Street West
Toronto, Ont. M5S 1P8

Czechoslovakia
Mr. Karel MRAZEK
Head of Department
Study and Typification Institute
Perlova 1
Prague

Mr. Vladimir PRCHLIK
Adviser
Research and Development Centre for
   Environmental Pollution Control
Voddrenska 2
81643 Bratislava

167

Denmark

Mr. Poul AHRENST
Chief of Section
Federation of Co-operative Housing in Denmark
Lindevangs alle 6
2000 Copenhagen F

Mr. Ole JENSEN
Danish Building Research Institute
Post Box 119
2970 Horsholm

Mr. V. JORGENSEN
General Manager
Federation of Cooperative Housing in Denmark
Lindevangs alle 6
2000 Copenhagen F

Mr. Ernst KRISTOFFERSEN
Head of Division
National Agency for Physical Planning
Ministry of the Environment
23 Holbergsgade
DK-1057, Copenhagen K

Mr. P. SCHAARUP-SORENSEN
Manager
National Organization of Non-Profit
Housing Societies
Tomsgardsvej 28
24001 Copenhagen N.V.

Mr. Olaf SMITH-HANSEN
Civil Engineer
Ministry of Housing
Slotsholmsgade 12
1216 K - Denmark

Finland

Mr. Dick A. H. BJÖRKHOLTZ
Paraisten Kalkki Oy
Stenbergsvägen 31
02700 Grankulla

Mr. Risto Kalevi MÄKINEN
Project Manager
Finnish National Fund for Research and
    Development (SITRA)
Uudenmaaankatu 16-20 B
06120 Helsinki 12

Mr. Reijo Yrjo Olavi MERIVAARA
National Housing Board
Ministry of Interior
Malminkatu 34, 00100
Helsinki 10

Mr. Pekka J. PAASIKIVI
Vice President
ORAS Oy, Rauma Naappukja 20

Mr. Olli A. SEPPÄNEN
Manager of Building Research
EKONO Consulting Engineers
Postbox 27
00131 Helsinki 13

Mr. Esko YLIKOSKI
Bureau Chief, Energy Department
Ministry of Trade and Industry
Rautatielaisenkatu 6
Helsinki 52

France

M. Hervé MATHIEU
Ingénieur - Directeur d'Etudes
Centre de Recherche d'Urbanisme
74, rue de la Fédération
75015 Paris

M. François PARFAIT
Directeur Général
Société Centrale pour l'Equipement du
    Territoire
4 Place Raoul Dautry
F-75741 Paris, Cedex 15

M. Raymond PARRAIN
Chef du Service Energie
Société Centrale pour l'Equipement du
    Territoire
4 Place Raoul Dautry
F-75741 Paris, Cedex 15

M. Maurice R. TRICHARD
Chef de division
Direction de la Construction
Ministère de l'Equipement et de
    l'Aménagement du Territoire
117 rue Jean Moulin
78300 Poissy

German Democratic Republic

Mr. Roland FREIGANG
Deputy Director of Department
Bauakademie der DDR
102 Berlin
Ministerium für Bauwesen
Scharrenstr. 2-3

Mr. Manfred SCHULTZ
Deputy Director
Institut für Ingenieur und Tiefbau
Winckelmannstrasse 315
1197 Berlin

Germany, Federal Republic of

Mr. Kurt TSCHICHHOLZ
Ministerialrat
Federal Ministry for Regional Planning
Building and Urban Development
Deichmanns Ave.
5300 Bonn-Bad Godesberg

Mr. Gerhard WAGNER
Diplom-Geograph
Bundesforschungsanstalt für
Landeskunde und Raumordnung
Michaelstr. 8
53 Bonn

Greece

Ms. Maria POLYZOU-SAVVAIDES
Director
Ministry of Coordination
790 Boylston Str. Apt. 44
Boston, MA 02199 U.S.A.

Hungary

Mr. Janos BRENNER
Deputy Director
Planning Institute BUVATI
Varoshaz 4. 9-11
Budapest V

Mr. Laszlo SZATHMARY
Head of Department
Ministry of Building and Urban Development
Beloiannisz u. 2-4
Budapest V

Iceland

Mr. Geirhardur THORSTEINSSON
Architect/Town Planner
Reykjavik-Community
Veltusund 3

Ireland

Mr. Patrick Joseph MINOGUE
Research Officer
An Foras Forbatha
St. Martins House
Waterloo Road
Dublin 4

Italy

Mr. G. SAGGESE
Professor
Politecnico di Torino
Strada dei Colli 11
Pino Torinese

Netherlands

Mr. Pieter W. van BAARSEL
Head - Research Department
Ministry of Housing and Physical Planning
Alkemadelaan 85
The Hague

Mr. Pier Hendrik JANSMA
Building Research Engineer
Ministry of Housing and Physical Planning
Boerhaauelaan 5
Loetermier

Mr. Gerard KOL
Civil Servant
Ministry of Economic Affairs
Bezuidenhoutseiveg 30
The Hague

Mr. Karel W. NIEUWZWAAG
Director
Rijksgebouwendienst
7 Kennedy Lane
The Hague

Norway

Mr. Pal E. HOLTE
Head of Division
Ministry of Environment
P.O. Box 8013
Nyntgt. 2
Oslo 1

Mr. Sven E. LUNDBY
Director
Norwegian Building Research Institute
Forskningsveien 3B
Oslo 3

Mr. Jens L. SEIP
Chief of Department
Royal Ministry of Local Government and
   Labour
Kommunaldepartementat
Oslo Dep.

Poland

Mr. Edward SWIRKOWSKI
Electrical Engineer
Institute for Organization, Management and
   Economics of the Building Industry
Filtrowa 1
00-611 Warsaw

Portugal

Mr. L. PAZOS ALONSO
Embassy of Portugal, Ottawa Canada

Sweden

Mrs. Ingrid ÅRLIN
Head of Department
Ministry of Housing and Physical Planning
Fack, S-10320 Stockholm

Mr. Bengt MATTSON
Senior Lecturer
University College
Karlstad
Skogstorpsgatan 3
S-65465 Karlstad

Mr. S. NORDSTRÖM
Head of Division
National Board of Public Building
Byggnadsstyrelsen
S 106 43 Stockholm

Mr. Sture PERSSON
Head - International Department
Ministry of Housing and Physical Planning
Fack, S-10320 Stockholm

Mr. Göte SVENSON
Ambassador
Ministry for Foreign Affairs
Box 16121
10320 Stockholm

Mr. U. THUNBERG
Head of Division
National Board of Urban Planning
Byggnadsbyran, Fack,
104 22 Stockholm

Switzerland
Mr. Olivier BARDE
P.O. Box 190
1227 Geneva

Turkey
Mr. Akin ERYOLDAS
Architect-Planner
Ministry of Construction and Resettlement
Ankara

United Kingdom
Mr. P. CLAYTON
Department of the Environment
Becket House
Lambeth Palace Road
London SE1 7ER

Mr. N. REES
Architect
Department of the Environment
Becket House
Lambeth Palace Road
London SE1 7ER

United States of America
Mr. S. CAVROS
Chief
Community Systems Branch
Division of Building and Community Systems
Energy Research and Development
  Administration
Washington, D.C.

Mr. W. T. COYLE
Program Manager
Architectural and Engineering Branch
Division of Building and Community Systems
Energy Research and Development
  Administration
20 Massachusetts Ave. N.W.
Washington, D.C. 20545

Mr. J. GOBER
Chief of Regional Planning Staff
Tennessee Valley Authority
Knoxville, Tennessee

Mr. Lenneal HENDERSON, Jr.
Associate Director of Research
Joint Centre for Political Studies
1426 H. St. N.W. Suite 926
Washington, D.C. 20005

Mr. Charles INCE
Executive Administrator of Energy Programs
American Institute of Architects Research
  Corp.
1735 New York Ave.
Washington, D.C.

Mr. Hugh MIELDS
Assistant Executive Director
U.S. Conference of Mayors
1620 Eye St. N.W. Washington, D.C. 20016

Ms. Yvonne S. PERRY
Deputy Assistant Secretary for Interprogram
  and Areawide Concerns
Office of Community Planning and
  Development
Department of Housing and Urban
  Development
7100 HUD Bldg.
7th and D Streets
Washington, D.C.

Mr. William J. RAUP
Program Analyst
Department of Energy
12th and Pennsylvania, N.W.
Washington, D.C. 20461

Mr. Oscar SUTERMEISTER
Principal Community Planner
Department of Housing and Urban
  Development
451 7th Street, S.W.
Washington, D.C. 20410

Yugoslavia
Mr. Peter NOVAK
University of Ljubljana
Faculty for Mechanical Engineering
61001 Ljubljana
Murnikova 2

GOVERNMENTS PARTICIPATING IN A CONSULTATIVE CAPACITY

Brazil
Mr. José VILAR DE QUEIROZ
Minister-Counsellor
Embassy of Brazil
255 Albert St.
Ottawa, Canada

Mr. Paulo WOLOWSKI
Secretary
Embassy of Brazil

255 Albert Street
Ottawa, Canada

Philippines
Mr. Nathaniel VON EINSIEDEL
Architect-Town Planner
Human Settlements Commission
TRC Building
Buendia Ave.

Ext. Makati
Rizal
Philippines

UNITED NATIONS

United Nations Environment Programme (UNEP)
Mr. Francisco SZEKELY
Regional Adviser
Latin America
Ave. Presidente Mazarik 24
piso 10
Mexico 5 D.F.

Centre for Housing, Building and Planning
Mr. W. GARCES
Deputy Director in charge of Research and
    Development
United Nations Headquarters
New York

SPECIALIZED AGENCIES

World Meteorological Organization (WMO)
Mr. Frank QUINLAN
Chief, Climatological Analysis Division
National Oceanic and Atmospheric
    Administration
Federal Building
Asheville
North Carolina 28801 U.S.A.

INTERNATIONAL NON-GOVERNMENTAL
ORGANIZATIONS

Building Research Establishment (CIB W67)
Mr. Per BAKKE
Assistant Director
Building Research Establishment
Bucknalls Lane
Garston
Watford
England

*European Insulation Manufacturers' Association
(EURIMA)*
Mr. Werner LINANDER
Secretary General
8, rue Nicolas Welter
Luxembourg

*International Confederation of Free Trade Unions
(ICFTU)*
Mr. Jim MACDONALD
Director, Social and Community Programmes
Canadian Labour Congress
2841 Riverside Drive
Ottawa, Ontario, Canada K1V 8X7

Mr. Seppo NOUSIAINEN
Canadian Labour Congress
2841 Riverside Dr.
Ottawa, Canada K1V 8X7

*International Federation for Housing and Planning
(IFHP)*

Mr. Peter H. OBERLANDER
Director
Centre for Human Settlements
University of British Columbia
2075 Westbrook Mall
Vancouver B.C. V6T 1W5, Canada

*International Institute for Environment and
Development (IIED)*
Mr. F. A. ROMIG
Energy/Architecture Consultant
International Institute for Environment and
    Development
3 Tanza Road
Hampstead
London NW3 2UA, England

Mr. J. D. RUNNALS
Environmentalist
International Institute for Environment and
    Development
3 Tanza Road
Hampstead
London NW3 2UA, England

*International Organization for Standardization
(ISO)*
Mr. Stanley KENT
Architect and Professor
University of Toronto
20 Denewood Crescent
Don Mills
Ontario M3B IM5, Canada

Mr. L. LOSHAK

International Real Estate Federation (FIABCI)
Mr. Philip D. P. HOLMES
President
Pemberton, Holmes Ltd.
68, rue des Archives
75003 Paris, France

Mr. J. T. Blair JACKSON
Executive Vice President
Canadian Real Estate Association
99 Duncan Mill Road
Don Mills
Toronto
Ontario, Canada M3B 122

International Union of Architects (IUA)
Mr. Jean-Louis LALONDE
Architect
1980 Sherbrooke St. W.
Montreal H3H 1E8, Canada

Mr. H. V. WALKER
Architect

World Environment and Resources Council
Mr. P. LACONTE
Director
University of Louvain
Belgium

World Society for Ekistics
  Mr. Alexander B. LEMAN
  Architect-Consultant
  Leman Group Inc.
  Consultants on Human Settlements
  87 St. Nicholas Street
  Toronto
  Canada M4Z 1W8

INTERGOVERNMENTAL ORGANIZATIONS
ATTENDING AT THE INVITATION OF THE
SECRETARIAT

*Organization for Economic Co-operation and
Development (OECD)*
  Mr. Ferenc JUHASZ
  Principal Administrator
  Environment and Energy Division
  2, rue André Pascal
  Paris 16e, France

LIST OF CANADIAN ACCREDITED PARTICIPANTS AND THE CANADIAN SECRETARIAT

Provincial Advisors
  Mr. Andrew ARMITAGE
  Director of Research
  Ministry of Municipal Affairs and Housing
  810 Blanshard Street, 4th Floor
  Victoria, British Columbia

  Mr. A. REGENSTREIF
  Assistant Secretary of the Housing and
    Urban Development
  Legislative Building, Room 50
  Winnipeg, Manitoba R3C 0V8

  Mr. A. R. HUGHES
  Managing Director
  New Brunswick Housing Corporation
  Bird Building, Industrial Park
  P.O. Box 611
  Fredericton, New Brunswick E3B 5B2

  Mr. A. VIVIAN
  Chairman
  Newfoundland and Labrador Housing
    Corporation
  Elizabeth Avenue, Elizabeth Tower
  P.O. Box 1816
  St. John's, Newfoundland A1C 5K5

  Mr. Arthur A. IRWIN
  Conservation Coordinator
  Energy Council of Nova Scotia
  1690 Hollis Street, 6th Floor
  Halifax, Nova Scotia B3G 2X1

  Mr. Bunley YANG
  Advisor
  Transportation and Urban Development
  Ontario Ministry of Energy
  56 Wellesley Street West, 12th Floor
  Toronto, Ontario M7Z 2B7

  Monsieur Claude ROQUET
  Conseiller spécial au sous-ministre de l'Energie
  1305, chemin Sainte-Foy, pièce 200
  Québec (Québec) G1S 4N5

  Dr. Harold J. DYCK
  Deputy Minister of Urban Affairs
  Department of Municipal Affairs
  1791 Rose Street, 3rd Floor
  Regina, Saskatchewan S4P 1Z5

Territorial Advisor
  Mr. N. MAC PHERSON
  Director
  Federal Liaison Bureau
  Government of the Northwest Territories
  Centennial Tower, Room 328
  400 Laurier Avenue West
  Ottawa, Ontario K1A 0H4

Federal Advisors
  Mr. W. A. CUMMING
  Vice-President, Laboratories
  National Research Council of Canada
  M58 Building, Room W315
  Montreal Road
  Ottawa, Ontario K1A 0R6

  Dr. E. F. ROOTS
  Science Advisor
  Department of Fisheries and Environment
  Ottawa, Ontario K1A 0H3

  Mr. A. G. WILSON
  Director General
  Technological Research and Development
  Department of Public Works
  Sir Charles Tupper Building
  7D Riverside Drive
  Ottawa, Ontario K1A 0M2

  Mr. David CRENNA
  Director
  Policy Development Division
  Central Mortgage and Housing Corporation
  Montreal Road
  Ottawa, Ontario K1A 0P7

  Mr. Graham ARMSTRONG
  Director of Research

Office of Energy Conservation
Department of Energy, Mines and Resources
580 Booth Street, 17th Floor
Ottawa, Ontario

Canadian Secretariat
Mr. Peter S. VAN ES
Executive Director and
Canadian Seminar Coordinator
Ministry of State for Urban Affairs
Ottawa KIA 0P6

Mr. Maurice RABOT
Ministry of State for Urban Affairs
Ottawa KIA 0P6

Mr. J. BARBER
Financial and Administrative Director
Ministry of State for Urban Affairs
Ottawa K1A 0P6

Mrs. M. MORRIS
Study Tour Director
Minstry of State for Urban Affairs
Ottawa K1A 0P6

Mr. Luc SICOTTE
Communications Director
Ministry of State for Urban Affairs
Ottawa K1A 0P6

Mr. W. B. GRIGGS
Natural Environment and Resources
Directorate,
Ministry of State for Urban Affairs
Ottawa KIA 0P6

Mrs. Barbara MALONE
Seminar Arrangements Director
Ministry of State for Urban Affairs
Ottawa KIA 0P6

Mr. M. H. JONES
Science, Environment and
Transportation Division,
Department of External Affairs,
Ottawa KIA 0G2

Mr. R. D. MUNRO
Portfolio Directorate for International
Affairs,
Ottawa KIA 0P6